ADVISING CHIANG'S ARMY

Also by Stephen L. Wilson

South Dakota Crusader: Francis Case's Road to Congress

Answering the Call: With the 91st Infantry Division in the Italian Campaign During World War II

SECOND EDITION

ADVISING CHIANG'S ARMY

An American Soldier's World War II Experience in China

STEPHEN L. WILSON

Joycliff Press | Saint Paul, Minnesota

Advising Chiang's Army: An American Soldier's World War II Experience in China

Copyright 2024, Stephen L. Wilson, All rights reserved.

Published by Joycliff Press, Saint Paul, Minnesota

ISBN 978-0-9789600-5-6 (paperback)
ISBN 978-0-9789600-6-3 (eBook)
Library of Congress Control Number: 2024909895

steve.wilson.wwii@gmail.com

No part of this publication may be reproduced, stored in a retrieval system, or transmitted, in any form or by any means, electronic, mechanical, photocopying, recording, or otherwise, without the prior written permission of both the copyright holder and the above publisher of this book, except by a reviewer who wishes to quote brief passages in connection with a review written for insertion in a magazine, newspaper, broadcast, website, blog, or other outlet in conformity with United States and International Fair Use or comparable guidelines to such copyright exception.

Cover Design by Lois Stanfield

Typeset by B. Cook

Publication of this Second Edition managed by AuthorImprints.com

For Phillip, Debra, Jane and John; and
in memory of their parents, Lois and Phil

Contents

Prologue 1

1. Commissioned Officer and College Man 7
2. Stateside Duty 11
3. From Milbank to Kunming 23
4. Joining Traveling Instructional Group No. 4 31
5. A Challenging Assignment 51
6. The Chinese Army and its American Advisors Hang On 77
7. Change in American Leadership 87
8. New Leadership—Mixed Results 99
9. Assigned to Central Command 113
10. The Kweilin Offensive 125
11. It's Over 135
12. From Kunming to Milbank 145

Epilogue 153
Photos, Maps, and Other Illustrations 173
Acknowledgments 229
Notes 233
Sources 267
Index 277

Prologue

It was his first deep-sea fishing trip. From a boat off the southern Florida coast, Phil was enjoying simply being on the ocean and looking back at the shoreline. Suddenly he hooked a fish that sent his line singing. The hook firmly set, the rookie deep-sea fisherman alternated between letting his prey run out the line and reeling it in. This back-and-forth tug of war continued for 50 minutes or so. The spirited fish finally tired, and Phil managed to get it into the boat. It turned out to be a 35-pound sail fish that was five feet long. Having grown up in a small Midwestern town—far from any ocean fishing—Phil was understandably proud to return to land with his trophy.[1]

The fishing trip was undertaken while Captain Phil Walter Saunders, an Infantry Officer in the U. S. Army, was in Miami, Florida, during the late summer in 1943. Miami was his last stop in the United States before travelling to his overseas assignment. Less than two months after he caught the sail fish and attended a dance with "all the belles of Miami" that evening, Phil and a group of American soldiers were ambushed by a Japanese unit on China's Burma Road.[2]

* * * *

Phil's father, Phil Crowley Saunders, was 18 years old when he began working for the Farmers and Merchants Bank in Milbank, South Dakota, in 1904. Milbank is a small town located in the northeastern corner of the state near the Minnesota border. It is the county seat of Grant County, which was established in 1873 and named in honor of American Civil War General and U.S. President Ulysses S. Grant. In 1917, Phil married Jean (also known as Jennie) Johnson. The couple had three children—Corinne, Gene, and Leola. In 1919, Phil became president of the bank.[3]

Tragedy struck the young family in 1926. In the early morning on Saturday, July 31, Phil was returning by automobile from Redwood Falls, Minnesota to Milbank. He was driving northwest on a state highway that followed closely along the Minnesota River. There was a heavy fog along the river bottom. About one-half mile east of Granite Falls, it appears that Mr. Saunders missed a bend in the road and angled his car toward the river instead. Realizing what had happened, he stopped the car before it went into the river, but his right front wheel extended over the river bank's edge. A newspaper account of this accident explained what happened next:

> All indications are that he then got out of the car, walked around to the left front side to ascertain the position of his machine, and in stepping on the steep edge of the grade lost his balance and grasped the fender of the car to save himself from falling into the river. As the car was in neutral and the brake not set, it did not hold on the grade but ran forward into the river, and that as it did so he was either struck by some part of the bottom of the car or the rocks in the river, which doubtless rendered him unconscious and unable to assist himself or get out from under the car and the water that he had fallen into, which was about two feet deep at that point, and his death resulted from drowning.[4]

The newspaper article went on to state that "his passing comes as a terrible shock to his family and relatives, and constitutes a distinct loss to the community and Grant County citizens generally," and "in his home life he had indeed been an exemplary husband and father, and when not actually engaged in the discharge of his business duties he was always found in the company of his family[.]"[5]

Jean was 41 years old when Phil died. Her daughter Corinne was seven, son Gene was five, and younger daughter Leola was four.[6] Shortly after her husband's death, she changed Gene's name to Phil.

Jean was forced to raise her three young children on her own. The family she raised would become very close to her and to each other.

* * * *

After graduating from Milbank High School in 1938, Phil attended the University of South Dakota in Vermillion. Four years later, he completed the Reserve Officers' Training Corps program at the University and was commissioned as a second lieutenant in the U.S. Army. His first 15 months in the Army were primarily spent taking a basic infantry officers' course at Fort Benning, Georgia, and then serving as a unit training officer in an Infantry Replacement Training Center at Camp Wheeler, Georgia.

Next, he was sent to China as a combat liaison officer with Generalissimo Chiang Kai-shek's Nationalist Chinese Army. The Chinese had been at war with Japan since 1937. Shortly after the attack at Pearl Harbor, the United States government formed a coalition with Nationalist China and established the U.S. China-Burma-India theater of operations. Army Lieutenant General Joseph W. Stilwell was appointed head of this theater. Generalissimo Chiang, the Allied Supreme Commander for the China theater, reluctantly accepted Stilwell as his chief of staff.[7]

As a combat liaison officer, Phil was responsible for advising the Chinese Army "in training, in supply, and in operations."[8] This assignment would prove to be challenging for a number of reasons.

When he arrived in China in October 1943, the Chinese Army was underfed, unfit, and underequipped. One statistic graphically illustrates this army's many problems: "The rate of loss by death or desertion of all Chinese conscripts in 1943 was 44 percent, or 750,000 out of a total of 1,670,000[.]"[9] Moreover, the Chinese displayed a general attitude toward war markedly different from their American advisors. Barbara Tuchman, in her classic work, *Stilwell and the American Experience in China, 1911-1945*, described that attitude as follows:

Retreat without orders and failure to take or hold a given position were habitual and inherent in the traditional Chinese idea of war as a kind of chess game of cunning and maneuver rather than a physical clash. For a commander to lose his life or his army was not gallant but stupid.

* * *

Chinese officers on the whole did not regard themselves as responsible for the outcome of the battle. Traditionally the military profession was not highly regarded, the Chinese theory being that "good iron is not used to make nails nor good men to make soldiers." . . . The Chinese commander was not a member of an institutional army like the Western officer. This led to placing loyalty directly in the person of the leader instead of submitting to obedience in a chain of command, with the result that divisional generals and even regimental colonels would frequently take orders only from Chiang Kai-shek himself instead of from their immediate superior[.][10]

With considerable American aid and constant prodding, these conditions and attitudes would improve as the war in China unfolded, but they provided substantial barriers to accomplishing American objectives in China.

Phil's experience in China also presented challenges on a more personal level. In addition to the obvious dangers posed by encounters with the Japanese, his living conditions were very primitive and unsanitary. Rats and pigs often shared the American soldiers' living quarters. Phil had frequent problems with an unruly stomach, which prompted him to request shipments of Pepto-Bismol from his mother on multiple occasions. Shortly before leaving China after the war was over, he was diagnosed with amebic dysentery and required to spend several days in the hospital to treat the disease. The weather offered extremes at both ends—the winters were so cold that Phil's unit resorted to sleeping eight in the same bed and burning their wooden furniture in order to stay warm. On the other hand, the temperature soared to 108 degrees Fahrenheit on April 12, 1944, and many other days were extremely hot. The rugged terrain required travel on horseback or by foot, and Phil's assignments involved frequent travel.

Phil served in China from early October 1943 until mid-September 1945. During his stay, American ground troops significantly increased, although the numbers were very small compared to U.S. ground-troop presence in other theaters. As of December 31, 1942 (10 months before Phil arrived), there were only 96 ground forces in China.[11] By August 15, 1945, that number had grown to 22,151.[12]

Phil's World War II experience, like all those who served during that most horrible conflict in human history, was both common to many and unique to him. This narrative attempts to explore that experience, primarily on the personal level.

CHAPTER 1

Commissioned Officer and College Man

Every student brings something to the campus. The sum total of these contributions leaves its imprint upon the University. The ideas and ideals of each of you are brought together in this institution. Here you test and weigh them. As a result, some are strengthened, others redirected, and still others are discarded. In other words, the experiences of four years in the University do change your outlook and philosophy of life.

* * *

Society is looking for men and women with ideas and ideals. The world needs leaders and followers with courage, faith, intelligent optimism, and a high sense of justice.

I sincerely trust that your experiences at the University will enable you to take your place of responsibility during the war and in the reconstruction. I wish you Godspeed.

I. D. Weeks

Phil graduated from Milbank High School in 1938. That fall, he enrolled at the University of South Dakota in Vermillion. At that time, 828 students attended the University. He majored in the pre-law program and was required to take the Reserve Officers' Training Corps (ROTC) Basic Course. This course, which lasted two years, consisted of two drill periods and one class period each week.

Showing himself to be "potential officer material," Phil was accepted into the ROTC Advanced Course his junior year. As an advanced student, he attended three classes, and two drill periods, per week. He received three hours of college credit each semester for the course, and the U.S. Government paid him approximately $7.00 per month.[1]

Lieutenant Colonel Joseph Church, professor of military science and tactics, headed the ROTC program. He was assisted by two officers—Major Ralph M. Wade and Major Frank E. Sims. Both were University graduates who joined the staff in 1940, and both served as assistant professors of military science. Staff Sergeant Albert Dixon and Sergeant James Throckmorton were also part of the University's ROTC department.[2]

The ROTC program included an annual inspection by visiting officers. This was a two-day affair, and it featured both classroom and drill inspections. During Phil's senior year, a "sham battle" was also conducted during the inspection. It attempted to employ new combat principles, included simulated use of rifles, mortars, and machine guns, and was conducted "in the most realistic fashion possible."[3]

On May 24, 1942, Phil and 24 other University seniors were commissioned as second lieutenants in the U.S. Army. Most of these newly-minted officers (including Phil) went into the Infantry, although a few transferred to the Air Corps and one into the Signal Corps.[4]

Apart from his participation in the ROTC program, Phil was involved in several activities during his last year at the University. He was elected President of the Student Senate—the University's 12-member student governing body. Under Phil's leadership, the senate worked with the school's administration to secure more tennis courts, obtain a scoreboard for the football stadium, and implement other minor improvements based on suggestions made in a student "gripe box." Sounding a lot like the politician he would later become, Phil noted that "we could never have accomplished the splendid results we did, had it not been for the combined efforts of students and administration."[5]

Phil also served as president of his social fraternity—Sigma Alpha Epsilon—during his second semester. He was one of two members selected by that organization to represent it on the Inter-Fraternity Council, which acted as "a link between administration and the fraternities."[6]

From an early age, Phil developed an aptitude and appreciation for entertaining a crowd. His membership in Strollers provided an outlet for this interest during college. The 1942 school yearbook described this group as follows: "Organizers of the annual . . . [vaudeville] show at the University, STROLLERS each spring emerge from their comparative obscurity to direct the show, give the patrons, some one thousand strong, a consistent good evening's entertainment, award prizes, lay plans for the coming year's show, pledge new members, [and then] dissolve completely." The yearbook also stated "Strollers are elected to membership on the basis of dramatic, musical, directing and journalistic ability."[7]

Phil's account of past Strollers performances included an "old Swede act Joe Foss and myself put on each year." His critique of this act: "It was terrible but it seemed to get results." He also recalled another performance that he described as "the highlight of the whole works." Details of this skit are sketchy, but it involved "an old broken down white horse in the middle of the stage" that "at the most opportune time. . . developed an excessive looseness of the bowels."[8]

The annual Strollers show for 1942 featured seven individual acts and two in-between-acts features that reportedly "brought down the house." Sigma Alpha Epsilon's act— "Pop's A Hellin" (a spoof on Strollers productions)—tied for first place with the Alpha Tau Omega fraternity's rendition titled "Nothing is On the Air" (a radio-television program). Such a result had never happened before in Strollers show history, and the two winners therefore had to split the $65.00 prize money.[9]

In addition to these activities, Phil was a member of the Law Association and the Political Science League. Based on his college record, he was named in *Who's Who in American Colleges and*

Universities. He was also honored as one of six Outstanding Seniors featured in the yearbook's *University Celebrities* section. The text accompanying his photograph stated:

> **PHIL SAUNDERS,** successful, conscientious student president, worked hard with the student senate "towards student betterment," sharpened campus interest in the potentialities of student self-government. Soft-spoken, but determined, Saunders merits the praise-word, "outstanding," applied to his work. By no means a one-field man, law-destined Saunders found time to work as a Stroller and serve as president of his fraternity.[10]

Phil left the University with many friends and fond memories. He would stay in touch with several University faculty members—and one student in particular—during the war.

CHAPTER 2

Stateside Duty

Gentlemen, here they come, the queen of battles, the infantrymen, the old foot sloggers. Twenty-five years ago at West Point, an old tactical professor used to say to us: "Never overlook the doughboy. A thousand years ago it was the foot soldiers who won and held territory and it will be the same a thousand years from now...." Look at 'em, the doughboys, God bless 'em.

George S. Patton, Jr.

After receiving his commission, Phil returned to Milbank to visit his mother and several friends. He stayed for one week. On May 31, he left for Omaha, Nebraska, to take a required physical. The next day, he passed the physical and officially entered "extended active duty" in the U.S. Army.[1]

During June 1942, Phil obtained a uniform and other equipment, began a series of tetanus shots, took an Army-required written test, filled out numerous forms, and made his way to Fort Benning, Georgia. This post, home of the U.S. Army's Infantry School, is located about three miles southeast of Columbus, Georgia, near the Georgia/Alabama border. It was named after Brigadier General Henry L. Benning, a Confederate army general who fought in the Civil War. The post was established as Camp Benning in 1918 and renamed Fort Benning in 1922. It is one of the Army's largest. During World War II, it included 197,159 acres. Almost all of this land is in Georgia, although a small portion extends into Alabama.[2]

Phil was sent to Fort Benning to take a basic infantry officers' course. The purpose of this training "was to give as much technical and tactical knowledge and skill as possible in a brief course [.]"[3]

After his arrival, he took a few days to become familiar with the post, meet his future classmates, and complete additional paperwork. He and approximately 200 other junior officers were eventually assigned to the Rifle and Heavy Weapons Company Officers' Course No. 42.[4]

The course began on Wednesday, July 8 and lasted 13 weeks.[5] It covered a variety of topics in a very concentrated, hands-on manner, focusing primarily on "weapons, materiel, small-unit tactics, and methods on instruction, administration, and leadership."[6] Most of these subjects were taught under the "block system," whereby

> each major subject occupied the student's entire time until it was completed, in contrast to the usual civilian practice of scheduling several subjects concurrently. In operation, all instruction given by a Weapons Department, for example, might be concentrated into a 6-week period, followed by a 3-week interval containing all training offered by a Tactics Department. Within the block of time allotted to the Weapons Department, shorter blocks were scheduled for each weapon. At the end of each block an examination tested the student's command of the subject covered. There his responsibility for the material ended, as did also his opportunity to practice it, except incidentally as the subject figured in subsequent phases of the course.[7]

The basic course also contained miscellaneous "minor" topics that had no relationship to each other. These subjects included "first aid, discipline, training management, administration, military law, and censorship."[8]

Major and minor subjects were presented by conferences, demonstrations, paper problems, and practical work. Officially, no "lectures" were given because "they were regarded as largely a waste of time, producing no sure results and deferring or curtailing really beneficial practical work" and "no amount of listening to lectures on how to fire a rifle would enable a man to fire it skillfully."[9] But in practice lectures (sometimes disguised as conferences) were frequently utilized because they could cover much more material in a short amount of time.[10]

The passage below provided an example of the common approach to instruction employed in Phil's basic course:

> The lectures were kept as brief as possible, although 2-or even 3-hour lectures were not uncommon in the larger schools, where one instructor had to do the work of ten. Whenever possible they were preceded and followed by demonstrations and sessions of practical work. In a typical arrangement for teaching marksmanship, the class would be assembled to hear a 10-minute talk on the prone position, during which the position would be demonstrated fully; then the class would practice for twenty minutes. This would be followed by a lecture and a demonstration of the kneeling position, after which the class would practice it. Rapid alternation of short periods of different types of instruction provided variety, sustained interest, and enabled students to put knowledge to use before it had been forgotten or submerged.[11]

After he had completed his first two weeks in the course, Phil wrote a letter to the *Grant County Review* (one of Milbank's two local newspapers) that described life at Fort Benning:

> As you know, this is the big infantry school, and it really is big too. They do a wonderful job down here, however, in teaching this war business. If a person doesn't know his stuff when he gets out of here there isn't much hope for him.
>
> I don't believe people on the whole realize what a terrific job it is to build a modern army. Seems like there is a million

and one things to be done before we can ever start operating. The spirit and morale of the men is wonderful—no complaints about anything and there are a good many things that are not so easy to take. Weather is awful hot and dry.

I hear we have a rather good crop up home. I sincerely hope so. All they seem to raise around here is trees, and of course armies. I am sure it won't be long now before our armed forces will be producing some results.[12]

Phil received specific instruction on all the basic weapons assigned to a Rifle Company and a Heavy Weapons Company. Both companies utilized individual and crew-served weapons. The Rifle Company's individual weapons included the M1 rifle (the unit's principal weapon), M1903 rifle (used to fire an antitank rifle grenade), bayonet, carbine, pistol, hand grenade, and antitank rifle grenade. This company's crew-served weapons were the light machine gun, 60-mm mortar, and automatic rifle. Like the Rifle Company, a Heavy Weapons Company's assigned individual weapons included the pistol, carbine, hand grenade, M 1903 rifle, and antitank rifle grenade. The Browning automatic rifle was an additional individual weapon for this unit. Its crew-served weapons were the heavy machine gun and the 81-mm mortar.[13]

After weapons instructions were completed, the course moved to tactics employed in both offensive and defensive combat. Lectures, demonstrations, and simulated exercises were used to teach these subjects. For offensive combat, Phil and his classmates were given lessons in approach march; reconnaissance and orders prior to attack; day and night attack; raids; attack in woods; and attack of towns, villages, river lines, and fortified localities. Lessons in defensive combat included general defense conduct; retrograde movements; defense in woods, towns and villages; defense of river lines; and defense against airborne operations. In the field-exercises portion of this instruction, the students took on all roles from private to commander, and such roles were rotated from one exercise to another.[14]

In addition to the training described above, the students themselves conducted daily drills and physical exercise. A small group of men in the class were selected, two or three days in advance, to prepare instructions from designated sections of Army Field Manuals on Infantry Drill Regulations or Physical Training. Each man was put in charge of the class (or a portion of it) for ten to fifteen minutes. During that time, he typically explained the drill or exercise, demonstrated it, had the group perform it, and then critically evaluated the performance.[15]

Phil graduated from the basic course on October 3, 1942. After doing so, he immediately reported to his next assignment at Camp Wheeler, Georgia. This facility was located in central Georgia about five miles southeast of Macon. Like Fort Benning, it was named after a confederate Civil War soldier—Lieutenant General Joseph Wheeler.[16]

The post was situated on 14,394 acres. It had also served as an army training camp during World War I and was closed after that war ended. The camp reopened in 1940. In March 1941, it was designated as one of four Army Infantry Replacement Training Centers in the United States.[17] As of late 1942, the principal function of these centers was

> the provision of loss replacements to established units in the United States and active theaters of operations. Loss replacements . . . were those provided to fill vacancies in units caused by transfer, discharge, hospitalization, or death.

* * *

> As mobilization approached completion and as the intensity of combat increased. . . [,] the greatest need was for combat loss replacements in active theaters of operation, rather than for replacements to fill and maintain at full strength units in training in the United States.[18]

Phil was assigned as a Platoon Leader/Trainer when he arrived at Camp Wheeler. There were roughly 60 enlisted trainees in his platoon, which was one of four platoons comprising his rifle training company. Four training companies were organized into a training battalion, and there were 17 such battalions activated and staffed at the post. Each rifle company was allotted six officers and thirty enlisted men called a cadre. All of the officers, and 18 of the enlisted men, served as instructors. This meant that the ratio of trainers to trainees was one to ten.[19]

Moving up the organizational chart, four battalions made up a training regiment. It is believed that the "extra battalion" at Camp Wheeler was either attached to one of the four regiments or functioned outside the regimental umbrella. Brigadier General Ambrose Robert Emery was the post commander.[20]

The training cycle lasted 13 weeks. During Phil's first cycle, which officially began on October 3 and ended on December 31, 1942, he acted as an assistant instructor and was directly supervised by a more experienced officer. Eight weeks into the cycle, he became Executive Officer for his training company, and one week later he was officially promoted to first lieutenant. In addition to conducting training sessions in the day, Phil frequently attended Cadre School at night. Here he was given additional instruction and review in the technical and tactical subjects to be taught later in the cycle. He also engaged in "trial teaching" before other instructors and their superior officers.[21]

The 13-week training cycle was further divided into three distinct phases, with each phase lasting about a month. During the first phase, the training focused on basic subjects. These included orientation; military courtesy, discipline, and articles of war; military sanitation, first aid, and sex hygiene; map reading; care of clothing and equipment; packs and tent pitching; individual tactics of the soldier; drill; inspections; and physical training. These fundamental subjects were primarily taught by lectures, practical demonstrations, and films.[22]

The trainee's most important piece of equipment was colorfully described in a booklet about Camp Wheeler's Infantry Replacement Training Center:

> The basic weapon of the Infantryman is his M-1 rifle. Immediately after he arrives at the IRTC for training he is issued one—it is his baby from then on. He cleans it, cares for it, carries it wherever he goes, and even sleeps with it. With just that rifle he is the most potent fighter the world has ever known. He is, as Ernie Pyle once said, "the guy wars can't be won without."
>
> The M-1 rifle is to the Doughboy what the lamb was to Mary. The two are inseparable[.][23]

The booklet also noted that "long before the trainee takes his M-1 rifle on the firing range he must be thoroughly familiar with its operation, and be able to disassemble and assemble it in the dark."[24]

During the second part of the cycle, the training shifted to technical subjects and became more diverse. The trainees took their M-1s to the firing range and learned how to shoot them from the prone, kneeling, sitting, and standing positions. Having studied the mechanics of other weapons (e.g. light machine gun, carbine, automatic rifle, and 60-mm mortar) during the cycle's first phase, the trainees now learned how to fire and maintain them. They were run through the camp's Waterbury obstacle course—reputed to be "one of the toughest in the world." They also received instruction in tossing hand grenades, in constructing hasty field fortifications and employing camouflage, and in defending against a chemical attack. Principles of parry and thrust were taught on the bayonet assault course.[25]

In the final phase of the cycle, the training concentrated more on tactical subjects, and the activities shifted into ranges and fields. The men were marched to the post's bivouac areas, pitched their pup tents, and conducted several "exercises" (also called "problems") over multiple days. This training emphasized small unit tactics in attack and defense.[26] Trainees were also required to negotiate the quick-firing reaction and the blitz courses. "The quick-firing reaction course consisted of lanes containing surprise targets which were engaged by the trainees, but it did not involve the negotiation of obstacles. The blitz course had no targets and required no firing by the trainee, but contained obstacles, explosives, and, during certain stages, overhead fire."[27]

Phil's first training cycle officially ended on December 31, 1942, although he was not at Camp Wheeler when that occurred. Having now been in the Army for six months, he was given a furlough in mid-December. During that break, he spent the Christmas holidays with his mother and sister Leola, who were living in the Admiral Hotel in Minneapolis at the time.[28]

In late December, Phil returned to Camp Wheeler to participate in another training cycle. It began on January 19, 1943, and he was assigned as Company Commander for his training company. This cycle occurred amid recent criticism that replacement training was not providing soldiers who were ready for combat.

The North African campaign, launched in November 1942, required many combat replacements. In early 1943, several high-level Army officers involved in that campaign complained that the replacements they received were "not satisfactory" for a number of reasons.[29] In partial response to those complaints, revisions were made to the infantry replacement training program at Camp Wheeler (and at the other three Infantry Replacement Training Centers). These changes were designed to make the training more realistic and relevant to soldiers who would be sent directly into combat after their training was completed. Thus in February 1943, three special battle courses—often referred to as "battle inoculation" courses—were introduced to the training regimen. These courses—named the close combat course, the village fighting course, and the infiltration course—"were introduced to prepare the trainee psychologically for experience with live ammunition and to accustom him to use his weapon under conditions more realistic than those on the range." And they "were conducted in carefully prepared and highly organized training areas, each designed to introduce the trainees to some phase of the sound and fury of actual combat."[30]

The close combat course evolved out of the quick-firing reaction and blitz courses described above. It contained elements from each of these courses, and its purpose "was to teach men to fire small arms with speed and accuracy at surprise targets while negotiating a broken terrain."[31] The surprise pop-up targets appeared without notice, and the trainee was required to quickly shoot them before moving on.

The village fighting course had three purposes:

> first, to train the individual soldier to work efficiently and to fire accurately at fleeting targets amid the noise and confusion of battle; second, to train the individual soldier in the proper techniques of street fighting, entering and clearing houses, jumping from roofs and scaling walls, and avoiding booby traps; and, third, to train the individual soldier to operate as a member of a team in the tactics of a small unit in clearing a village.[32]

Camp Wheeler's "village" was a replica of a German small town, with a main street, houses, and two-story buildings.[33]

One of the last courses taken in the revised training cycle was the infiltration course. This course "did not lend itself readily to realistic tactical training or a tactical situation." Its purpose "was primarily to accustom men to overhead fire and to the noise and effect of near-by explosions. Stress was laid on the proper techniques of moving forward under fire and negotiating barbed-wire entanglements."[34] Negotiating the infiltration course was described in the Camp Wheeler booklet in dramatic terms:

You come out of the dugout, hugging the earth with a passion.

B-O-O-M!

You stop dead. Immediately in front of you is a crater and you're being showered with sand. It gets in your mouth, your eyes. You pull your rifle closer to you. Gotta keep it clean. If it isn't in condition to fire when you finish the course, the lieutenant may make you run the course again.

The machinegun bullets are just a deafening discordant series of tones—like somebody pounding one piano key endlessly. You make your way further, through barbed-wire entanglements, over logs, down ditches, shrugging along, pulling your body with you. You swear actual combat could never be like this.

Slowly you realize you are being conditioned to combat—for the first time you are actually under fire. You look around at your buddies. You grin at them, and it's reflected in their faces.

Then you go on some more—for 75 yards. Only it seems like that many miles—just pulling your body along towards what looks like all of the Sahara Desert ahead, dotted with thorny ribbons of torture.

Then finally you're at the end. You grope around, eyeing the torn fatigue jackets of your buddies. Then the lieutenant calls you together.

"All right, men," he says grinning. "That wasn't so tough, was it?"[35]

On March 4, 1943, Phil received his designated military occupation specialty (MOS) as a Unit Training Officer. This specialty was described as follows: "In an Infantry Training Center in the United States, responsible for administration and tactical training of a company of Replacement trainees." Starting the next day and for the remainder of this training cycle, he returned to serving as his company's Executive Officer.[36]

Other significant developments occurred in March 1943. The training program was modified again. At the end of the cycle, all trainees were now required to take three days of field training that "included a 20-mile march, squad and platoon exercises, and enforcement of ration and water discipline."[37] Sometime after March 5, Brigadier General Reginald William Buzzell replaced Brigadier General Emery as commanding officer at the post.[38]

Phil took an active role in training his men. That role apparently led to his involvement in an accident in March. Although the article did not explain how it happened, the *Grant County Review*'s March 18, 1943 edition noted that "Lieut. Phil Saunders . . . recently had the misfortune to sustain a fractured leg and some fractured ribs. At latest reports he was getting around on crutches."[39] No information was located that told how or for how long this injury affected Phil's ability to perform his duties. But his officer qualifications card indicated he continued as a trainer for the rest of the second cycle.[40]

Phil's third and final training cycle at Camp Wheeler began on April 13 and ended on August 10, 1943. He served as a Company Commander for this entire period.[41] On June 5, Major General Albert E. Brown assumed command of the post's Replacement Training Center.[42] Shortly thereafter, the training cycle was extended from 13 to 14 weeks. In this new cycle, the field training was increased to ten days.[43]

On June 22, Phil was promoted to captain. The *Grant County Review* noted this fact and indicated he had fully recovered from his injuries sustained in the spring.[44] And because he had now served in the Army for over a year within the continental United States, he was also awarded the American Theater Ribbon.[45]

Due to its permanence, Camp Wheeler developed training areas that were highly efficient and realistic. One example was the Camouflage Demonstration Area located in Woods "E" at the Camp. As of June 1943, the area seated 280 men, so it could accommodate an entire training company at one time. It had eight separate installations that displayed various uses of the "flat top" and other methods of camouflage. The flat top was "a garnished net, either rope or chicken wire, stretched tightly over an installation or weapon parallel to the ground, and not over six feet from the ground," and was "perhaps the most common method of camouflaging objects from aerial observation." Installation No. 1 displayed a flat top over a machine gun position with the net constructed too high. Installation No. 2 featured a quick opening embrasure (small slit through which gun can be fired) that would allow a machine gun's use in anti-aircraft fire. In Installation No. 3, the flat top was folded back to allow sufficient clearance for mortar fire. Installation No. 4 demonstrated a spider hole "set up" on an 81 mm mortar. In Installation No. 5, a 37 mm anti-tank gun was covered by a flat top. Installation No. 6 had a drape propped away from a vehicle. Installation No. 7 had a flat top camouflaging an ammunition dump. And finally, Installation No. 8 showed how natural camouflage could protect a command post from air observation.[46]

An additional change to the training program was made in June. Overhead artillery fire was added as another battle course. A field artillery battery was stationed at Camp Wheeler to expose the trainees to this fire. The purposes of this course were "to demonstrate what a concentration of artillery fire actually was, to build confidence in trainees in their own artillery, and to convince them that artillery fire not be feared."[47]

Phil was quite satisfied with his 10-month assignment at Camp Wheeler and believed he gained valuable experience by teaching the trainees how to become combat soldiers. When his last cycle ended, he was eager to go overseas and put his Fort Benning training and Camp Wheeler instruction experience to the test.

CHAPTER 3

From Milbank to Kunming

If you think riding an airplane is pleasure you are mistaken.

Phil Saunders

When Phil finished the third training cycle at Camp Wheeler, he was granted another furlough before being sent overseas. He drove to Milbank in mid-August. There he spent a few days visiting his mother, his sister Leola (who worked for International Harvester Company in St. Paul, Minnesota, and came to Milbank soon after Phil arrived), and long-time family friends. He left Milbank on August 22 and made a brief stop in Minneapolis before flying to Miami, Florida.[1] While in Florida, he enjoyed the deep-sea fishing trip and dance mentioned above. He also filled out forms related to his overseas assignment, attended briefings on the war situation in the China-Burma-India theater, and was given vaccine shots for cholera, yellow fever, and typhus.[2] On September 10—his twenty-third birthday—Phil began the long journey to China.[3]

His first stop was at a U.S. Army air base in Brazil. He found it to be a "rather nice" post. On a warm September night, he saw Charlie Chaplin in *The Gold Rush* at the post's outdoor movie theater. Phil noted that this film was "popular back in 1926." The closest town had "40,000 people and 6,000 of the women are prostitutes," making most of the town "off limits" to American soldiers. Mules pulling carts provided a common means of transportation, although "a good many American made automobiles" were also present. Phil related that "the thing I miss most of all is papers and magazines—not a damn thing to read—for God sake if peace is declared someday please write me or we never will stop this foolishness[.]" He also made the following comment concerning his ultimate destination: "Heard from different sources today that we are on some special emergency mission to the far East—but all I know for sure is that it is far[.]"[4]

Phil left Brazil in mid-September. He flew across the Atlantic Ocean and over "tiger country" in west and central Africa. After making a brief stop in Egypt, he continued east to an Army camp in northern India. Arriving there on September 20 "after three days of hell and high water," he described the air travel in less-than-glowing terms:

> What a trip. If you think riding an airplane is pleasure you are mistaken. You can't sleep, eat nor do any of the other essential things.
>
> I wish you could have seen me get off the plane this morning. I looked like the black natives sure as the devil—I'll bet they thought I was a lost relative, whiskers an inch long, and my uniform so dirty that it is still standing up.

On the positive side, Phil noted "they really treat us swell around here—can't do a damn thing without some native boy helping you."[5]

The camp he was staying in was built

> by the English about 30 years ago. The buildings are about 100 yards apart so the damn thing is spread all over the devil—we have to walk about three miles to the mess hall even. If we don't have an appetite when we start we certainly have one when we get there. The food is getting a little bad now, but it is as good as can be expected I guess[.][6]

After being there for about a week, Phil noted that his Army commanders

> have changed our clothing order about ten times now—First they say we are going to cold climate—then two minutes later

its hot climate—then a few days later it is cold again—Our foot lockers and barracks bags won't get to us in China so it looks like if we go north we will have to buy all new winter uniforms—It beats me[.]⁷

A few days later Phil was issued his "field equipment" and started to get his legs in shape "by running a few miles this afternoon. The running, I might add, will now continue daily until we reach our final post." He bought some long underwear because he was told "it gets rather cold in China where we are going[.]"⁸

Phil also noted that "people are starving to death by the hundreds just a few hundred miles from where we are—you probably have heard about it over the radio. The natives around here seem to think nothing of seeing a few dead bodies in the street[.]"⁹ He was likely referring to the Bengal famine of 1943, where at least three million people died from starvation and malnutrition in India's Bengal province—located in the northeastern part of the country.¹⁰

In early October, Phil began the last leg of his journey. While still in India, he visited the Taj Mahal in Agra, a city in the province now known as Uttar Pradesh. This Islamic tomb was designated as one of the Seven Wonders of the World. Shah Jahan had it built from 1631 to 1653 and dedicated it to his third wife Mumtaz Mahal. The monument was constructed entirely out of white marble brought from several locations in India and Central Asia. Many different varieties of precious and semi-precious stones were used to create spectacular inlay work on the walls and ceilings.¹¹ Phil described the jewel and gold inlays as "most beautiful."¹²

He also visited an American field hospital before leaving the country. While there, he "talked with one boy who was rather badly mashed up ... He was from Cody, Wyoming and has a big café out there—I told him we had been through there in '38 and so we had quite a discussion about Yellowstone & things in general[.]"¹³

Phil's last night in India proved to be memorable:

> I wish you could have seen where we stayed last night—ye Gads—It was some old broken down hut in the middle of the desert . . . rats started to run around—and then about 11 o'clock an old cow came walking through—at 2 this morning a little old train came puffing by and set the straw roof afire, but the natives were not a bit alarmed as it happens every time the train goes by—We got to laughing so hard I can still feel it[.][14]

The trip from India to southern China required flying over "the Hump"—nicknamed for the 15,000 foot-high Himalayan mountain chain. It has been described as a "villainous and forbidding . . . stretch of terrain" and "probably the most hazardous flight route in the world."[15] Phil's flight passed "right over a Jap air field," but his plane was not attacked.[16]

He finally arrived in Kunming, China on October 6—25 days after he left Florida. Kunming is the largest city in the Yunnan province. It served as the provincial capital during World War II. The Yunnan province is located in southern China and borders on Burma and the former French Indochina.[17] Kunming is also the starting point for the Burma Road—a nine-foot wide, 715 mile, single-lane highway that connects Kunming to Lashio, Burma.[18] Phil described the Kunming area as being "very beautiful . . . with big mountains on all sides."[19]

Prior to Phil's arrival, the U.S. Army had established various headquarters in Kunming. The Army's Services of Supply (SOS)—originally set up in India in 1942 to "take necessary action required to push equipment and supplies through to General Stilwell and to assume all supply and administrative functions in India necessary to successful functioning of his command"— had its China headquarters here.[20] In addition, the American Y-Force Operations Staff Headquarters—discussed in detail in Chapter 4—was located in Kunming. Finally, the Fourteenth Air Force, created by presidential order in March 1943, was also headquartered here.[21]

By the time Phil got to China, its wartime-government capital had been moved to Chungking. This mountain city is located at the confluence of the Yangtze River and its main tributary (the Kialing River). It is in the Szechwan province and is about 390 miles northeast of Kunming. Generalissimo Chiang Kai-shek's headquarters were here. So were General Stilwell's—under the name "Headquarters, American Army Forces, China, Burma and India."[22]

Now that he was stationed overseas, Phil was subject to the U.S. military's censorship rules. These were set forth in War Department Pamphlet No. 21-1 dated July 29, 1943. This pamphlet was titled **"When You Are Overseas—These Facts Are Vital."** Its introductory section stated that

> CENSORSHIP RULES ARE SIMPLE, SENSIBLE. – They are merely concise statements drawn from actual experience briefly outlining the types of material which have proven to be disastrous when available to the enemy. A soldier should not hesitate to impose his own additional rules when he [is] considering writing of a subject not covered by present regulations. He also should guard against repeating rumors or misstatements.

It then lists the following *"**ten prohibited subjects**"*

1. Don't write military information of Army units – their location, strength, materiel, or equipment.

2. Don't write of military installations.

3. Don't write of transportation facilities.

4. Don't write of convoys, their routes, ports (including ports of embarkation and disembarkation), time en route, naval protection, or war incidents occurring en route.

5. Don't disclose movements of ships, naval or merchant, troops, or aircraft.

6. Don't mention plans and forecasts or orders for future operations, whether known or just your guess.

7. Don't write about the effect of enemy operations.

8. Don't tell of any casualty until released by proper authority (The Adjutant General) and then only by using the full name of the casualty.

9. Don't attempt to formulate or use a code system, cipher, or shorthand, or any other means to conceal the true meaning of your letter. Violations of this regulation will result in severe punishment.

10. Don't give your location in any way except as authorized by proper authority. Be sure nothing you write about discloses a more specific location than the one authorized.

The pamphlet went on to explain the proper way to address letters, the requirements for a return address, and how the letter is to be mailed. It then discussed related subjects (e.g. V-mail, cables, and radiograms) before addressing the last two subjects—***Talk*** and **Capture**. With respect to ***Talk***, the pamphlet stated in part that "SILENCE MEANS SECURITY. – If violation of protective measures is serious within written communications it is disastrous in conversations. Protect your conversation as you do your letters, and be even more careful. A harmful letter can be nullified by censorship; loose talk is direct delivery to the enemy." Regarding **Capture**, the following guidance was provided:

> Most enemy intelligence comes from prisoners. If captured, you are required to give only three facts: YOUR NAME, YOUR GRADE, YOUR ARMY SERIAL NUMBER. Don't talk, don't try to fake stories, and use every effort to destroy all papers. When you are going into an area where capture is possible carry only essential papers and plan to destroy them

prior to capture if possible. Do not carry personal letters on your person; they tell much about you, and the envelope has on it your unit and organization.

The pamphlet ended with this simple directive: "**Be sensible; use your head**."[23]

Phil's first letter to home after he got to China gave initial impressions on several subjects and described early experiences in this most foreign land:

> At the present time we are fairly well inside the Chinese border. We have had no contact with the Japs as yet, but it won't be long now. These Chinese do not have a great deal of equipment or arm[aments], but individually speaking they are good soldiers—The biggest difficulty is the fighting between the various war lords against the government itself—you really would be surprised if you knew the inside story of this mess over here. We have to guard our supplies very closely or they will steal it and run like hell.
>
> I thought India was dirty, but ye gads you should see how the people live here. This afternoon I actually saw two pigs in a Chinese kitchen—and by God they were alive and residing there. The cities are even worse—millions & millions of poor, dirty, people everywhere you look—and most of them live in the gutters which are a hell of a lot cleaner than their houses—but regardless of how poor and dirty they are most of them are very happy and have a wonderful sense of humor. They think Americans are O.K. and we are treated with all the respect in the world—when we go down the street you would think a circus was coming, as they will follow you by the hundreds.

I have learned to eat with chop sticks and they are really quite the thing. We get Army food so far—and damn good eggs.

I have been on the Burma Road a number of times—and it looks just like it is pictured in the movies; and you should see how these Chinese drive—just like old man Lockhart—They don't give a damn for anything—and you [go] down the hills full speed and around hair pin curves even faster—From now on I am doing my own driving [.]

It is rather cold at night where we are at the present time—but I have 4 big blankets and have winter clothes also. One would really be surprised what you can get use[d] to[.]

In our spare time we have been trying to learn the Chinese language—It is rather simple and they say in 2 or 3 months you can speak it fairly well.

* * *

I suppose by now it is almost winter in the States—If I ever get home again and hear anyone complain about anything I will hit them over the head with the nearest chair—you just have no idea how lucky you are.[24]

After spending about a week in Kunming, Phil was ordered to leave the city and undertake his first assignment in a remote area of the Yunnan province.

CHAPTER 4

Joining Traveling Instructional Group No. 4

It should be borne in mind that in addition to training, all U.S. Army personnel have a diplomatic function—namely to convince Chinese troops and officers of the value of our type of training, and to win over their goodwill. Often this is not easy, because of the newness and strangeness of the whole project to the average Chinese, and because of the difference in racial characteristics. As a rule Chinese are receptive and well-disposed toward Americans, as they know we have no ulterior motives and no desire to acquire unfair advantages or any form of aggrandizement in China.

* * *

Since we will for several years be working with the Chinese Army, hardships and discomforts should be shared and understood; thus building up bonds of personal as well as official friendship.

Memorandum to all Chiefs of Instructional Groups from Colonel Frank Dorn

The Y-Force (also known as the Yoke Force) consisted of Chinese troops in Yunnan province. Under the so-called 30-division plan, drawn up in 1942, Americans were to train and equip these soldiers for combat against the Japanese. The troops to be included in this plan were "those of the Chinese Expeditionary

Force, stationed on the western or Salween River front, those of the Yunnan Provincial Troops stationed on the southern or French Indo-China border and around Kunming, and those troops of the National Army which were stationed in the south and around Kunming."[1]

On April 29, 1943, the American Y-Force Operations Staff (YFOS) was established at Kunming by verbal order from Lieutenant General Joseph W. Stilwell, commander of the U.S. Army Forces in the China-Burma-India theater (CBI).[2] This verbal directive was followed up with a written order in June. That order designated Colonel Frank Dorn as the YFOS Chief of Staff. Three other officers were appointed as his assistants. The order also described this unit's general mission:

> The Y-Force Operations Staff, and such other officers and enlisted men as may be attached from time to time, will work in liaison with the Chinese Staff of the Y-Force, and will be charged, under theater direction and supervision, with the training, organization and equipment of the Y-Force, as well as establishing priorities for Y-Force supplies to be . . . [brought] in by air. The Staff will supervise the Infantry and Field Artillery Training Centers at that station, co-ordinate their activities, conduct their relations with the Y-Force, and transmit to the Forward Echelon Headquarters for action any requisitions for personnel and supplies, and any matters that have to be referred to the Chinese Government or to U.S. agencies on any matters that cannot be settled on the spot. It will also formulate plans for supply and operations, and assist the Chinese Staff of the Y-Force in every way possible.[3]

It soon became apparent that instruction at the Infantry and Field Artillery Training Centers (located near Kunming) could not meet all the training requirements. Accordingly, by the end of June, a joint Chinese/American plan proposed having Army schools in the Y-Force. In mid-1943, there were four Chinese Group Armies stationed in

Yunnan. They were designated by the Roman numerals V, IX, XI, and XX. Each Group Army had its own commanding general. The planned Army schools

> were to be supervised by a joint Chinese and American committee, with sub-committees assigned to each Group Army to supervise training, to inspect and enforce training regulations and orders, and to examine the results of training and recommend improvements. These sub-committees were set up as Traveling Instructional Groups, staffed by Chinese and American officers and American enlisted men. Four groups were ready to begin operations early in August, 1943.[4]

Because General Chen Cheng (Commanding General of the Chinese Expeditionary Force and assigned supervisor of the training program) was absent from Yunnan in early August, the program did not start until about September 1. One month later, all four Traveling Instructional Groups (TIGs) were in the field. TIG No. 1 had been assigned to XI Group Army, TIG No. 2 to XX Group Army, TIG No. 3 to V Group Army, and TIG No. 4 to IX Group Army.[5]

As of October 1943, the Chinese command structure for training its army in Yunnan was exercised through Generalissimo Chiang Kai-shek's Field Headquarters (commanded by Governor Lun Yung), the Headquarters for the Chinese Expeditionary Force (commanded by General Chen), and the commanders of the four Group Armies.[6] On the American side, the command structure ran from the Chinese Training & Combat Command (commanded by Lieutenant General Stilwell) to YFOS headquarters (headed by Colonel Dorn), to the four Traveling Instructional Group commanders/chiefs.[7]

When Phil arrived in Kunming, he reported to the YFOS Headquarters. On October 11, he and 11 other U.S. Army officers were ordered to proceed from Kunming "to such places in Yunnan Province as may be necessary for them to carry out their orders" and "report upon arrival at destination to Col PHILIP H ENSLOW[.]"[8] Colonel Enslow was Commanding Officer/Chief of TIG No. 4 which, as noted above, was assigned to the IX Group Army. This Group Army consisted of a headquarters unit and two separate Chinese armies—the 52nd Army and the 8th Army. Both of these armies contained three divisions. The IX Group Army Headquarters was located in Wenshan, a city 150 miles southeast of Kunming and about 40 miles from the French Indochina border.[9]

On October 16, Phil and the other officers assigned to TIG No. 4 began their journey to Wenshan. They did not get very far before being ambushed. Phil described his first encounter with the enemy in a letter written a day after the incident:

> I consider myself very fortunate in being able to even draw breath after what happened yesterday—I can't tell too much what happened, but we were trying to get to our assigned unit over the Burma road when suddenly we were ambushed and all hell broke loose; but . . . I finally got my gun in action. We got 5 of the devils and wounded a few more, but we lost a gas truck and had 5 casualties in our group. All of the damage I received was a hole through my helmet which I didn't happen to have on at the time—needless to say. We had to turn around and come back because our truck was badly shot up and the damn road was blocked, but we will try again in the near future and this time we'll make it hell or high water—They caught us about as unprepared as the Navy at Pearl Harbor[.][10]

The next day was a Sunday, and Phil attended a church service at the YFOS Headquarters compound in the morning. Joseph Stilwell and Louis Mountbatten visited the compound that day. Lieutenant General Stilwell acquired the nickname "Vinegar Joe" when a subordinate drew a caricature of him arising from a vinegar bottle after Stillwell gave the subordinate a harsh performance review.[11] By the fall of 1943, the 60-year-old general held the following positions:

Commanding General of U.S. forces in the CBI theater, Deputy Supreme Allied Commander in Southeast Asia, Commanding General of the Chinese Army in India and its field commander in Burma, nominal Chief of Staff to Chiang Kai-shek for the China theater, chief of the Chinese Training and Combat Command, and Administrator of Lend-Lease to China[.][12]

He was "a slight figure, lean and bony, five-foot-nine, with short-cropped gray-black hair, a hard, lined, decisive face and a deceptive appearance of physical fragility. He was in fact as fragile as steel wire." Stilwell's motto was "*Illegitimati non carborundum*, personally translated as 'Don't let the bastards grind you down.'"[13]

Vice Admiral Lord Louis Mountbatten was the Supreme Commander of the Southeast Asia Command (SEAC) created in 1943. (SEAC was an Anglo-American command that operated in Burma, Ceylon, Sumatra, and Malaya.) Mountbatten was a cousin to King George IV and had been a successful British naval commander before undertaking this assignment. One writer described him as a "dashing, forty-three year old" who "had proved he could unite soldiers of many flags to one cause" and "loved aggressive battle plans."[14]

A few days after they were forced to return to YFOS Headquarters, Phil and his group made their second attempt to get to their post at Wenshan. This time they were successful. The journey provided several unique experiences and further insights about the Chinese:

> We had to almost build the road . . . as we went along. Came through some parts where we were about the only white men ever to venture into the stuff—We talked to a number of the Chinese people in these districts and most of them have never heard of Japs—didn't know there was a war on—and [it was] the first time they had seen a truck—They use water buffalo to plow with, etc.—I now know how people lived and worked in the Stone Age. These little villages have no communications with the outside world whatsoever.

* * *

> In going through a little town yesterday I wish you could have seen the excitement we caused. The streets were so narrow we had to almost take the buildings with us. Hundreds and hundreds of people followed our trucks—others on top of buildings and just all over everywhere—We were very pleased at our reception to say the least.
>
> We stayed at a French Hotel one night—all the rooms were filled so we slept in the dining room.... As we sat down to eat supper we had fine damn plates—They would fill one—you would eat that—they would take it away & then fill the other & etc late into the night—Really makes it interesting as you don't know what is coming next.[15]

The group encountered Japanese troops again, but this time "we had too much fire power along—so they were quite peaceful. These little devils are very poor fighters, they won't attack unless they have a 20 to 1 advantage."[16]

When Phil's outfit arrived at its destination, the quarters turned out to be quite rustic: "At the present time we are staying in some old Chinese barn. Handy as hell—We use one corner for the toilet—another for our food—the other two corners are missing as is the wall, so we have plenty of fresh air."[17]

Over the next few days, Phil was given written materials that set forth YFOS Headquarters' view on how the TIGs should approach working with Chinese officers, explained the TIG overall assignment, and described the training program in place at the time. A memorandum from YFOS Headquarters (quoted from at the beginning of this chapter) stated in part:

> All U.S. personnel must make an effort to see the Chinese point of view, which may be in complete accord with our own.

Before demonstrating our method, it is highly advisable to ask to see theirs. Then convince them, if you do not agree, that your own is the better—by demonstration and explanation. Do not in your enthusiasm to get things done, push too hard. If you do, you may force the Chinese with whom you are working, to draw back, rather than to come forward. Be ready to compromise, rather than insisting on upsetting a conviction which probably has been acquired in battle.

Do not make comparisons, unless they are favorable, between Chinese and American equipment or methods. With almost no resources the Chinese have hung on in a six-year war against an enemy which has been better prepared, better equipped, and better organized. They feel a justifiable pride in this achievement. Without intending to do so, you may offend friends and Allies. Similarly, the standard of living in the Chinese Army has been lowered by difficult war conditions. From our point of view they are poverty stricken. When you encounter this condition on visits of either an official or social nature, be careful <u>not</u> to express a feeling of pity, or any feeling that may be construed as pity. You should express praise that Chinese officers have been able to endure hardships for such a long period of time, and still maintain their determination to resist and drive out the invader. . . .

Always bear in mind that the officers with whom you are working, have had considerable experience under extremely difficult conditions. Their feelings and convictions should be considered, and wherever possible their advice accepted. We are in China to work <u>with</u> the Chinese Army; not to work <u>on</u> it.

(underlining in original).[18]

A document titled "Travelling Instructional Sub:Committees: Information for American Personnel" explained the TIG organizational structure:

* * *

b. The Travelling Instructional Group (T.I.G.) is a committee of Chinese and American officers appointed for the purpose of supervising training and recommending improvements therein. It is responsible to the Commanding General C.E.F. [Chinese Expeditionary Force].

c. The Travelling Instructional Sub-Committees work under the T.I.G. These subcommittees are composed of American and Chinese officers and are sent out to the Group Armies. Under the direction of the Group Army Commanders, they will supervise instruction, make training inspections, enforce training regulations and orders, and make recommendations for improvement of training. They will make frequent visits to the Armies assigned to the Group Army.[19]

That document also gave a general description and purpose of the training program:

* * *

(1) Training within the Armies consists of the Army Infantry Schools and unit training. The purpose of the Army Schools is to prepare officers, non-commissioned officers and key privates to be instructors for their respective units. Programs, schedules and training literature have been prepared both for the Army Infantry Schools and for unit training.

(2) At present, sub-committees have authority only to supervise the Army Infantry School training, but it is anticipated that authority will be extended to include unit training.[20]

Before Phil's group arrived in Wenshan, TIG No. 4 consisted of eleven American officers, eight American enlisted men, and at least four Chinese officers. This group was accompanied by a three-member Weapons Maintenance Team (one American officer and two American enlisted men). So Phil's group basically doubled the number of American officers assigned to either TIG No. 4 or Weapons Maintenance Team No. 4.[21]

The Army Infantry Schools—set up for members of IX Group Army—provided separate training for Chinese officers and non-commissioned officers. The Officers' Course was generally described as a "comprehensive twenty-eight day course in Infantry subjects." The course curriculum consisted of:

1. 8 days of training in the student's principal weapon with the student group divided into the following subgroups:

    Rifle

    L.M.G. [Light machine gun] and [Thompson] submachine gun,

    Heavy machine gun,

    Trench Mortars,

    Antitank rifle and rocket launcher.

2. 8 days of training in the other basic weapons (2 days in each weapon).
3. 10 days of tactical training.
4. 2 days of signal training.
5. 28 days.—Total

Each school will have three classes for [160] officers so that at the end of 84 working days 480 officers will have been graduated.[22]

The non-commissioned officers' course was shorter and more specialized:

> Classes of 160 non-commissioned officers each will take a weapons course lasting ten days. The entire ten day period will be devoted to training in the specialized weapon of the non-commissioned officer concerned. Each Army Infantry School will have eight classes for non-commissioned officers so that at the end of 80 working days 1280 non-commissioned officers will have been graduated.[23]

Phil was designated as a Liaison Officer in TIG No. 4. It appears that he supervised and inspected Army Infantry Schools (later designated as Officers Weapons Schools and NCO Weapons Schools) at the IX Group Army Headquarters in Wenshan from the time he joined TIG No. 4 until the end of 1943. During this period, he also traveled to other schools in the southern part of the Yunnan province—most likely to supervise or inspect schools for the 8th and 52nd Armies.

Phil described the condition of the Chinese troops in stark terms:

> I just wish to God you could see the pain and suffering these poor Chinese soldiers go through each day—The Japs have taken their homes—most of the units have men with legs, arms, eyes, ears and what have you amputated from battle wounds, but yet they keep right on going, smiling, fighting for their very lives . . . —If I ever complain about one damn thing again I hope someone will hit me right between the eyes.[24]

On October 26, Lieutenant General Stilwell visited the men at TIG No. 4 Headquarters. Phil and a few others got to talk with him, and Phil was quite impressed with the CBI Commanding General: "He really is a brave soldier and one hell of a good man—Everyone likes him a lot."[25]

One day later, Phil finally received several letters from the United States. It was the first mail delivered to him since he left Florida almost seven weeks earlier. The letters were from his mother and sister Leola, his once-removed cousin Hilfrid Johnson, Dr. J.A. Jacotel (long-time family friend from Milbank), Carl "Rube" Hoy (University of South Dakota's athletic director, head basketball coach, and head track coach), and Marshall McKusick (dean of the University's Law School). Through this correspondence, Phil learned that his sister Corinne was pregnant with her first child, the University had about "300 or 400 cadets" enrolled at the school, and Mrs. Jacotel had pretty much recovered from a severe headache.[26]

Phil's "free time" activities toward the end of October included haircuts, a shower, and a basketball game:

> We had a hair cutting evening last night—ye Gads you should see us today, but it's still better than having it long... We took a shower last night too—filled our wash basins up and then threw the water on one another—you would be surprised how wet you can get that way[.]

> We also played the Chinese [in] basketball the other day, but they had too many men for replacements and gradually but definitely beat us—besides I am getting just too old for that game. They really are swell sports and the crowd enjoyed the game a great deal.[27]

His group also engaged in conduct that thoroughly confused their allies:

> We got a little silly today—In fact, the Chinese think we are crazy as hell—We had long underwear on—coats, hats, overshoes and what have you when we went to bed—One thing lead to another and we ended up doing chorus steps with songs out in the middle of nowhere[.]

* * *

One of my roommates is now playing Tarzan while the other is imitating Mrs. Roosevelt—if Leola was only here to play the piano. We keep from going completely nuts this way.[28]

An American war correspondent joined the group in late October. But he was unable to objectively report his observations because "the Chinese government won't allow him to take any pictures and they censor everything he writes." Remarking on these restrictions, Phil concluded that "in a way it's a good thing no one knows the truth of this situation."[29]

During the second week in November, Phil learned one reason why he and others in his group had not received any mail since late October. Someone in New York had decided that "our addresses are not proper" because "he didn't like just getting an A.P.O. number;" and he decided to return the mail to its senders. Phil thereafter included a more detailed address to his correspondents to remedy this situation. He also wrote a letter to Chan Gurney, U.S. Senator from South Dakota, which told the senator about the slow and unreliable mail service in China.[30]

Apart from his frustration with the mail service, Phil gave these updates in a November 10 letter to his mother and sister Leola:

Things have been very quiet the last days so we have been busy eating and sleeping. Sounds good—but it isn't worth a damn. The weather is getting awful cold now, but then just think what old Washington went through at Valley Forge—and besides we have even got overshoes now … Big five buckle ones like we used to wear—remember? Also got me a G.I. stocking cap—and it is really warm[.]

* * *

> We have just about got rid of our fleas—We poured kerosene on each other—a person would be surprised how many you kill that way—soldiers of course[.]
>
> You should see how these Chinese wash our clothes—ye Gads they just beat hell out of them—We were afraid our soap would run out, but my God we haven't been able to wash[.][31]

Two days later, Phil relayed another story that demonstrated how unreliable the mail service was:

> One Lt. over here had a letter saying that his wife just got back a Xmas package she mail[ed] last Oct.—in 42—so you can see how efficient the damn system is—Lots of our mail planes have been shot down by Japs so that may be the reason we haven't received any[.][32]

In mid-November, Phil's group "received a big new Signal Corps radio, so we can now get the news once in a while—also got some hard moldy biscuits—but they even taste good to us." At this point, the TIG No. 4 members were receiving their supplies by pack horses, "so you can see what a job it is to get anything at all[.]" The group got some new neighbors: "Three nice big pigs—and they are only ten feet from our front flap." And the men undertook activities to remind them of home: "Last night a few of us got together and sang Xmas carols. It sounded like hell to the listeners, but damn good to us."[33]

Phil's closing comments in a November 15 letter indicated his interest in, and concerns about, becoming a first-time uncle:

> Any recent developments on the situation in Washington?—I mean Corinne. Old Uncle Phil will be waiting for the latest report. I certainly hope it isn't twins—ye gads that would drive her nuts wouldn't it?

* * *

I hope Corinne has a girl—I would hate like hell to have a nephew of mine go through this living hell.[34]

The first snowfall occurred on November 19. It prompted Phil to remark on the cold weather:

Tonight we can bank up our bedding walls with . . . [the snow] and keep the damn wind out—cold as the devil the last few days. In fact we go to bed with a hell of a lot more on than we wear in the day time. We laughed at old Lt. Nelson last night, he had on a wool stocking cap—gloves, & overshoes. Just like Emil[Johnson—Phil's grandfather] used to do.

* * *

I really don't see how these Chinese live in this cold weather. Most of them have no shoes, no clothes to speak of—no blankets, and not a stick of wood to build a fire. Out of one Chinese army they lost around 5000 men due to sickness—graves all over hell.[35]

The Monday before Thanksgiving provided some relief from the weather: "It got a little warmer today and it really feels swell." Phil's unit probably engaged in combat during the night on November 21: "The boys started playing dirty last night so it's our turn tonight."[36] A few days later, TIG No. 4 "moved a little bit south so the weather is a bit warmer, but still awful cold at night."[37]

Thanksgiving Day 1943 was celebrated with a not-so-traditional turkey dinner. Phil and his good friend Captain Irwin L. Nelson (whom, for unknown reasons, Phil often referred to as Mow Em Down Nelson) were the cooks. Here was Phil's description of the cooking process:

We had canned turkey for Thanksgiving. It was really good too. We only had one difficulty and that was no one knew how to cook it, so good old Uncle Phil and mow em down Nelson volunteered for the job. The oven consisted of a G.I. helmet and we used old shoes for wood. At one time in the process we laid down enough smoke to hide a whole damn division, in fact half of the meal was cooked with our gas masks on. The outstanding dish consisted of a homemade pudding. We made up two big bowls of it and at the conclusion of the meal we had two big bowls left. So the only thing it spoiled was the bowls, it ate holes right through them.[38]

Another incident occurred on Thanksgiving Day that could have come straight from Mort Walker's *Beetle Bailey* cartoon strip: "We have just got two jeeps in this part of China—In other words just two cars for hundreds of miles around—and I'll be damned if they didn't run into each other[.]"[39]

As of late November the Chinese had not been very successful in fighting the Japanese: "Don't believe any of those reports you hear about the fighting in China. We get the hell kick[ed] out of us every time we turn around, but it will be our turn someday soon—we hope."[40] A week later, Phil again alluded to contact with the enemy: "We had a big time with the little bastards the other day."[41]

In TIG No. 4's new location, the letter mail delivery had improved somewhat. But packages were another story:

> It is best not to send me anything unless I ask for it, because very seldom does any of it ever get here. Our supplies have to come by pack train (mules) some of the way, and most of the mules either run away or our little yellow friends shoot them.[42]

In early December, Phil replied to a letter he received from Phyllis Dolan. Miss Dolan was a long-time friend from Milbank. Her father owned and published the weekly *Grant County Review*, and she contributed a column titled "Ain't It Awful!" under the pseudonym "X.Y.Z." Phil's letter began by noting that "I haven't received the Review as yet, but the news in your letter will help a lot until it gets here." He then described how his group dealt with the cold weather:

> At the present time it is really cold over here. I have put on everything I can get a hold of, but it seems like I have reached the law of "Diminishing Returns," because if extra clothes keep me warmer I have yet to notice it. When we retire for the evening it is always the biggest military maneuver of the day by a long ways. And the only difference between our going to bed clothes and our day uniform is that at night we put on our heavy overshoes. Lately we have even used a community bed system, that is we pool the blankets, covers, burlap, & etc. of about eight men and then place them all together as to resemble a big bed. There are, however, a number of draw backs to this Chinese way of sleeping. In the first place everyone must face in the same direction, and if one decides to turn he must discuss it with the entire bunch so that all may have an equal chance. Another difficulty is that someone is always getting out or getting in, and usually in that process the covers, blankets, straw, & etc. fly in all directions. However, the biggest difficulty as I see it is this. As you know any army diet consists of beans—ours is no exception, and in preventing the head from freezing it is absolutely necessary to cover that part of the body with the blankets, and when these two conditions are put together and the natural reaction takes place, well—it takes about two hours of the morning's fresh air to come out of it. We can't complain too much, however, as the poor Chinese soldiers have only one blanket for about every 5 men.

And Phil made this comment about the food:

Food, of course, is another one of our chief concerns. I hardly suggest that no one attempt to serve rice to anyone coming back from China. One Lt. from Michigan puts it this way—"If my wife ever mentions rice to me as a breakfast dish—the afternoon headlines will read—(Maniac Slays Mate)." I am sure that statement expresses our sentiments on the food situation.[43]

As previously mentioned, Phil sent a letter to Senator Gurney that complained about the slow mail service. This complaint was independently confirmed when the letter took over five weeks to reach its recipient. In his reply, the senator acknowledged that "it does take a long time for your mail to come this way, and I am at a loss to understand it[.]" He then added:

> Your letter has given me a chance to talk personally with the Secretary of War on the matter of mail for our forces in faraway places, and especially in China, and I have insisted that they take all necessary steps so that you fellows will be better taken care of in the future.

Senator Gurney also offered these words of encouragement:

> Certainly you are doing a good job over there, and I am thinking that more equipment and facilities of all types will be coming to you during the winter months, so that 1944 will go a long ways toward whipping the Jap rats.
>
> People in South Dakota are working hard, have had big crops, and are getting good prices, and you can be assured the one thing they want "mostest", as Amos and Andy would say, is for this war to come to a victorious conclusion, so that our boys can come home.[44]

In mid-December, some Chinese generals gave a "little banquet" for Phil's group. During that event, the Americans "were given commissions in the Chinese Army—along with the Chinese service bar[.]" Phil enjoyed the food and the unique way it was presented:

> The food was really good—They just sit it in the middle of the table and everyone dives in with chop sticks flying all over hell. No one has a plate so when you finish your place of activity looks like Grand Central Station—Along with the food they also serve ching ba juice—which you must drink along with the Chinese officers—and the only difference between it and American varnish is that it is white in color—I always managed, however, to spill about 90% of it so I came out after 15 rounds in very good condition—However, some of the other boys didn't come out of it for about 3 days afterwards—This dinner fortunately was a short one—some of them they tell me last for 12 to 14 hours—believe it or not—(No wonder the Japs are beating the hell out of them.)

After dinner all the Americans "had to give speeches," and, according to Phil, "the food was much better than the speeches."[45]

A day or so after the banquet, Phil's unit once again moved to a new location:

> I just finished driving an old broken down Dodge truck about 150 miles, and most of it through the mountains—It took me 3 days and I was lucky at that. Mow em down Nelson had to hang on the fender all the way and pour gas in the carburetor as the line was filled with dust. At the end of the trip we had to pour mow em down Nelson in bed as <u>he</u> was filled with dust.

(underlining in original).[46]

Joining Traveling Instructional Group No. 4

During this same time period, Phil and other members of TIG No. 4 received a memorandum from YFOS Headquarters that contained observations made "during the present Burma offensive now being conducted by American-trained Chinese units." The memo began by making positive comments about the Chinese performance:

1. Elements of this Army have been in continuous contact with the enemy since November 1, 1943. Our troops have shown that they can and do stand toe to toe with the Japanese and are their superiors in ability to sustain hardship.

    a. Our supply system has proven superior to theirs. We have unmistakable evidence that the Japanese in November were forced to live on bananas, jungle roots, and food stolen from natives, whereas our troops have never been without food or ammunition.

    b. Our air force has destroyed enemy supply installations and caused great casualties. Not even one enemy plane has attacked our forces.

It then admitted "that the enemy has out-maneuvered and out-witted us in the jungle. Many of our men have died bravely, but not intelligently, and hence we have not extracted from the enemy the maximum casualties. We learn by mistakes. <u>We must not repeat them.</u>" This comment was followed by a list of mistakes "made in the past month." After discussing these mistakes in some detail, they are summarized on the memo's last page:

1. Incorrect and insufficient offensive action.
2. Improper defensive measures.
3. Lack of fire control discipline.

4. Lack of patrolling.
5. Improper sanitation.
6. Failure of commanders to lead their troops <u>around</u> rather than straight against enemy positions.

The memo concluded by noting "All members of this command will be given the necessary instruction and training concerning the points listed above, under supervision of unit commanding officers, in order that the fighting efficiency of our forces will be improved." (underlining in original).[47]

Phil hoped that his unit would get a "chicken or duck" for Christmas dinner. He was less than optimistic about receiving any Christmas presents because "the story is circulating now that the Japs shot down the plane bringing over Xmas presents. They get the biggest pleasure out of doing things like that."[48] No letter has survived (and may have never been received) that described Phil's first Christmas overseas.

During the week between Christmas and New Year's Day, he spent one day in bed with a stomach ache—"it seems everyone has a stretch of it about every 2 weeks;" a few flakes of snow fell that "didn't amount to anything—thank God;" and his group had played "a little Rook lately— The boys put $1.00 on each game—I win more money that way." As 1943 came to a close, Phil was looking forward to having dinner with General Gow on New Year's Day because "[t]hat means some fairly good food."[49]

CHAPTER 5

A Challenging Assignment

It is to raise the hopes and capabilities of this ally that American personnel has come to China. It is up to that personnel to help, to train, and to infuse new spirit into her armies. If the result is short of this accomplishment, we have failed in the mission assigned to us by our own Government.

Memo for all Yoke personnel
from Brigadier General Frank Dorn

The food served at General Gow's New Year's Day Banquet was not quite what Phil expected:

The first dish . . . was described as the guts of a cow. The next dish was boiled livers, next came fried duck . . . then we had eggs . . . and we finished with the universal dish of those damn peanuts. Mow Em Down used to be a butcher in Iowa so he could give me a dish by dish account as the meal went along. Incidentally the affair ended up by Mow Em Down telling the general how American hamburger is made.[1]

In addition to attending the banquet, Phil received a new assignment on January 1st when he became a Liaison Officer to the 52nd Chinese Army. Thirteen other Americans from TIG No. 4 (nine officers and four enlisted men) were also assigned to this army. The "principal duties" of the U.S. Liaison Group were "supervision of Army Schools and Division Unit Training; Group administration; and Group Supply." An unknown number of enlisted men from the 993rd Signal Operations

Company were added to the Group "for radio communications purposes[.]"[2]

In early January, it had

> been a little warmer lately, but we still have all the clothes on we can get. We haven't seen a great deal of action now for some time, so we spend most of our time teaching the Chinese to use Am. Weapons[.] . . . Along with teaching the boys I also give them a little current events beforehand. . . . Yesterday—just joking I said "Last night Japan surrendered to the victorious Chinese armies," the class leader immediately rose and said let's stop this talk and get on with the lesson.[3]

During this period, it was evident that Phil and his group did not have much to keep them busy: "I never realized before that time went so slow—seems like there is 48 hours in each 10 minutes."[4]

Things got more interesting the next week when Phil's group traveled south:

> I have just spent a few days down on the French Indochina border—it really was a hell of a trip with these damn stubborn Chinese mules. The Japs have very few troops down there and I don't believe they will be coming this way any further (we hope).

> We could stand on one side of the river, which separates the borders, and look over into Indochina which the Japs hold. The river is only 50 feet wide so we could see the little rats very plainly. Just about each day our P 40s from the American 14th Air Force bomb and machine gun the hell out of them, and our position on the other side of the river makes a grandstand seat for each performance.

* * *

The mountains we had to pass over were extremely high. The best way we found was to hang onto the mules tails and let them pull you over. One of my Sgts. got blisters on his feet so we had to leave him at a small village, and picked him up on our way back[.][5]

While in this area, Phil's group rescued a person who appears to have been a Frenchman. (The letter describing this operation "looks as if the censor burned out the information he did not feel should go through or as if the letter has been rescued from a fire."[6]) In any event, here is the surviving portion of Phil's letter on this subject:

... who was looking out for that country's interests in Indochina; hell of a good egg. The Japs had a reward of $10,000 for him and the Chinese $15,000, so he was really in one hell of a mess. He lived for the most part in the underbrush along the river & with an American Lt. who has an outpost along the border. We brought him back with us dressed up as an American soldier so he could get past the Chinese front lines. From here he is going to North Africa to join the fighting French located there. His folks for the most part were killed when the Germans took France in 1940.[7]

By mid-January, Phil had received "a good many Xmas cards from people back home," including Rube Hoy, I.D. Weeks, Marshall McKusick, and J. Herndon Julian (vice president and Dean of Student Affairs) from the University; Sergeant Hanks (his first sergeant at Camp Wheeler) and several officers he served with at Wheeler; Mr. Smith (his "old mail carrier"); Hilfrid Johnson; and several others. In addition, he got the letter from Senator Chan Gurney cited in the previous chapter. The senator "also sent me a number of air mail stamps. (You can always tell when election is getting near)—I wrote back to him and explained some more damn foolishness going on over here so old Chan and myself will probably turn out to . . . [be] buddies."⁸

As winter dragged on, Phil continued to struggle with the weather: "Nights are still very cold. It seems like the colder it gets the more coffee I drink—it's around fifteen cups a day now so I certainly hope it doesn't get any colder."⁹ In late January, he attended another social event given by Brigadier General Liu Yu Chang, head of the 52nd Army's 2nd Division. This gathering included after-dinner entertainment:

> After the dinner we attended a Chinese play, and I'll be damned if they didn't make us get up and sing some songs—4 of us. The worst voices in the whole China, but we tore down the house nevertheless. It seemed that wasn't bad enough so Major Gallo—a Dr. from N.Y., insisted on singing a solo—His selection was "I'll take you Home Again Kathleen." The tune sounded like Dixie and the words I have never heard before—he ended up by whistling—ye gads. (It was just like Corinne and Miss Dolan at the ladies aid.)¹⁰

The next day Phil was scheduled to "speak before a bunch of Chinese generals on the 'War in General and What China Must Do.'"¹¹ It is unknown how this speech was received.

By the end of January, the 52nd Chinese Army had moved from its prior location in Wenshan to an area located northeast of that city.¹² It had also completed its Army School training in the Officers and NCOs Weapons Schools; and it had begun conducting unit training.¹³ The unit training

> consists, in general, of training in basic, tactical, and technical subjects. Principal subjects are: Disciplinary Training; Military Sanitation; First Aid and Hygiene; Marching; Security Measures; Camouflage; Signal Communications; Care of Material; Care of Animals and Stable Management; Intelligence Training; Rifle

Marksmanship; Night Operations; River Crossing; Air-ground Liaison; Compass and Map Reading[14]

YFOS Headquarters rated the morale of Chinese troops involved in this training as "Fair to Good" and their health as "Fair."[15]

Phil received a few Christmas packages in early February. They must have contained food because he noted "that box Leola sent was very good indeed—It lasted about 10 minutes. Thanks a lot." He requested his mother or Leola to

> please send me some pills for indigestion or pills that will relieve gas—This damn food really mixes things up and lately we have been having some trouble keeping it down. Ask some druggist what would be best—I am awful sorry I have to keep asking for things but that is the only chance we have of getting anything.[16]

Sometime during the second week of February, Phil was involved in a medical emergency that went far beyond anything he had ever experienced:

> The other night a Chinaman came tearing into my tent half crazy and pulled me over to see his friend who was having an attack of appendicitis—and after looking the boy over I went and got the Am. horse doctor, the only thing that even comes close to a doctor for hundreds of miles around here; this particular Vet. works in Missouri on the racing dogs and horses of the big tracks there--& he has been in a number of movie shorts taken of those places—Well anyway Dr. and I decided that the only thing that would save his life would be an operation—so we carried the poor devil over to a straw hut—cleaned it up the best we could—got a number of flashlights candles and what have you and in general got ready for the

legal execution, and naturally this being my first operation I was somewhat nervous. Dr., however, was very cool as he has killed hundreds of animals before. Anyway we finally got things all set, and the Dr. washed up along with the instruments. The first problem was how to put the man to sleep—Dr. had some medicine that worked on horses but he wasn't so sure it would work on a Chinaman—so the Dr. insisted that we just hit him in the head, but after talking the situation over with our staff, which included one 1st sgt., one G.I cook, and a Chinese horseshoe-er, we decided that the medicine that would put a horse to sleep would do likewise for the Chinamen..., so the Dr. shot a little of it into him—It worked very well... The next problem was this—the Dr. didn't know the exact location of where to make the incision—so everyone present pointed to where they thought it was, but the location varied to such a large extent that the final decision was to make the cut about 18 inches long and then use the hunt and poke system which the Dr. said he used very successfully on pigs. As the Dr. made the cut blood flew all over the place, but we were told it would prevent infection, so with our now red uniforms we rested at ease for the Doctor's next move, as we did the Dr. continually explained to us the difference between a horse and a human being—after this lecture the operation went on. With a long piece of wire with a hook on the end he now started to hunt—First came out a hunk of brown stuff—the smell identified it. Next a little black object, but after a staff consultation it was decided that it was the liver so the Dr. pushed it back in. In the next half an hour all those present witnessed seeing most of the organs of the human body being pulled up one by one with the added explanation of the Dr. "Nope, that isn't it." A short while later the situation became so desperate that the Dr. read a few chapters from one of his old text books, while the staff took turns trying to locate the appendix. Shortly, however, with enlightened knowledge from his books, the Dr. returned and pulled out something undiscovered before—We all decided that was it so the Dr. cut it out and put him back together—Two days later the Chinaman was still sleeping from the horse medicine, but today there are signs of recovery. All those who witnessed the operation pray to God each evening that they will never have appendicitis.[17]

About a week later, Phil attended a course put on by the Fourteenth Air Force:

> I just returned from a few days course given by the 14th Air Force—It was very interesting and I believed I even learned some things—it was so simple. Their objective is to get bases in China so they can actually bomb Japan itself, but all supplies must be flown over the hump so they barely get enough gas to maintain fighter protection—I am glad old General Chennault is on our side[.][18]

The "General Chennault" referred to in the above statement was Claire L. Chennault. He was a retired U. S. Army Air Corps officer who came to China in 1937 as Chiang Kai-shek's private advisor. In 1941, with the approval of Chiang and President Roosevelt, Chennault formed the American Volunteer Group (AVG). The AVG, which became known as the "Flying Tigers," was made up of about one hundred U.S. civilian volunteers recruited to fly the P-40 pursuit airplanes that China had recently bought from the United States. In July 1942, the AVG was integrated into the U.S. Army Air Forces as the China Air Task Force. Chennault was recalled to active duty as a brigadier general and put in charge of this new unit. Eight months later, President Roosevelt disbanded the China Air Task Force and put Chennault in command of a new Fourteenth Air Force in China. Roosevelt also promoted Chennault to major general and expanded the newly-created air force's fleet of fighter and bomber aircraft.[19]

Sometime during the latter half of February, Phil's and Irwin Nelson's .45 caliber automatic pistols were stolen. Although it cost only $35 to replace this weapon, it was rumored to be worth $1,500 on the black market.[20] An officer in TIG No. 4 investigated the thefts. His conclusion was identical in both cases: "Investigation has revealed that this officer had no knowledge of the serial number of the pistol. It is therefore felt that this carelessness on the part of the officer is justifiable reason to hold him pecuniarily responsible for the pistol and equipment."[21] But this recommendation was not followed by YFOS Headquarters, which found that

1. No regulation requires officer to know the serial number of his individual weapon, altho it reflects considerable doubt on the sense of responsibility of the officer concerned.

2. It appears that all reasonable precautions for securing the weapon were taken.

3. Captain Saunders [and Captain Nelson are] ... hereby relieved of all responsibility for this equipment.[22]

Phil's group celebrated George Washington's birthday with a dinner featuring baked duck. The ducks were procured by the men themselves: "We came upon a whole bunch of wild ducks yesterday—so we took out our tommy guns and burned up some of the Government's amm[unition] and got 2 of them[.]"[23] They then embarked on a six-day trip "along the front" on horseback. That journey proved especially difficult for Captain Nelson: "Mow Em Down is really in bad shape—All his belongings were on a pack mule and the damn animal fell over a big cliff taking everything with him. He really will look funny in just shorts."[24]

In late February, Phil related another incident involving the Fourteenth Air Force's B-25 airplanes: "2 bombers were forced down near here the other day—planes were wrecked, but crews came out

O. K. – We fed them up and gave them enough horses to pack them back to their home base. Another half million dollars of American tax payers money gone to hell[.]"[25] At least one of the planes had salvage value, and YFOS Headquarters later granted TIG No. 4 authority to "proceed with salvage operations." It was "authorized to retain for your use the items mentioned in your radio. All other salvageable material is to [be] returned to this headquarters for delivery to the 14th Air Force." The group was also advised that "your engineer officer should be placed in charge of salvage operations to determine what is suitable for return. Any parts of the ship not returned should be completely destroyed."[26]

As of March 1, the cold weather finally appeared to be ending. "It's fairly warm over here now—In fact we took off our long underwear, and it was the first time in 3 months." On that day, one of Phil's fellow American officers temporarily left the group. "Capt. Ward, a boy that has been with us a long time, left for the front in Burma this morning. We certainly hated to see him go, but he will get us some valuable information and experience." TIG No. 4 also got some new equipment: "We have got some brand new weapon carriers now with 50 caliber machine guns on them so in the future these damn bandits won't interfere with our convoys."[27]

* * * *

Phil and Allen Wilson were SAE fraternity brothers in college. They also were fellow ROTC cadets—with Phil in the class one year ahead of Allen. Allen had a younger sister named Lois, who was a freshman at the University of South Dakota when he was a junior and Phil a senior. Herman W. Frankenfeld, better known as "Frankie" and described as one of the University's "most congenial men," was the University's Registrar while both Lois and Phil were in college.[28] He became friends with them while they were students. Frankie wrote to Phil after Phil went to China, and in early 1944, he suggested to Lois that she do the same. Lois followed this suggestion, and Phil responded to her on March 4. In that letter, Phil congratulated her on recently becoming an aunt, told her that his older sister was "expecting in April," and asked for Allen's address. He also stated: "I receive letters from Frankenfeld very often and he keeps me fairly well informed as to what is happening around the campus. Rube Hoy writes often also, and I certainly enjoy his letters."[29]

Phil went on to describe his China experience in very broad terms:

> We are having a big time over here in this God forsaken China. I have been over here for about six months now, and we really have had some interesting experiences to say the least. These poor devils over here live in the worst conditions possible, it's really a mystery to all of us how they can even exist. We hope to have big things happen over here in the near future, and preparations for the main show keep us busy most of the time.

His letter ended by asking Lois "what are you majoring in . . . ?"; stating "As I recall you should be a junior this year—am I right?" (He was); and noting "I certainly hope after this war is over Allen will go back and finish his law course—We really used to have some swell times."[30]

* * * *

In early March, YFOS Headquarters issued a memorandum that discussed, among other things, the policy goals YFOS hoped to achieve by employing Chinese interpreters:

> We have now, and will have in rapidly increasing proportion, a definite contact with . . . [young Chinese people] through interpreters. These young men will be from the universities and solid middle classes of China. As university students they are giving up possible future careers to serve in the most suitable manner the joint war effort of our two countries. Some have

already been assigned for our use. Within the next year many hundreds, and later thousands will be attached to the U.S. Army agencies.

These young men represent the future of China; and during the next thirty years will have supplanted the power cliques, the incompetent, and the selfish in posts of control. Our attitude towards them now will have very great repercussions in the future relations of our two nations, and indirectly on the future peace in the Pacific basin.

For these and the many connected reasons, which should be obvious to American personnel, it is desired that this group of young men be handled with thought for the future. They are under military discipline which they understand. But if they are convinced at this time of our sincerity and good intent, they in turn will become the ambassadors of the future between our two peoples.

In order to improve mutual understanding, classes in English for interpreters will be conducted regularly. Interpreters will be taught the use of weapons and how to fire them. When practicable they will be taught how to drive and take care of American vehicles. They will be given reasonably short talks at regular intervals on American governmental principles, the reasons for American methods, our people, our internal geography, and our geographical position with relation to the rest of the world. Talks should be informal, allow time for questions, need not be detailed, but should present the true picture in order that these young men may judge for themselves as to how our type of modernized civilization may be adapted to the future needs of China. In turn they should be asked to talk to American personnel on such aspects of China as individuals may know.

Informal monthly reports will be submitted to this Headquarters on the progress of this project. Further suggestions will be welcomed.

This memorandum will be read by unit and subordinate commanders to all officers and enlisted men of their commands.[31]

Phil's experience with his interpreter was very positive:

> I talk with the Chinese through my interpreter—He is a young smart fellow who escaped through Jap lines from Hong Kong when they moved in. He really is a swell little boy and I wish I could take him back with me. I know enough Chinese now to get the bare necessities of life, but beyond that I run into various difficulties. Mr. Whang knows English . . . and I would say is the best damn Chinaman in this forsaken hole.[32]

On March 6, TIG No. 4's "doctor decided that it was time for shots—yellow fever—and all that stuff, so right now our arms are stiff as the devil and most of the boys have retired for the night."[33] Two days later, Phil was once again a victim of theft:

> Some son of a _____ [blank line in original] got into my stuff last night when I was asleep, and stole my wallet—They only got one dollar, but my identification cards—pay card—a battle certificate and some other official papers were in it. Please send me another one right away—about the same kind if you can find one. . . . Thanks a lot. I think I can get most of my papers back from Washington.[34]

Also on March 8, YFOS Headquarters issued a bulletin that addressed a number of subjects. The first one pertained to censorship. With respect to this topic, the bulletin stated:

1. The following amendments to current censorship regulations are announced for the information and guidance of all concerned:

a. Mention may be made of service in China, Burma or India. <u>No smaller geographical localities may be mentioned except where specifically authorized by this Headquarters.</u>

b. Mention may be made of service with troops of our Allies. <u>No mention may be made of specific duties, assignments, or locations, of either the writer or allied troops. Mention of the branch of service of allied troops to which writer is attached is also prohibited.</u>

c. Mention may be made of incidents arising out of association with members of Allied forces. <u>No mention may be made of incidents of friction, unfavorable comparisons, ridicule, or criticism.</u>

d. Mention may be made of living in jungle and of living conditions. <u>No mention may be made of places, complaints, location of bivouacs, or movements of troops.</u>

e. Mention may be made of combat experience. <u>No mention may be made of units involved, localities, losses in personnel and materiel, atrocities, wounded, or accounts of escapes.</u>

f. Mention may be made of captured Japanese personnel and materiel. <u>No mention may be made of time, place, numbers, identifications, or units making capture.</u>

g. Mention may be made of our weapons and those of our Allies in a general way. <u>No mention may be made of specific classifications, calibers, characteristics, or of any weapons not yet used in combat in this Theater.</u>

h. Mention may be made of having seen the Theater Commander. <u>No mention may be made of specific time or place, and always in past tense.</u>

(underlining in original).[35]

Two weeks later, YFOS Headquarters expressed its concern in writing about criticisms of the Chinese Army coming from Yoke personnel. Indeed, Phil had previously made criticisms of this nature—at least in his letters to home (which probably violated censorship rule c. above). For example, he had remarked "We just don't seem to be able to get these bastards to do any fighting"; "the damn Chinese are about as bad as the Japs"; and "these devils are even more bull headed than the Norwegians."[36]

The first of two memorandums from Headquarters regarding criticism of the Chinese Army was addressed to "All Y-Force Units," and its subject was "Attitude of Yoke Personnel." This memorandum stated in part:

1. There has been an increasing amount of adverse comment and criticism of the Chinese Army by Yoke personnel that can only reflect undesireably /sic/ in their work and relations with Chinese personnel. There is the possibility as well, that if this unfavorable comment continues and comes to the attention of the Chinese—as it will, the discovery may result in a lowering of their morale and effect their desire for offensive operations.

2. In order that all personnel may have a more complete understanding of the conditions that have produced undesireable /sic/ conditions in the Chinese Army, the attached memorandum will be read to all officer and enlisted Yoke personnel.[37]

The above-referenced "attached memorandum" began by noting the Chinese Army's victory in northern Burma proved that "given proper rations, equipment, training and leadership, the Chinese soldier as a soldier is the equal of any soldier in the world." It then stated that the "mission of Yoke personnel is identical with that of American instructor personnel in India," but that "limitations on the air flow of supplies makes it impossible to equip troops in Yunnan as completely as those in India." It also listed a number of reasons why the Chinese troops in Yunnan had not performed as well as those trained in India. These included a "shortage of food in China as a whole" that "compels the Chinese soldier in China to live on the barest essential necessities of life," "extremely low pay and the demands of growing families with rising costs and seven years of poverty," and the fact that "even before the Japanese attack on China in 1937, Chinese Armies have been starved for heavy equipment, ammunition, and much of the paraphernalia which is considered essential for combat armies." Due to these factors,

> discouragement of the [Chinese] Army and the people is the natural result. Since the army has had insufficient heavy weapons and ammunition, it has not been able to strike back. Morale has been badly effected /sic/; since pay and rations are poor, enlistments are low and desertions are high; lack of medical supplies and trained personnel have engendered indifference to a bad situation; and lack of action has bred incompetence among many officers.

The memorandum ended with these comments directed to American soldiers:

> a. For those who stop to analyse their situation with respect to Chinese troops with whom we are working, such an attitude [of disillusionment growing into resentment and bordering on condemnation] is against all of the principles of fair play of which Americans like to boast. We are in China to help the armies of a people who through thirty four years of revolution, civil war, political upheavals, and a crushing invasion have become the world's underdogs among nations.

b. It can be expected that the most high-minded Americans will be impatient, disappointed, and even discouraged at times. The unthinking will be inclined to condemn their immediate Chinese associates.

But before any reaction is allowed to govern our thoughts; it would be unfair not to recall that China has lost several millions of soldiers in casualties; she has lost tens of millions through starvation, Japanese oppression and mass murders; she has lost access to all raw materials; practically all of her industry; she has woefully inadequate food production; a wrecked financial structure; and a discouraged people.

It is to raise the hopes and capabilities of this ally that American personnel has come to China. It is up to that personnel to help, to train, and to infuse new spirit into her armies. If the result is short of this accomplishment, we have failed in the mission assigned us by our own Government.[38]

During the morning on April 1, "the Chinese had a mass execution ... It seems a few of them stole a few bullets, so the general just up and decided they should be shot—These old boys just don't believe in courts and lawyers." Phil also related that "a Chinese general gave me a nice silk banner the other day—I think it would cost 89 cents in the states, but it [is] nice and I appreciated it a lot nevertheless," and "we were able to get some Army K rations a few days ago. They really aren't bad at all. Even a cereal in the breakfast unit with powder[ed] milk."[39]

Two days later

we covered 38 miles on the back of a horse up and down mountains. The Rockies in the states are just gradual inclines compared to these damn things.

We got started at 8 o'clock and everything was going fine until Nelson got his horse wrapped around a tree.... A few miles further on my horse developed the diarrhea, and of course every time a movement took place it was necessary for him to stop. This happened about every 20 yds. and became quite a source of irritation for both the people in our party and the horse's hind end.

We passed through one little village about noon and we had to stop and call on the magistrate, and in so doing he insisted that we stay for dinner[.]

Once again Captain Nelson had trouble keeping his belongings safe:

Towards the end of the afternoon the pack horse carrying Nelson's baggage went over a cliff, but the only thing that went to the bottom was a small little box. I really thought the damn thing was full of gold the way he carried on, so we had to stop and get ropes to lower him down and get the damn thing. When I found out the only thing in it was cool aid I could have shot him, but our ammunition is getting rather low.[40]

During the first half of April, TIG No. 4 moved into a small village believed to be somewhere in the southwestern part of Yunnan province. On April 12, the temperature reached 108 degrees Fahrenheit. The next day, "Mow Em Down saw ants, or something, crawling around in his stool ... so we are going to send him back to our field hospital."[41]

The group experienced a complaint shortly after arriving at its new location:

It became very necessary the other day to build a road block across a path running through an old woman's back yard. She came steaming out hollering and carrying on something awful, saying that our construction would spoil her damn garden. The Chinese officer argued with her for a few minutes and then got the general—He told her that for the use of her land the Chinese would be very thankful, and besides if she said one more word he would shoot her himself. The road block was then built. (A great democratic country I keep telling myself.)[42]

Phil provided colorful descriptions of his living quarters in the village, where "the things that happen to us shouldn't happen to a dog."

> The Chinese General had to move Mrs. Sun Ti Lou out of her hut to give us a place to stay. That caused, of course, various difficulties. . . . Her 2 pigs refused to leave; and furthermore they decided to make their home under our eating table and hell and high water won't make them move. We really don't mind them so much now as they are very friendly pigs and with the rats and fleas that go with them it keeps us from getting homesick.
>
> Mrs. Sun Ti Lou also has a gigantic water buffalo, and the old gal insists that the damn thing be allowed to eat the nice grass growing right outside our door. You would be surprised how hard it is to step over those damn animals, but he does keep a lot of Chinamen from tearing in and out.
>
> Lately we have also been having trouble with Mrs. Whang So Gee. It seems that for the past 25 years she has been throwing her dish water and that sort of thing over the wall into our front yard. The water buffalo, of course, is most delighted with this practice, but after taking a most unexpected shower every 20 minutes for the past two weeks we decided to put in a complaint. She was most cooperative with us, now she throws the same content on our roof which leaks. . . . This new

system of disposal, however, has its advantages as it does keep the furniture from drying out along with our beds, and the pigs have a big time rolling around in each puddle.[43]

TIG No. 4 also participated in Chinese Army defense drills:

> The army, in this section of China, has the civilians practice right along with them in the defense against Jap paratroopers. Their job being to clear out the huts of all people and belongings and move them to the top of a nearby mountain. Our hut, naturally, comes within their jurisdiction. So about twice a day the alarm sounds and immediately 20 or more Chinamen come tearing in and start hauling stuff around, I usually end up with the kitchen stove and one or two foot lockers, but nevertheless after 30 minutes or so we get things under control and start to the mountain with ... [the] Chinese and their house hold belongings. After 2 hours of walking almost straight up we reach the mountain top, at which time all ... Chinese gather around us to have a look at our stuff[.] ... After mingling with our dear friends in this sort of way for 2 or 3 hours in the burning sun or the down pouring rain, the all clear signal is given and we pick up what's left and start back, but in the excitement and confusion of it all there seems to be a mutual exchange of belongings. ... This constant drilling for such an enemy attack is very valuable of course, but the water buffalo in front of our door does take an awful beating. Every time he hears the alarm now he becomes very pale and says to himself "My God here we go again."[44]

The cooking arrangement—and its effect on Phil's ability to get a decent night's sleep— also produced detailed comments:

We have two soldiers doing our cooking for us. The food isn't so bad, but the kitchen is located right in the middle of the hut which doesn't work out so well. For one thing they insist on doing their butchering at 2 or 3 o'clock in the morning[.] ... One would think that the least you could get would be some nice restful sleep, but it just doesn't work out that way at all. After the final execution the boys then make a nice big fire and at the same time lay down a smoke screen[.] ... At this time you can do one of three things, put your head under the covers, which isn't much better because most of our diet is made up of beans; 2nd put on your gas mask, but if you go to sleep with it on you will wake up dead, 3rd pick your bunk up and go out in the front yard, but this isn't so good either as the water buffalo takes up most of the space and the birds seem to use the rest of it for their dumping ground.

Usually by the time breakfast is ready the smoke has cleared out somewhat and you are so tired it is then possible, by missing breakfast, to get a few minutes sleep.[45]

In an April 23 letter to his mother, Phil indicated that he was somewhere in Burma and would be spending "a few days" there. The letter suggested his work had become significantly more active: "The activity is picking up over here to beat the devil. The harder we push the rats in the Pacific the rougher they seem to get in these parts. Right now they are concentrating on trying to take back our advanced bases all up and down the line, and they are doing a fairly good job of it."[46]

By late April, Phil had returned to the small Chinese village in southwestern Yunnan. From there, he reported on the physical and mental health of two fellow officers:

The boys back at our field hospital found Mow Em Down to be in rather bad shape so he is on his way back to India to get some kind of special treatments.

One of our commanding officers went nuts last night—Before we could get ahold of him he all but tore the place apart. Sometimes I wonder where the dear father is keeping himself.⁴⁷

The next day

An air force was supposed to drop some of our supplies . . . but they were a little off the beam and most all of it went in the damn river and floated down to the Japs. I suppose if the dear defense workers back home knew about that we would have a few more strikes or a congressional investigation[.]⁴⁸

Perhaps as a substitute for the food it did not receive in the air drop, Phil's group "had roast dog for dinner" that night. It turned out to be "really not bad at all."⁴⁹

Sometime during the spring of 1944, a new commanding officer was assigned to Phil's group—Colonel Paul R. M. Miller. Phil described him as "an old West Point Colonel . . . really a tough old boy who knows about everything in regard to the army."⁵⁰ Colonel Miller wrote the following in a note to Phil dated May 2:

My dear Saunders—

Congratulations on a job well done! Maj. Larkin reports an excellent job [next word or phrase cut out of note] on your part!

You may well feel proud of your part in earning the praise of the Division Commander and Chief of Staff.

Feel assured that full official notice has been taken of your efforts to assist in attaining desired standards.

Sincerely,

Paul R. M. Miller, Col., F.A.

The censorship rules must have prevented Phil from describing what was involved in the "excellent job" referred to in Colonel Miller's note. All Phil said was that the note related to "some work I have just finished."[51]

In mid-May, Phil's teeth "started to act up something awful," so he traveled to YFOS Headquarters to get them "fixed up." The dentist there was able to do whatever was necessary to relieve the tooth pain. And Phil was glad to be back in Kunming for other reasons:

> It's really nice to get up here again and get some good . . . Am. food. The other night I also saw a G.I. movie—first one in 7 months—ye Gads even they are getting short of men. I didn't see one male in the whole picture that wasn't at least 72 or 3 years [old].

During this visit to "our main Hdqs.," "the Japs came over and dropped a few eggs . . . It's getting to be an almost daily affair I understand."[52] And he finally received word that his niece Nancy was born on April 23rd. Phil was delighted to get this news: "I am more than happy that things turned out the way they did, and especially happy that it was a girl." He also informed his sister Corinne and brother-in-law Jim that

> at the present I have a medic with me who used to be a baby specialist in L. A., so if any unexpected problems come up be sure and write me all about it and I will get the approved solution from him. Of course you realize a <u>baby specialist</u> is <u>very</u> valuable over here. Ye Gads.

(underlining in original).[53]

Phil eventually made his way back from YFOS Headquarters to his group's location in the field. Rain made the return trip a very slow one—on one of the days it took "five hours to cover 20 miles in a jeep."⁵⁴ After checking in with his unit, he spent the last part of May and early part of June

> out looking around at things, and with the rain it wasn't very pleasant to say the least. These little trails get awful slippery and most of the time you are either flat on your face or on the way down. It's very obvious now that the Japs want to finish up this war with China before it gets too hot for them in the Pacific—and we expect them to throw everything [at us], including the kitchen sink, in order to complete their goal over here this summer.⁵⁵

A new threat against the Americans had also surfaced: "We got word the other day from the Chinese Govt. that many Jap agents have entered this area with the mission of doing away with <u>all</u> Americans. I am not in the least bit worried . . . [but] it does make things rather interesting[.]" (underlining in original).⁵⁶

Phil was overjoyed when he heard about the allies' successful D-Day invasion in France:

> We just received word over our little radio that the second front in Europe has been started. We all are so happy that we don't know what to do. Some of the boys over here haven't prayed for years, but I am sure we all asked the dear father this time to do his part in keeping the deaths as low as possible. It's very obvious that nothing can happen over here until the Germans are taken care of. Our main Hdqs. station is sending us news twice a day now, so we will be able to keep fairly well up on the situation. Our chaplain has a pray[er] meeting once a day and so far the attendance has been 100%. We all take our hats off to the boys who we know darn well will not fail in their missions whatever they might be. Most of the boys here

feel somewhat guilty in that they cannot help, but our time will arrive someday we hope.

And on a personal note, he also reported receiving duplicate copies of all the papers stolen from him in early March.[57]

In mid-June, Phil received two packages and several letters from relatives and friends in the United States. One of the packages contained pills sent from a local pharmacy (Phil had requested pills that relieved indigestion in early February). These added to the considerable number of pills he was already taking:

> Every night now before we go to bed we have to take certain pills—sulfa guanidine for stomachs, quinine for the prevention of malaria, my vitamin pills, and now 2 more boxes of pills—so each night I take around 9 pills before going to bed and there isn't a damn thing the matter with me. It just goes to show you. By the way those pills you sent me what are they <u>supposed</u> to do?

(underlining in original).[58] Among the letters was one from Mr. Phillippi—his local banker. In that letter, "Mr. Phillippi said he had read my description of the appendix operation on the Chinaman and wanted to know how he turned out. I really don't know how he is, but I bet a million he is as dead as [a] door nail."[59] Shortly thereafter, Phil got a letter from Frankie indicating that he too had read about the operation in the Vermillion newspaper. Phil's reaction: "Ye gads things certainly get around these days."[60]

At this juncture, Phil sounded more optimistic about developments on the battlefront:

> We have been earning our money lately with all kinds of jobs, going here and going there in this darn rain and mud isn't so easy. We were all very happy to hear about the B-29

raid on Japan the other day. These Chinese boys have done an excellent job in holding those advanced air bases from the Japs. Things are certainly looking better all the time and our hopes are high for a complete victory sometime in '45 if the good father stays with us.

I have a number of boys with me now who were in the invasion of the Aleutian Islands and N. Africa—a few of them have been shot up rather badly but darn good boys all the way through. They don't get excited over anything and I don't believe they would fear if the devil himself moved in[.][61]

On June 18, Phil was "auth[orized] to wear one Bronze Star . . . on [his] Asiatic Pacific Service Ribbon." This service ribbon was awarded to those who served in the Asiatic-Pacific Theater (which included all of Asia) during World War II. The Bronze Service Star (also referred to as a "battle star," "campaign star," or "engagement star") was presented for his participation in the "China Defensive" campaign. He was also awarded the 52nd Chinese Army Service Medal for his work with that army.[62]

Near the end of June, Captain Nelson returned to his unit: "I guess they fixed him up fairly decent—he lost about 50 lbs., but it came off in the right places[.]" With respect to allied combat operations,

> there seems to have been considerable trouble around these parts to coordinate air and ground attacks—so the old man called a few of us into one of our field Hdqs. and we have to go to school for 6 days. The air corps insist that the Chinese are shooting down Am. planes and ground forces insist that the only people they hit are our own troops. So all and all the relationship between the two aren't so hot right now and the results are much worse because of it.[63]

On June 28, "an order came out . . . from General Stilwell that no one would remain in this area longer than 24 months, so I only have 14 more to go—ye Gads. We hope that after the war in Europe it will be reduced to 18, but it's rather wishful thinking I do believe."[64] Phil's hope that his stay in China would be reduced to 18 months did prove to be "wishful thinking."

CHAPTER 6

The Chinese Army and its American Advisors Hang On

Don't believe all the crap in the papers about the terrible serious situation over here. It's bad, but not many Americans are affected. At least if China surrenders no Americans will be left here. I just don't see how these poor devils can last much longer.

Phil Saunders

Effective July 1, 1944, Phil was given a new assignment. He was now the Executive Officer for the liaison group attached to the 2nd Division in China's 52nd Army. As previously noted, General Liu commanded this division. Its headquarters were at Sinkai, a village believed to be located near Wenshan. When Phil was assigned to this unit, its estimated strength was 7,300 Chinese soldiers. This number was 4,160 less than the planned-for strength of 11,460 men.[1]

Shortly after being assigned to the 2nd Division, Phil attended the American air ground school at one of YFOS's field headquarters. When he returned to his camp, he discovered the Chinese leadership had decided that American troops needed more security in their area. This was a laudable goal, but it caused some unanticipated consequences:

> The General got worried about our safety the other [day] so now he has about 25 guards, 4 to 10 machine guns and most everything else stationed around our hut, and the guards have rigid orders about letting people in and out. The other

night one of the boys got the runs, but by the time he finished convincing each guard that he wasn't a Jap agent it was just too late. A few nights ago we came home from a late meeting and we almost had to go into an attack formation before we got in. I noticed this morning they were digging a big wide ditch around the place and filling it with water so in a few days it will be necessary to have a battleship and a couple of destroyers to either come or go.[2]

After serving as a captain for over a year, Phil was understandably interested in being promoted to major. But "General Stilwell has a rule that one must be in grade at least 18 months before getting a promotion, so at the best I have another 5 months, and they are a damn hard thing to get then." Nevertheless he decided he could afford to support the war effort with his captain's salary:

I took out an $18.50 war bond the other day—I will get one every month and it will be sent to the bank, comes right out of my pay each month so it's handy as the dickens. I really should have been getting more of them all along I do believe.[3]

In the third week in July, a B-29 airplane on its way back to India was forced down near Phil's location. The crew was brought to his unit, together with one of the plane's valuable assets: "We got a 20 m. gun from . . . [the airplane] for our anti-aircraft protection. . . . The boys tell me it works like a million and can hit most any target."[4]

During the night on July 27

it rained so hard and so much that the west wall of our little old hut washed away—so we now have plenty of fresh air and can get a first-hand view and smell of Mrs. Sun Lou Yen's pig pen. I went over the other day and tried to tell her how to raise pigs so we could at least look at nice fat pigs, but she says that all

Americans can do is to make machinery—so I told her one of these days I would turn out a corn binder and give [it to] her.[5]

In early August, Phil explained to his mother and Leola why his letters took so long to reach the United States:

> We had our mail dropped from an airplane day before yesterday and I got one letter from you postmarked July 5.
>
> If you could see this damn country around here you wouldn't wonder any longer why my mail is 3 weeks apart. I write every time the mail goes out, usually we have to send a horse convoy out every 3 weeks and that's the only way we can send mail out. We want to build an airport so a plane could land and pick up our mail as well as deliver it to us, but we just don't have enough equipment to build it or enough soldiers to protect it from the Japs.[6]

Five days later, Phil received four letters from his mother. He learned that she likewise received several of his letters "all at once," and he concluded "that's the way it will be depending on the planes flying over the hump."[7]

On August 9, it appears that Phil's unit was attacked. But in compliance with the censorship rules, he referred to the event in very general terms: "All hell broke loose for a short while this morning, but things seem to have settled down a little now."[8] That same day, Phil noted "that when a reporter asked F.D.R. how things were going in China, he said just two words—'not good.'"[9]

Two unconnected events occurred at Phil's unit during the night of August 20: "One of the boys was cleaning his sub-machine gun . . . but forgot to unload it—you would be surprised to see what a nice hole it made in his foot"; and "our goat had a crop of little ones. . . . The Doc. was up all . . . night with her and she was the worst patient he has ever had."[10]

In addition to receiving several letters from Rube Hoy, the rest of the Hoy family decided to write Phil as well. In the latter part of August, he received a letter from Mrs. Hoy (Hazel) and her three children: Carleton, age 15, Richard, age 13, and Nancy, age 9.[11] Although that letter's content is unknown, Phil said it was "real nice of them" to write to him.[12]

At the end of August, Phil noted that his living quarters had become somewhat cramped:

> We are so crowded in our little hut at the present. I have in my room a doctor from N.Y.—a bomber pilot from Wis.—an engineer from Calif. and a poor broken down dentist from Florida. If I ever had a chance to get an education this is it. Our place gets just like it does up at Anderson's when everybody starts talking and nobody listens.

He also stated that "just about every day I get to talk to a few French officers and they all seem to speak better [English] language than most of us."[13]

The *Grant County Review*'s August 31, 1944 edition contained a front-page story titled "Capt. Phil Saunders Is Instructor Of Chinese Troops Under Stilwell." Among other things, the article described Phil's duties in China:

> Captain Phil W. Saunders, son of Mrs. Jean Saunders of Milbank, is now serving in China. Capt. Saunders is actively engaged with the Y-Force, which is headed by Brig-General Frank Dorn and under the command of General Joseph W. Stilwell, instructing Chinese troops in the use of American weapons and modern tactics.
>
> His job also includes serving as liaison officer to the Chinese forces in combat. For the past year this force has been engaged

on this mission and has also been furnishing certain arms and ammunitions to the Chinese and giving them advise /sic/ on matters of strategy.[14]

In a contemporaneous letter to Allen Wilson, Phil described his duties somewhat differently than the *Grant County Review* article did:

> At the present I am with a Chinese front line unit tearing around most everywhere—We always seem to be on the move and it's always in the same direction—backwards. We get one can of C ration a day and for the rest it must come from the land and it just doesn't exist. About all these poor bastards have are a few worn out rifles and a couple beaten up M.G.s [machine guns] per Bn. [battalion].[15]

The 2nd Division still had not reached the manpower numbers its planners had envisioned. By August 31, 1944, its estimated strength had increased from 7,500 to 9,753. Although this estimate showed the division gaining in numbers, it still had 1,707 fewer men than were authorized for this unit.[16]

In early September, Phil received word that he had been promoted to major. He "certainly was surprised to say the least" because under his understanding of Stilwell's policy described above, he could not get a promotion until after he had served at least 18 months as a captain.[17] He relayed this news to his mother and Leola in a September 5 letter:

> I got my promotion to a Major a few days ago—I certainly didn't expect it for at least another six months, but old Colonel Miller really went to bat for me. I get a $60 increase a month also which won't hurt any I am sure. I'll be getting about 400 bucks a month now which is probably more than I'll make as a lawyer for 20 years.[18]

Phil had obviously developed a positive relationship with his commanding officer. And the two seemed to enjoy ribbing each other: "Our old West Point Col. says I am the youngest Infantry major in the army, but I tell him what a wonderful guy he is so I guess he has to say something. Actually neither one of us are worth a damn."[19]

The good news about the promotion contrasted with the harsh conditions Phil now experienced: "We have been on the move again but have a few days of rest at the present," and "our living conditions are going from bad to worse. We only get 1 can of C rations a day at the present and our little old pup tents leak like the dickens." But on the optimistic side, he noted "this phase of our activities should stop in a few weeks if all goes well."[20]

In mid-September, Phil thanked his mother for sending him a bottle of Pepto Bismol. He reported that it "really does a nice job on my stomach" and asked her to send more.[21] Five days later, he cancelled this request because in the interim, he received three more bottles that his mother had sent several weeks earlier. Despite having this medicine, Phil mentioned that he had "been a little sick the last few days, but I am afraid I won't die now as I seem to be eating a little right at the present."[22]

Phil also reported that "the Japs have started a new drive into southern China so our business right at the present has picked up a great deal. They have got the Chinese outnumbered about 5 to 1 so it will probably be the same old story—<u>retreat</u>." (underlining in original).[23] In response to this threatened action, Phil "got an addition to my command today—another carload of Chinamen God only knows how many there were."[24]

As of September 24, 1944, the Chinese 2nd Division's estimated troop strength was 9,700—53 fewer men than it had at the first of that month.[25] Seven days later, that strength estimate was down to 7,500, suggesting that the division experienced significant casualties during the last week of September.[26]

A presidential election was held in 1944, and the CBI theater issued information and guidance regarding "Soldier Voting." That directive provided in part:

* * *

2. The policy of the War Department is to assist and encourage soldiers, eligible and desiring to vote in the election, to exercise that privilege, and to expedite absentee balloting procedures to the greatest extent practicable and compatible with military operation.

3. The policy of this Theater will, in general, be that voting is considered to be compatible with military operations whenever local conditions are such that soldiers are able to prepare, send, and receive personal mail, and commanding officers will be guided accordingly. However, no soldier will be ordered to vote or marched to the voting place; and no commissioned, warrant, or non-commissioned officer will attempt to influence any soldier as to his choice of candidates. The responsibility for affording to every soldier and attached civilian eligible and desiring to vote in the election the means and opportunity to do so, and for providing the necessary facilities and information, falls on commanders at all levels, but particularly on company and similar unit commanders. They all must be imbued with individual responsibility for the conscientious execution of this policy. Designation of soldier voting officers does not relieve commanders of any portion of this responsibility.[27]

Phil received his "war ballot" on September 21, and he "voted for the first time" that day. Although he did not specifically name the candidates for whom he voted, he did reveal his political leanings: "think I'll be a Republican." He also shared the latest rumors circulating among the men in his unit:

If the war in Europe ends soon there is talk of cutting our time down to 18 months. In that case I could do the rest of my time standing on my head. If the situation over here gets any worse there is a lot of talk of taking us out of China—It's getting just a little too hot under the present circumstances.[28]

Two days later, Army Headquarters in the CBI theater distributed a memorandum titled "Morale in C-B-I Theater" and classified as SECRET. The memo, issued by command of General Stilwell, was sent to seven commanding generals of various units in the CBI theater and to the Chiefs of Staff for the "Y" and "Z" Force Operations Staffs. It enclosed portions of a document named "A Morale Study in the C-B-I Theater" (earlier sections of this document had been provided to CBI Headquarters in July); a Supplementary Report titled "What do American Soldiers in CBI Theater Comment About"; and "A Summary of Main Findings and Corrective Action to Be Taken." This morale study "was conducted among a scientifically selected, representative cross-section of troops in the C.B.I. Theater [.]"[29]

The memorandum summarized the main findings, conclusions, and recommendations included in the study. Overall, the findings and conclusions indicated morale was low in the CBI, and corrective action was needed:

* * *

3. This report indicates that the soldier in this theater thinks:

> a. That present non-commissioned officers are not fully capable, or are even the best available.
>
> b. That officers are not exercising the leadership qualifications necessary to a good command.
>
> c. That officers are not showing sufficient interest in the welfare and well-being of the troops under them.
>
> d. That his mess is not as good as it could be under existing conditions.
>
> e. That he is often improperly assigned.

4. Further, the report indicates, judging by what the soldier thinks, that in many instances:

> a. The soldier doesn't know why we are fighting.
>
> b. The soldier doesn't know why he is here.
>
> c. The soldier hasn't been made aware of his importance, or of the importance of his job and unit in this theater.

5. It is desired that each addressee take an active personal interest in the matters listed above. It is realized that this report is based on what the soldier says he thinks, but the indications are considered to be too strong to be shrugged aside as a "soldier gripe."

6. It is realized that this headquarters is at fault in not emphasizing the dissemination of "Why We Fight" information. Action is already underway to correct this fault, and in the near future, a series of articles showing that we are basically fighting for self-preservation, and showing the importance of each man in the theater in this fight, will be published. These publications will be designed to assist commanders of all units and installations in disseminating this vital information. However, it is desired that action not be delayed waiting on these publications.

7. It is requested that you give your personal attention to determining the status, within your command, of the conditions covered in paragraph 3 above. Should the soldiers' opinion be corroborated by your findings, the corrective action necessary is obvious—instruction and supervision by senior more experienced officers; demotion, reassignment, or reclassification where necessary.

8. It is desired to emphasize the necessity to bring command pressure to bear to correct existing deficiencies indicated by this report.[30]

Phil's assessment of the men's morale was consistent with the overall conclusion in the study cited above. But he had a different explanation as to why this situation existed in early October 1944:

> Our morale at the present is low as the devil in that the European war has slowed down so much. I hate to think what will happen over here if the Germans hold the boys during the winter. I also noticed in "Time" [magazine] that the rotation policy had been all but discontinued so it will probably be the Golden Gate in [19]48 after all.[31]

American troop morale would eventually improve, but it generally continued to be low for the remainder of 1944.

CHAPTER 7

Change in American Leadership

"THE AX FALLS," Stilwell wrote on October 19. "I am recalled." The next day, at 5:00 p.m., Stilwell had one final meeting with the "Peanut." Both sides mouthed the necessary hypocrisies: Chiang claimed that he regretted everything that had happened, and Stilwell asked him to remember that he had only ever acted for "China's good." Chiang offered Stilwell the Grand Cordon of the Blue Sky and White Sun, the highest honor that China could offer a foreigner: Stilwell declined it. ("Told him to stick it up his___!"). Four days later, on October 24, Stilwell took off for Delhi. He would never again set foot in China.

Rana Mitter

In mid-October, Phil noted that "it's starting to get cold as the dickens here again. I hate to think of another winter in China, but it kinda looks that way right at the present." He also reported on a recent visit to a U.S. installation in the field:

> A few days ago I was eating lunch on top of a mountain where we have an American outpost. The clouds were so damn heavy up there that about every ten seconds they came floating through the hut and we couldn't even see one another. I was only able to get one quick look at the food throughout the entire meal, but it was rather good nevertheless. The Air Corps is supposed to drop them supplies once each month, but the

last time they hit the landing ground was back in 42 so the boys didn't have a hell of a lot left. It's a great war.[1]

A week later, Phil had this to say about the weather and the current strategic situation:

We have had a lot of rain once again so it makes all operations very difficult. We are all hoping that the boys land on the East coast of China darn soon as another three months of Jap advances will wash us completely out of here.

The Air Force was supposed to fly in a small projector with a movie this afternoon, but things didn't work out just right so I suppose it will be another few months before we see anything but defeated Chinamen.

He also added a note regarding the food situation:

By the way I got another box with peaches and chicken soup—Thanks a million. They taste awful good. We have to be very careful how we eat American food after eating this Chinese junk for so long or we get sick as the dickens. The change is just too great they keep telling me.[2]

* * * *

Phil and his unit were unaware that a change in American leadership at the highest level was about to be implemented. That change marked the end of the rocky relationship that existed between General Stilwell and Generalissimo Chiang Kai-shek since the two met each other in 1942. They had several disagreements on how to best conduct the war against Japan and how to best employ Chinese troops and American resources in that effort. Stilwell increasingly referred to Chiang as "Peanut"—his code name originally intended for use in official radio messages.[3]

In the fall of 1943, Chiang made repeated specific requests to President Roosevelt to have Stilwell recalled and removed from the CBI. But Stilwell had the support of General George Marshall, the U.S. Army Chief of Staff, and Henry Stimson, the Secretary of War. In addition, Lord Mountbatten, upon being introduced to Chiang in October 1943, made it clear he "could not proceed with plans to use Chinese forces if their American commander of the past two years was withdrawn."[4] Accordingly, Chiang decided to back down on his recall requests for the next several months.

Chiang's desire to oust Stilwell from the CBI resurfaced in 1944. The situation reached the boiling point in September, when Chiang made it clear that he would not allow Stilwell to command the Chinese Nationalist Army, and "he wanted Stilwell relieved of all duties inside CBI and SEAC: effective immediately."[5] During the next three weeks, high-ranking American officials, including Secretary of War Stimson, Chinese Ambassador Clarence Gauss, and Army Chief of Staff Marshall tried to negotiate an agreement with Chiang that would keep Stilwell in the theater. But Chiang "refused to budge."[6] Moreover, by October 1944, Stilwell had little support in the CBI or SEAC. Even Lord Mountbatten, who had insisted Stilwell remain in command the year before, no longer stood by him.[7]

Given these circumstances, the American war leaders decided Stilwell had to go. On October 19, General Marshall sent Stilwell an advance radio message that he would be immediately recalled to Washington.[8] After a final meeting with Chiang on October 20 (briefly described at the beginning of this chapter), Stilwell spent the next few days making farewell visits to various locations in the CBI. Then, on October 24, he arrived in Delhi for his last stop in the theater. "Two days later, Vinegar Joe Stilwell climbed aboard one more air transport and—after thirty-two months of constant fighting in pursuit of the impossible—he departed India for the long trip to Washington. 'Shoved off—' he wrote, 'last day in CBI.'"[9]

When the decision was made to recall Stillwell, it was further decided that

> the China-Burma-India theater of operations was also to be dissolved and reconstituted into two new theaters. The first, India-Burma, was to be commanded by Stilwell's capable chief of staff, the American General Daniel Sultan. The region's second theater would be China, with the American General Albert C. Wedemeyer taking command of all American forces there and becoming Chiang's new chief of staff. (Taking Stilwell's SEAC duties would be Stilwell's supply second in command, Lt. General Raymond A. Wheeler.)[10]

General Wedemeyer—46 years old and Deputy Chief of Staff for the SEAC during the past year—arrived in Chungking, China on October 31 to begin his new assignment.[11] He

> was a highly educated and elegantly tall man. He had a thick and rich head of silvering black hair, the aquiline facial features of a movie star, and a self-assurance that verged on monomania. . . . Priding himself on his insight and affability, he planned to use "honey instead of vinegar" in relations with Chiang and—as a gentlemanly start to that—he'd already locked away all files and communications pertaining to Stilwell and Chiang, vowing not to read them until the war was over.[12]

Stilwell was "infuriated" by this appointment. He "felt that . . . [Wedemeyer] 'thinks well of himself,' which ranked perhaps the ultimate Stilwell criticism of character."[13]

* * * *

Not surprisingly, the situation in China did not change immediately after General Stilwell was recalled. In an early November letter to Lois, Phil gave this account of how things were going in the country and made a prediction about his own future there:

We have been in sort of a whirlwind ever since Gen. Stilwell was removed. It doesn't make much difference what they try it just doesn't work over here. Most of the roads and trails are extremely crowded with refugees streaming back to the few remaining Chinese cities. When they see Americans they yell—cheer—some even will tear your clothes off thinking we will be able to take back their homes. Actually all we can do is give them a little food and walk backwards with them.

This Chinese language is really the stuff. Every ten miles they speak a different dialect so our interpreters can't even understand what's going on.

* * *

I expected at one time to be back in school by 46 but the way things are looking now it would be safe to add about ten to that figure.

Have you heard the good news?!! After two years overseas we get to spend 21 days at home before being sent over again. Now isn't that big hearted of the War Dep't.[14]

A few days later, he provided this brief assessment of the recall: "Things are in a heck of a mess over here at the present and the removal of Gen. Stilwell won't help much."[15]

In a November 7 letter to Corinne, Jim, and Nancy, Phil enclosed "a letter from a Chinese kid which I thought you might find interesting." That letter was written in Chinese with an English translation hand-printed above and below the Chinese characters. The translation read:

Dear Brave American Soldiers:

You are fighting on the front to resist the Axis powders /sic/. We thank you very much. Recently you come to China to fight for us and supply us with a lot of ammunition. In this way we cooperate to fight against the Axis. We will win before long.

Frequently the teachers tell us that how hard and bravely you American soldiers fight. We are touched very much while hearing of it. Thus after the victory is obtained we'll go together to maintain the peace of the world. Wishing you victory.

> Your Chinese little friend Cheng Hein-Hein.
> girl 8 years old 3rd class
> Address: Primary school, Central University
> Sa Pen Pa Chung King.

Phil's November 7 letter also asked "how did you vote today?" and added "most of us hope old Frank will get beat, but I don't suppose so."[16] The next day, he reluctantly acknowledged F.D.R.'s victory: "We just heard that old Franklin got elected for another term and most of us are awful disappointed."[17]

In a short letter to his mother written on November 15, Phil reported that he was "awful busy the last week"; he had "been having a heck of a time keeping peace in my bunch between the Chinese and Americans lately. No matter what comes up they seem to argue about it"; and "our mess officer was able to get us several ducks the other day so our Thanksgiving should be a big success."[18]

Two days later, the YFOS was disbanded, and "the American officers of the old Y-Force . . . became the Chinese Training and Combat Command [CT & CC], the China Theater equivalent of a theater ground force[.]"[19] In early December, the CT & CC was issued an operational directive. It provided that the

> mission of CT & CC CT[China Theater] was to render staff assistance and battle liaison to Chinese armies south of Yangtze River; to assist in training of Chinese Armies involved

in plan for defense of Kunming area; to increase the combat effectiveness of Chinese armies.[20]

Phil summarized these developments as follows: "By the way please notice my new address—C.T. & C.C.—The mission of Y Force was finally completed so now all we have to do is stop the Japs from taking all of western China—just a small detail you know."[21]

By December 1, Phil had arrived at a new U.S. Forces Rest Camp. He described it in glowing terms:

> At the present I am spending the first few days of my leave at our big Rest Camp. Boy is it nice up here. Food is wonderful—movies once a night, and a beautiful lake to fool around on in the day time. I will have two weeks altogether before reporting back to my unit.[22]

Four days later, he was "still taking it easy at the rest camp," and he told about his recent activities there:

> Last night we saw Sweet and Low with Benny Goodman—night before that The Lady in Dark with Ginger Rogers. Seems awful strange to see movies once again.
>
> At the present I am staying in a room with three colonels and two majors and what a heck of a time we have. To top it off they stuck three baseball players in with us. Luke Sewell, manager of the St. Louis Browns, Paul Warner outfielder with the N.Y. Yankees, and Dixie Walker who played with the Dodgers. We stayed up till three o'clock last night talking baseball with them. Sewell said he used to hunt out in S. Dak. but couldn't remember Milbank.
>
> You should just taste the hot cakes they make up here. . . I ate sixteen of them for breakfast the first morning. The capt.

in charge out here says that's the record. A couple days ago we had pumpkin pie for supper also. It wasn't as good as the ones you make but it was edible nevertheless. Only bad feature out here is the mail—They don't deliver out here at all so won't hear from you until I get back to my outfit.

Saw two red cross girls yesterday—first white women in months. They like to be called girls I understand, but I am very sure they were at least fifty or more.

While he was enjoying his experiences at Rest Camp, Phil provided a bleak assessment of the Chinese army's defense system: "The military situation here is most desperate indeed. It looks like we will have to get out or else."[23]

Phil returned to his unit the next week. Despite the Chinese having some success on the battlefield, he still believed they had not become an effective fighting force:

At the present I am back with my unit after spending 10 days at the Rest Camp. Suppose[d] to stay 2 weeks, but the situation around these parts is too hot for much resting. We feel rather good, however, in that the Chinese were able to push the Japs back around 40 miles in the last few days—wonders will never cease I guess. I would like to be able to give you the real low down on these damn Chinamen, but it wouldn't be wise. They are just not interested in fighting anybody but themselves and they do a poor job even at that.

On the positive side, he had this to say about a symbolic reminder that Christmas is coming: "I wish you could see our nice little Xmas tree—it's Chinese of course but even at that it's really not bad. The decorations are not too extravagant but at least we don't have to fool around with those darn lights."[24] A few days later, he noted that "the darn thing shed the other day and all that's left is the trunk, but it's still good looking."[25]

In mid-December, Phil described friction within his living quarters apparently brought on by the cold weather:

> Right at the present I am having a very difficult time with my roommate. It seems we ran out of wood several days ago and he insists on breaking up our furniture to keep our little old mud stove operating. When we moved in the Chinese General was kind enough to let us have a few chairs, tables, two wooden beds, and many other small items, but as I look around all that's left is a broken down old wash stand and I expect that to go most any time now.[26]

The U. S. Army responded to the winter cold by issuing sleeping bags. Phil described this item as being quite capable of keeping one warm but having a negative side as well: "Only trouble with them is that you can't move once you get into the darn things. Mow Em Down had to give his away because it took [too] long to get out of it when nature calls."[27]

One week before Christmas, Phil's letter to Lois provided an assessment of the Chinese troops' performance that was much more positive than the one quoted above:

> At the present most Americans in this part of the world are rather happy. Some of the Chinese units to which we have been attached were able to stop cold the latest drive into Western China and even in a few places were able to push them back several miles. Wonders will never cease I guess. The Ledo road through Burma has been just about completed so we expect to do at least somewhat better with all the supplies that should come over it.

In that letter, he also reported receiving "a swell letter from Rube Hoy, Mrs. Hoy and all the kids. Certainly nice of them[.]" Finally, he ended by noting he was not especially busy that day, but it was wise to create the opposite impression: "Must run along now. Nothing important to do as usual, but in the army one must at least appear to be busy at all times, so I'll just pick up a little piece of paper and start tearing around looking for somebody."[28]

Phil and his unit had an enjoyable Christmas celebration. "Last night we celebrated Xmas in a big way. Most of our boys were in from their front line positions to help out, so all in all we had a great time." Their Christmas day dinner consisted of pineapple juice, kosher dill pickles, roast breast of young tom turkey with cranberry sauce, mashed potatoes, asparagus, blueberry and mincemeat pies, assorted candies, rolls with butter, and coffee. His unit also received word of a welcome pay raise:

> Somebody got big hearted up in our main Hqs and gave all of us over here a $30 raise a month. We used to get $90 a month to pay for our food and now its $120, when actually the prices of food have gone down somewhat. Nice Xmas present don't you think?"[29]

This pay increase applied to all officers, warrant officers, and enlisted men "assigned or attached to the Chinese Training and Combat Command, United States Forces, China Theater."[30]

In a December 26 letter to Leola, Phil updated his sister on the war, the weather, and his continuing struggles with his sleeping bag:

> At the present the war situation looks much [better] over here. About all we are doing is sitting on our tails and just waiting for developments. Been cold as the dickens in these parts lately. I am using four G. I. blankets now and trying to get about four more of the darn things. The other night I got into my new sleeping bag and in the morning couldn't get out of it[.][31]

On New Year's Day, the dinner was a welcome repeat of the one served at Christmas. In addition, "each man got five extra cartons of cigarettes. From what we hear the people back home aren't getting many of them. The War Dept. must have had a change of heart because in the last few months we have been getting anything and everything." Phil also reported receiving 21 Christmas cards "so far." In addition, he shared the latest rumor regarding continued service in China: "The latest hot dope from Hqs. is to the effect of having to serve 3 years over here before being eligible for rotation back to the States." The prospect of such an extended tour did not seem to bother him: "As I look at it, as long as the war is going on and they keep giving me $15 a day I can well afford to spend a couple more days, months, years or what have [you][.]"[32]

CHAPTER 8

New Leadership—Mixed Results

The Chinese Combat Command (translated by Chinese as "Chinese-American Liaison Command") includes all U.S. personnel assigned to Chinese combat forces in the field.

* * *

U.S. officers will find it necessary to make suggestions and recommendations to the Commanders of the various Chinese units. These will be constructive in nature and will be made in a spirit of helpfulness and cooperation.

Memorandum to All U.S. Officers Concerned from
Lieutenant General A. C. Wedemeyer

Phil began the year 1945 in the same way he did in 1944—by attending a Chinese dinner party. This event was held on January 4, and Phil described it to Corinne and Jim in colorful detail:

Our Chinese Generals had all of us over to their place for a party. I am sure you just have no idea what one goes through at one of those things. You drink what they call gin ba juice, and when they say gom boy one must consume a glass full of it—means bottoms up, actually it's nothing but degenerated gasoline. On the seating situation the thing really gets complicated. Usually at one small round table they will put at least twenty five people, one dish of food is brought in at a time and placed in the middle of this arrangement. At this moment it's best to grab your chopsticks and prepare for battle because after everyone has smiled and bowed to one another the terrible confusion of trying to get some food gets underway. It's very difficult, however, to get very much to eat. In the first place one must be exceptionally clever with the chop sticks as our allies have been practicing with them twice a day for the last 5,000 years. I usually get speared in both eyes on the opening dish or at least drop them seven or eight times, and then when I do finally round up something no one else will eat there is always some darn fool who yells—<u>gom boy</u>!! at which time one must re-fuel with that gin ba juice, bow, smile at one another and then start all over again. The Chinese table manners are also rather strange. It's considered in the best of society to spit all food, bones, tea, or anything else you don't especially like, right out in the middle of the table. Of course after the third dish it then becomes impossible to distinguish the difference between the food that has been partially digested and the food that hasn't, but really it doesn't matter a great deal as there is absolutely no difference in taste between the two. At these free for alls it's also most necessary that you compliment the host at every opportunity. This, however, is not as simple as it sounds. In the first place you must talk through an interpreter and generally about 95% of them don't understand what you are talking about, but if by any chance the interpreter does understand you will then endeavor to convey your compliment to the host. However, the Chinese language has at least two hundred different dialects and it never fails but that the interpreter and the host speak opposite dialects; coupled with the above circumstances the party, by this continual gom boying, has become so loud that even if one had understandable communication it would still be impossible to hear one another. So in every case the supposed compliment ends up by all smiling at one another once again and muttering to yourself what a hell of a mess the whole thing is. Later on if you are especially fortunate there is a chance of getting back to your own room where you can devour a delicious can of cold American C-ration.

(underlining in original).[1]

In early January, Phil received several Christmas packages from his family and long-time Milbank friends. He also got more Christmas cards and felt "completely overwhelmed with the tremendous holiday spirit." In addition, his unit was rewarded with a rare break in the winter weather: "Yesterday it was 80 degrees above here and all of us were very comfortable walking around in our shirt sleeves."[2]

On January 8, the Chinese Training and Combat Command "was split into two separate and component parts: Chinese Combat Command (Prov) and Chinese Training Command (Prov) (CCC (Prov) and CTC (Prov))."[3] Phil was assigned to the CCC (Prov).[4] Its mission was "to advise and assist the staffs of the Chinese units to which its personnel were attached in planning for and execution of tactical operations and training."[5] The boundaries of this command included "all of unoccupied China west to China-Burma border, south to French Indochina border, and east to Japanese-occupied areas."[6]

In late January, Major General Robert B. McClure became the commanding general of the Chinese Combat Command, replacing Brigadier General Dorn.[7] A few days later, the CCC (Prov) was divided into six sub-areas: the Eastern, Central, Kwangsi, Southern, Western, and Reserve Commands.[8] Phil's unit continued to serve in the liaison group for the Chinese army's 2nd Division and was considered to be part of the Southern Command.[9] This command's geographical area was located directly south of Kunming on the Indochina border.[10]

On February 11, Phil wrote to Lois that he

just returned from a two weeks pack trip up and down the lines—Boy oh Boy I've been cold before, but nothing like this before. I guess the Chinese don't know what a fire is because I didn't see a darn one on the whole trip. How these poor people live with the few old rags they have is a mystery to all of us.

He also noted that activity has recently increased in the China theater:

With the completion of the Ledo road [American-built road beginning at Ledo, India, that connects to Burma Road at Mong Yu, Burma] things are really starting to move over here. We certainly could use a lot more American personnel than we have over here now. Supposed to all be rotated after our 2 years are up, but they are giving us that crap about being unable to replace us now that this Theater is getting so important. Same old army stuff you know.[11]

A week later, Lieutenant General Wedemeyer issued a "Letter of Instruction to All U.S. Officers Serving with the Chinese Combat Command." This document basically described how General Wedemeyer expected American officers to conduct themselves in the CCC. Among other things, it noted that this command "includes all U. S. personnel assigned to Chinese combat forces in the field"; its "Commanding General . . . and necessary staff . . . will be located at Kunming or in close proximity . . . to the Headquarters of the Chinese Supreme Field Commander"; and its mission "is to assist and advise Chinese Commanders of each echelon to which assigned, and to guide Chinese training, supply, and tactical operations." Wedemeyer's letter also provided that "United States Officers on duty with Chinese Combat Command will not exercise command over Chinese forces," and the Americans' degree of influence over these forces "is entirely dependent upon each individual's tact, patience and professional knowledge." According to the letter, "the basic responsibility of the

United States Officers . . . is to determine the status of the Chinese forces with which they are serving and to ensure that the U. S. resources which are being expended upon the various units are utilized against the enemy in the most effective manner." To ensure that this responsibility was met, the officers were required to submit periodic reports "as to the status of the health, morale, training, condition of uniform and equipment, adequacy of the food ration, combat effectiveness and leadership." The letter further stated that "U. S. officers will find it necessary to make suggestions and recommendations to the Commanders of the various Chinese units," and it set forth a detailed procedure (including written reports to higher authorities) that had to be followed by both American officer and Chinese commander if the U. S. officer's recommendations were disregarded.[12]

Finally, the document ended with this "general" reminder:

Each officer is a representative of the U.S. Army and the American people. He is under constant surveillance of a representative portion of the Chinese people. Accordingly, and in consonance with the mission in paragraph 3, above, each officer will:

a. Conduct himself in such a manner as to reflect credit on the U. S. Army and his country.

b. Maintain a high standard of appearance and personal habit.

c. Create a friendly cooperative spirit through tactfulness and perseverance.

d. Increase his value and effectiveness through personality, knowledge, thoroughness and sense of duty.

e. Require enlisted personnel under his command or control to adhere to those same principles.[13]

In a short letter addressed to "Dear All," written by flashlight, and dated February 23, Phil noted that he had "been on the move once again so things have really been up in the air," and the "weather is cold as the devil." He also added that he hasn't "had any mail from you for about a month"; he had "a wonderful bunch of men with me in my new outfit so it's really a pleasure to be around them"; and "we had a break down in our own transportation system the other day so had to ride a short ways on an evacuation train. Never do I hope to see sights like that again."[14]

By early March, Phil had received three letters from his mother and older sister, and "things in general are looking much better . . . now, but most all Americans over here are doing the work of about ten which seems to be just average."[15] This latter observation was consistent with the U.S. Forces Rear Echelon unit's assessment of the current situation:

> Difficulties in transportation limit the number of U. S. military personnel that can be brought into and maintained in China. Consequently, every individual must be kept at the highest point of technical efficiency and physical condition. These limitations on the strength of the command require a corresponding increase in the amount of work which must be performed by the individual, however, positive measures will be taken by each commander to insure that adequate time for relaxation is afforded to all members of his unit.[16]

And it did not look like Phil would be returning home any time soon:

> The War Department says no one over here will return to the States until there is a proper replacement for all scheduled to go. With the big shortage now present it doesn't look so good. Getting so used to this life over here it really doesn't seem like I have ever lived anyplace else. Isn't it terrible?

Phil also wrote about recent contact he had with another allied soldier. Conversation between the two turned out to be a challenge: "Had a French officer call on me the other night. What a time we had understanding one another. Used a Chinese interpreter who could speak a little French as the last resort. Each word took about 20 minutes before we all agreed."[17]

In a March 7 letter to Leola, Phil asked her for a favor:

> Wish you would do something else for me. My interpreter has been with me for about a year and a half now—real good boy. He wants a watch [in] the worst way and of course can't get one in this wilderness, so would appreciate it a lot if you could pick one up some place and send it to me. Enclosing a check for $40—Don't pay any more, also sending a list of some of the things he wants in the watch—Really doesn't make much difference. He has gotten me out of almost impossible situations several times so I would like to do him at least one favor. Maybe you could send it by first class mail.[18]

A March 19 letter to his mother, Corinne, and Jim relayed sad news and reminded them of war's ultimate cost: "Do you remember Terrence McCay?—a boy from Salem S. Dak. I went through the Un[iversity] with. He was killed on the Western Front at Xmas time. Makes one wonder doesn't it?—Also Arlo Olson—Leola liked him."[19]

Terrence C. McCay took the same pre-law course that Phil did at the University of South Dakota. He was a member of the Delta Tau Delta social fraternity, the Delta Theta Phi law fraternity, and the Law Association. He became a commissioned officer after completing the ROTC program at school. While serving in Italy, he was wounded at Salerno and again at Anzio. He received the Combat Infantryman's Badge for participating in active ground combat. On January 4, 1945, he was killed in action while serving as a first lieutenant in France.[20]

Arlo L. Olson, from Toronto, South Dakota, attended the University from 1936 to 1940. He and Phil were both members of the Sigma Alpha Epsilon social fraternity, and Arlo also received his commission through the ROTC program. After graduating in 1940, Olson worked in a bank for a year before joining the Army in 1941. While leading an infantry company as a captain, he died in Italy on October 27, 1943. He was posthumously awarded the Medal of Honor (the nation's highest military honor for valor in battle) for actions he took during his company's drive across the Volturo River and advance to the summit of Monte San Nicola.[21]

By the spring of 1945, war casualties from Phil's hometown area had significantly increased. Starting with its February 22 edition, the *Grant County Review* included a column titled "Grant County Honor Roll." It had five categories—Killed In Service, Died In Service, Wounded In Service, Missing In Action, and Prisoners Of War. The soldier's name and hometown were listed under each category. In the Honor Roll's first appearance, 22 men were listed as Killed In Service, 1 had Died In Service, 24 had been Wounded In Service, 2 were Missing In Action, and 8 listed as being Prisoners Of War.[22]

With a few exceptions, the Grant County Honor Roll was updated on a weekly basis from March 1 to August 2. An additional category—Injured In Service—was added starting with the paper's April 5th edition. The Honor Roll's final list included 27 men Killed In Action, 1 Died In Service, 52 Wounded in Service, 5 Prisoners of War, and 1 Injured in Service.[23]

Back in China, it had become "real nice and warm in our sector of operations" by mid-March, and Phil stated that "one of these days I'll even go so far as to take off my long underwear."[24] The warm March weather was soon followed by rain: "We have been having rain rain and rain for the past four days now. Can't seem to get any socks over here so am having Leola send me some. All the clothing goes to our great allies you know." Phil had also become frustrated with those allies:

This Chinese outfit I am with at the present will drive us all completely nuts I am sure. One minute the General tells me the Japs are three hours away and the next minute they are thirty miles the other side of some damn river. Wish I could write more about these things.[25]

On March 20, General Wedemeyer visited Phil's unit "with just about all the brass in China." Phil described the American Commanding General as "a swell old boy [who] just completed 2 years in the South Pacific before landing over here."[26] In a short speech given to the men, Wedemeyer "said a lot of nice things about us, but I am afraid it was not all the truth."[27] That same day, Phil received photographs of his niece Nancy. He noted that "she certainly is good looking and really growing up in a hurry. Suppose she will be having dates by the time I get back."[28]

The next day, Phil inspected a Chinese Field Hospital. It was an eye-opening experience:

Wish you could have gone with me on my inspecting trip through a Chinese Field Hospital today. About as many pigs and chickens in the place as soldiers. In one ward they had collected about ten people with broken legs, no attempt was made to set them and the American medical officer with me suggested they all be killed immediately rather than just passing out in degrees. Absolutely shameless.[29]

A letter to Lois dated March 25 indicated Phil and his fellow American soldiers recently obtained something that reminded them of how lonely they were:

Aren't we lucky?—Our Special Service Officer sent us down a phonograph today with several popular records. Only trouble is I am going to have to send the darn thing back because every time someone plays it all the rest sit around with big tears in their eyes. I guess after 20 months of this stuff most anyone would get just a little lonesome.

* * *

There is that darn phonograph again—pardon me while I cry along with the rest of the boys.—No kidding either.

Phil's letter also asked Lois "when is graduation this year?" and added that "you certainly have made a splendid record in your four years at the Un[iversity]."[30]

Indeed she had. A Business Administration major, Lois was elected student body president in the spring of 1944 and served in that position during her senior year. Under her leadership, the student senate initiated plans to convert the Union Building into a student center, revised the University constitution, sponsored a drive for the World Student Service Fund, and expanded the Thanksgiving holiday from one day to two.[31]

When she was a senior, the students elected Lois as Miss Popularity (better known as "Miss Pop"). According to the *1945 Coyote* yearbook, Miss Pop is "one of the greatest honors that can be bestowed upon a University woman."[32] During that year, she was also one of seven students chosen for Mortar Board (women's honorary group selected "on the basis of scholarship, service and leadership") and one of ten included in *Who's Who Among Students in American Universities and Colleges*.[33]

Throughout her four years in college, Lois was a member of the Kappa Alpha Theta social sorority. She served as its secretary in her senior year. As a senior, she also belonged to Guidon—a women's group organized as "Company A" that supported the military and received rifle instructions from the University's Military Department.[34] Finally, at varying points in her college career, Lois was a member of the Spanish Club, the Business Administration Association, the

Varsettes (a women's "pep organization"), Playcrafters (a theater organization), and Alpha Lambda Delta (national honor society for freshmen women).[35]

In late March, Phil made a short trip to the Chinese Combat Command Headquarters. The trip featured decent food and a forgettable movie:

> Just returned from a short airplane ride. The old man up the line got a few more of his great ideas the other morning so sent a plane down to pick [us] up. Took us 2 ½ hours to fly back whereas by pack horse it takes days. Really was nice getting back to at least a little civilization once again. We had potatoes, bread, meat, pie and all the trimmings for our supper. Then a movie, what junk they are sticking the people with now days. Ain't it awful? At breakfast the next morning we had oatmeal and cornflakes—damn near killed myself. Got back to my outfit around noon time and of course partook in the usual can of cold C-ration . . . Wouldn't be bad at all if we knew where the Japs were, but we have no way of finding out and the Chinese just aren't interested.[36]

April 1st was Easter Sunday, and Phil had to be reminded of that fact: "Somebody said this was Easter Sunday. Haven't had any religion for so long it's almost impossible to keep track." He expressed some irritation at having to comply with General Wedemeyer's newly-implemented reporting policy: "This new bunch of people we have in Hqs. are report crazy. Have about 10 men filling out papers all day long and it's all they can do to keep up with things."[37]

Three days later, Phil again mentioned his frustration with the Chinese unit to which he was attached:

> Wish you could have been in these parts yesterday. A handful of Japs shot off ten cents worth of fire crackers and the outfit

I'm with retreated 30 miles before it even looked back. Then the mugs in Washington want to know why we can't get going on the offensive.

Not much chance getting home this spring—maybe late fall if all goes at least 10% the right way. 2 years is much too long here.[38]

A letter to Lois dated April 8 gave a more optimistic view of the military situation, although Phil continued to question his Chinese unit's logistical capabilities:

The way things are going in Europe it just can't be too long now. Aren't the boys over there doing a wonderful job? Our Commanding General is now coming out with the dope that after the Germans are licked it will be just a short time before our lost replacements will start arriving. More good news now days.

* * *

Odd as it may seem military matters have gone rather well over here of late. Of course we don't have a Gen. Patton with 50 thousand tanks to tear around with, but the old ox carts nevertheless are right in there making a few yards every once in a while. The other day some darn fool got the bright idea of moving our so-called troops cross country instead of [using] the trail. About five seconds from the starting point we got mixed up in a village rice field and I am sure you have never heard such an agitated stir in all your life. Men, women, kids by the hundreds... came swarming out to inform us of our mistake. I ended up right in the middle of all of it, and I'm afraid we had numerous situations straining diplomatic relations to say the least.

New Leadership—Mixed Results 111

Phil ended this letter with the following post script: "When and if I get back to the States this summer I certainly would like to see you. Would you mind too much?"[39]

President Roosevelt died on April 12, 1945. He was succeeded by Vice-President Harry S Truman. Here was how Phil reacted to this unexpected event:

> The death of the President certainly was a great blow to all of us. It seems like no one realized before what tremendous faith we had in him. It's most difficult to even imagine his death at a more inopportune time in our country's history. Isn't it too bad people can't learn to say nice things about a man while he is living instead of waiting until he is dead.[40]

One week later, the *Grant County Review* featured a front-page article that was titled "Commander-in-Chief Stricken" and accompanied by a familiar photograph of the President. The article stated, among other things, that he was "deeply loved and admired by millions of Americans, while ardently hated by others"; that he was "the one man above all others upon whom millions based their greatest hope for establishment of a workable peace organization as the outcome of this war"; and that "never in the history of this country has one of our citizens been accorded the acclaim and tribute the world over that was accorded him."[41] And after noting the president died in April, the authors of *Time Runs Out in CBI* had this to say regarding FDR's involvement in the China war:

> President Roosevelt had taken a keen personal interest in the conduct of American affairs in China, and had kept many of the threads in his own hand. From 1942 to the fall of 1944, he had sent several special emissaries to China, and kept in touch with the Generalissimo and his entourage through many informal channels. Roosevelt had also been firm in his support of General Chennault in the disputes over strategy in China.[42]

On April 15, Phil wrote to Lois that "the situation is as confused over here as it's possible to get. No one seems to know who is fighting who and what side they should be on. Had a chaplain come in the other day and even he was in serious doubt." Phil also noted that his efforts at achieving cleanliness seemed to have backfired:

> Had very little to do yesterday so I decided to take a shower—first one in three months; ended up by catching cold. Also took my blankets out for a bit of air and sunshine and the result was I couldn't sleep a wink. Just nothing like the primitive filth and poverty.[43]

In sum, as of mid-April 1945, Phil's and other Chinese units had achieved mixed results in their efforts to defeat the Japanese. Phil was encouraged by some of those efforts but discouraged when the Chinese failed or refused to engage the enemy. Although he didn't know it at this time, he was about to be transferred to a new command that would conduct offensive action in a different part of China.

CHAPTER 9

Assigned to Central Command

The following named Os are asgd to Central Command, CCC (Prov) and WP via first avail T fr APO 627 to such places in China as may be necessary for them to report to the CG, Central Command for dy: Maj PHIL W SAUNDERS 0446777 Inf [.]

Travel by Govt owned mtr vehicle, rail, animal, air T, or any other avail means of T is atzd.

Special Orders, Number 105

As previously mentioned, six sub-areas of the Chinese Combat Command were established in late January, 1945. Among the six was the Central Command. It consisted of four armies (the 73rd, 13th, 71st, and 94th), and each army contained three divisions. The Central Command, with its 12 divisions, was one of the four commands created to be "an offensive force." (The other three "offensive force" commands were the Western, Reserve, and Eastern. They contained a total of eight armies and 24 divisions. General Ho Ying-Chin had overall command responsibility for all 36 divisions, which were collectively referred to as the ALPHA force.)[1] The Central Command was located north and east of Kunming. This area included Kweiyang, the capital of Kweichow province, which was described as a "vital road center ... from which roads lead to Kunming and Chungking." It also extended to smaller towns east of Kweiyang, some of which were located in the Hunan province.[2]

On April 21, Phil was assigned as a Liaison Officer in the Central Command.[3] The next day, he sent this update from Kunming:

Right at the present I am in the moving process once again. For a few days I'll be here at Combat Command Hqs. then push off again in another direction where the Japs now seem to be making their main effort. This morning I bought $25 worth of clothing. Didn't have a heck of a lot left, but in fairly good shape right now. Going down to the hospital this afternoon to have my eyes checked over—Do believe I need glasses—also having my stomach looked at. Seems like most everyone has some trouble with the digestion system over here.

Went to the Red Cross building here in Kunming last night. Really swell. Had a steak—ice cream, and most of the trimmings. Civilization is certainly wonderful.[4]

In late April, Phil reported he was

still hanging around Kunming but hope to push off shortly. These Headquarters people are a pain in the ___ [blank line in original].

I was out to see the eye Doc yesterday and guess I'll have to wear glasses for reading now.

Been hot as the dickens around here lately. Do believe I'll have my head shaved one of these days.

The latest dope from the War Dept. is that rotation is no longer, but at the end of our 24 months overseas we will be sent home for 45 days. This of course will all be changed at least ten times by next week.[5]

On May 2, Phil provided this description of his journey from Kunming to a convoy camp located somewhere in the Central Command Area:

Pushed off the other day from our main Hqs. so right now business is picking up. Roads are terrible and the jeeps ride like a Ford. Last night we had to dig in so it wasn't too comfortable, but tonight we are staying in a convoy camp and it's not bad at all. Going to get out my long underwear again as the mornings and nights are cold as the devil. Driving along this afternoon we saw a good many dead Chinamen lying along the road. Most of them soldiers. They seem to make no effort to dig a grave for them whatsoever. After a while one gets used to most everything I guess.

Certainly looks like Germany is done for now. If everyone gets down to business maybe the Japs will get the business this year also.

No lights at this dump and its getting awful dark so that's all for now.[6]

A day or two later, Phil arrived "at one of our big bases of operations" after "a lot of wear and tear on the hindquarters."[7] (According to contemporaneous Army records, it appears this "base" was the 94th Army headquarters, located at either Chenyuan or Chinghsien. Chenyuan is approximately 120 miles east-northeast of Kweiyang, and Chinghsien is about 80 miles southeast of Chenyuan. Kunming is roughly 380 miles from Chenyuan and 450 miles from Chinghsien.)[8] Phil explained that "we were sent out here to make contact with the Japs, but no one seems to know where they are. " He also reported that "we did have our first air raid in a long time last night." The climate in his new area was highly variable: "In one spot it's warm as the devil and then you go five miles further on and it's cold enough for polar bears." Finally, this letter from his new location ended on an optimistic note: "Looks to me now like there is a very good chance of the Japs being licked this year. Lots of strain on them from most every direction."[9]

Phil's travel the next day included riding on a Chinese train to an American convoy camp. When he and his group of Chinese soldiers arrived at "the so-called R.R. station," they were met by "at least 35 coolies," who all "grabbed a portion of something and then all started off in different directions." Phil

> rushed over to the Chinese ticket agent and tried to ask him what train we were supposed to get on, naturally he couldn't understand me and I couldn't understand him so we started putting on demonstrations for one another. I would grab a nearby bundle of some sort, then try to pronounce the name of the town we were headed for and at the same time start in the direction of one of the trains.

After several unsuccessful attempts at this form of communication, "the old ticket agent informed me that he couldn't see over ten feet in front of him so he thought maybe the demonstration method was rather useless." Phil agreed with him, and "as we terminated the activity, the . . . [Chinese] spectators gave us a most gratifying ovation."[10]

Phil spent the next two hours recovering most of his packed belongings that the coolies had dispersed throughout the train yard. Then, with the help of a Chinese conductor who spoke a little English, he and his group were finally able to get on the right train. But before it left the station, "apparently some passenger got the brilliant idea that the flat car in the rear of the train should be in the middle, so naturally we immediately started switching things all over the place." This switching operation took another 30 or 40 minutes and "was completed by the passengers and bystanders." After that was done, the train finally began its journey. Phil's description of the train trip ended with this paragraph:

> After 22 hours of similar activity we did reach our day's destination which was a gigantic grand total of 38 miles from

the starting point of confusion. When we first reached the American convoy camp people would just stare at us and then mutter something about how terrible and how long we must have been in the front lines.[11]

By May 12, the headquarters for the Central Command's 94th Army had moved about 70 miles further east and relocated at Wukang.[12] The next day, Phil was designated as a Chief of Staff in the 43rd Division of the 94th Army.[13] General Mou Ting-fang commanded this Army. Colonel George L. Goodridge was assigned as its American liaison officer.[14] The 43rd Division had approximately 10, 000 men.[15] When Phil got this assignment, Chinese units located in the Central Command Area had a "Generally satisfactory" combat efficiency rating. (Ratings for other command areas were either "Unsatisfactory," "Satisfactory," or "Very satisfactory," with some areas receiving mixed ratings for various units comprising that command.)[16]

On May 13, Phil noted that he had

> been traveling once again for the last three or four days. Talked with 5 Japs some of the more advanced units captured a few days ago. They seem very willing to give us most any information we desire.
>
> The German surrender was certainly wonderful news to all of us. I think in a few months the whole picture will have changed a lot, even these people over here seem to be getting on the ball. Imagine that.[17]

Two days later, he reported that "the much talked about Chinese counter offensive has gone rather well of late and naturally we all feel good about that." He also referred to one of his recent discussions with a Japanese prisoner: "I had the opportunity of talking with a Jap officer. . . [we] captured. I do believe they realize now what a terrible mess they are in. This fellow seemed to be well educated and spoke English rather well."[18]

Phil received a letter from Lois on May 21—29 days after she wrote it. He was very happy to hear from her:

> Your swell letter of April 22 reached me last night, and it certainly came at the right time. The last few days it's done nothing but rain and we had to be out tearing around in it getting nowhere so all in all I was feeling very low. Hearing from you made me feel a lot better.

Phil's response to Lois's letter also shared his post-war plans and thoughts about what life would be like once the war was over:

> After I get out of the army I would like very much to finish law school.... It's going to be awful hard to settle down and study once again no matter how I look at it. How about giving you a little practice in shorthand when I get back? I know just how you feel about typing. I took it in High School until the poor teacher just gave up.
>
> Most all of our discussions start and end on the subject of life after the war. I think everyone realizes that we all face a period of re-adjustment that maybe won't be so easy in a lot of cases, but all I want is a chance to at least make an attempt before I start getting [an] old age pension.

Phil's letter added this P. S. "Certainly glad you can't see me now—We have had to live off the land the last week and we all look like the very devil. Rather proud of my beard, however."[19]

On May 25, Phil wrote to the editor of the *Grant County Review*. Among other subjects, this letter included comments about American troops returning home and Japanese continued resistance:

A good many of the men in this theater are now on their way home as a result of the new point system the war department has set up. Most of them have been overseas for three or four years so I am sure they are worthy of all the breaks coming to them.

Looks to me like the war with the Japs is going to take a long time yet and I am afraid a lot of casualties, if they continue to fight like they have on Okinawa. In the last two weeks I have had an opportunity to talk to several Jap prisoners of war and they all seem to agree that they have lost the war, but at the same time are stupid enough to continue their fanatical resistance to the very end. One of the captured officers admitted that our present air and naval blockade has made shipping between China and the home island impossible. We always ask them about the 'death march of Bataan,' and the 'rape of Nanking,' but naturally none of them know anything about such horrible and hideous atrocities.[20]

That same day, Phil received a wrist watch from his sister Leola. This was the gift he had asked her to purchase for his interpreter back in early March. It was very much appreciated: "A couple of days ago I received the watch you sent. It arrived in excellent condition and I certainly do thank you for all the trouble you must have gone through to get it. It's really nice, and my interpreter went almost wild when he saw it."[21]

The next day, Phil "had to go down the road and inspect the quarters of some men we have stationed there." He was shocked by what he found:

Just couldn't believe that white people could live the way they were. Dick Savage had a palace compared to this hole. After making the inspection I had a little formation at which everybody stood at attention for ½ an hour and I think we now have a complete understanding of what is to be done.

In the letter that discussed the inspection, Phil also elaborated on how the point system—referenced in his May 25 letter to the editor—was being implemented: "Lot of people going home under this new point system. Trouble is they want to get rid of these sixty year old colonels and keep the younger blood—and they're doing it."[22]

Near the end of May, Phil recommended to his mother that she read "a nice little article" in "the May 14th edition of Time Magazine" that told "about the success of our recent sideshow."[23] That article stated:

> Even in tragic China the war picture grew brighter for the moment. Japanese commanders, their communications harassed by locomotive-busting Fourteenth Air Force pilots, had been sweeping aside light, ill-armed Chinese troops to smash the U.S. air bases one by one. But last week they tried for Chihkiang, 300 miles east of Chungking, and ran into something new and hard.
>
> As their columns moved westward from the Paoking area, northward from Chengpu, the usual ragged Chinese armies were suddenly stiffened by U.S.-equipped units, tough and battlewise. The Japs, who had set out on a mere punitive expedition, found themselves fighting a hard, draining battle.
>
> For the Japanese this was a foretaste of the future. The days of easy victories in China were fast passing. Exultantly Lieut. General Albert C. Wedemeyer, able commander of American forces in China, could promise his men that, with the end of the war in Europe, "our turn is coming."[24]

On June 1, Phil reported that

we will be having it rather easy the next several weeks—Going into a period of training and reorganization before pushing on. They tell us the eyes of the world are now upon this theater so we must produce outstanding results. At the present time replacements are coming in from the States thick and fast, but no one seems to be going home in spite of it.

He also mentioned receiving a letter from his "good friend Nelson," who "is out running around in the hills someplace having a big time."[25]

A week later, his unit "had to move a short distance" and it "seems like every time we get somewhat settled down some darn fool will always decide it's time to move again." At this point, "all the boys that had 30 months in overseas have now gone home. So it looks like the rest of us will have a chance when our time is up."[26] Shortly thereafter, he stated "My lord is it ever hot in this terrible place. I thought it used to warm up in Ga., but nothing like this—Would give a million dollars for just one little hunk of ice." He also added that "new officers coming over from the States most any day now. Most of them seem to be in the tank corps which won't do us a damn bit of good. Japs seem to be pulling out of South China so I suppose the Chinese will be claiming great victories now."[27]

* * * *

The MARS Task Force—also known as the 5332d Brigade (Provisional)—was activated on July 26, 1944. It consisted of two American regiments (the 475th Infantry and the 124th Calvary) plus the 1st Chinese Separate Infantry Regiment. Brigadier General Thomas S. Arms was the first MARS Task Force commander. He was succeeded by Brigadier General John P. Willey on October 31, 1944.[28]

This unit successfully participated in offensive actions that took place in Burma in late 1944-early 1945, and it was instrumental in reopening the Burma Road to China in late January 1945.[29] After victories had been achieved in Burma during that spring, MARS Task

Force members were moved to China to reinforce the Chinese armies fighting there.[30] By mid-June, a company of MARS men had become attached to Phil's unit. In separate letters to Leola and to his mother, he made it very clear that these troops were not helpful:

> I've got a company of the Mars Task Force attached right at the present. Nothing but a bunch of foolish kids. Last night I understand a few of them were running around naked in the small village located near here. I never realized before how many good for nothings we had in this army.

and "I suppose you know now that the Mars Task Force is in China. What a terrible mess they are. If our Armies coming from Europe aren't any better than this outfit, they might just as well keep them at home."[31]

Military historians who have examined the MARS troops' performance in their new assignment have voiced similar criticisms:

> Estimates varied sharply as to the usefulness of these Americans once they had arrived. For example, the MARS soldiers were two representative regiments of U.S. infantry, who in combat had done all their superiors asked of them, and done it well. On arrival in China they were expected to act as liaison personnel and instructors for Chinese troops. But many of MARS personnel did not have either the background or the temperament to act as teachers and advisors. The G-3 [Operations Section], Central Command, later testified that only 17 or 18 percent of the 900 MARS men assigned to Central Command were usable in their new roles. The rest, he thought, were simply a burden. Yet they needed about 500 tons of supplies every month, tonnage that would if converted to ammunition be enough to maintain a Chinese army for thirty days.[32]

* * * *

In a short letter to his mother dated June 20, Phil noted that it is "still hot as the dickens"; that "we have been getting some darn good food of late. We are now off per diem and getting Govt. rations instead which seems to make a big difference"; and that "lot of the boys going home now days, but they tell us some of us are essential so will be be held for a while longer." He also added that the "June 4th issue of Time Magazine has got a real good article in it about the situation over here."[33]

The referenced article was titled "CHINA: The New Army." It began by describing recent Chinese victories, and then provided extensive background information about "the commander of all the U.S. forces in China and Generalissimo Chiang Kai-shek's chief of staff—Lieut. General Albert Coady Wedemeyer." Next, the article described Wedemeyer's and Chiang's efforts to create "a new Chinese Army." It noted

> Wedemeyer and his staff have received unprecedented cooperation from the Generalissimo. . . . How well Lieut. General Wedemeyer has succeeded in the diplomatic part of his job was indicated last week when Generalissimo Chiang Kai-shek accepted an invitation to be Wedemeyer's guest at supper. Not since he became President of China has Chiang ever accepted such an invitation from a foreigner. But the Generalissimo has a good reason to be grateful. The new army forged by Wedemeyer is clearly superior to anything ever seen in China. Few can appreciate better than Chiang Kai-shek how much this new army will strengthen his Government for the internal and external trials that lie ahead for China.

Lastly, the article explored the "Political Implications" of China's recent victories. That analysis contained this prescient passage:

To her allies (the U.S. and Britain), the Chinese successes meant that the advance units of China's potential military might were slowly, doggedly beginning to move forward along the long road to Tokyo. Politically, the Chinese successes foreshadowed the emergence of China as a Far Eastern power whose political destiny might well prove to be the political destiny of democracy in Asia and in the world.[34]

On June 24, Phil wrote that "we will be leaving our truck road in a few days, so mail from this way might be a little slow for a while. Our only transportation now will be the legs."[35] This trip turned out to be Phil's most physically demanding activity of the war, and it was followed by his most significant combat experience.

CHAPTER 10

The Kweilin Offensive

Major PHIL W. SAUNDERS . . . is awarded the Bronze Star Medal for meritorious service. . . . During the KWEILIN Offensive of July 1945, he assisted materially in expediting the movement of supplies, ammunition, and rations for both the Chinese and Americans. . . . [In] the midst of the Campaign he assumed the duties of combat liaison with one of the Regiments of the [43rd] Division pressing the attack upon the city of KWEILIN[.]

Citation accompanying General Order No. 67

Kweilin is a city located approximately 475 miles straight east of Kunming. During World War II, it was the capital of Kwangsi province. By 1944, Kweilin's suburbs contained one of the U.S. Fourteenth Air Force's largest bases. By the fall of 1944, the Japanese were directing their forces toward Kweilin. In late October, Chiang "'assured'" General Wedemeyer that the Chinese army could hold the city "'for at least two months.'" But on November 10, the Japanese took it in one day. Before the enemy arrived, "Kweilin's hundreds of thousands of citizens had . . . evacuated the city by packed rail cars, in boats, and on foot." Moreover, members of the Fourteenth Air Force "abandoned and demolished all 550 buildings on their air base, taking every gallon of gas and every piece of equipment they could carry with them before blowing up or burning what remained." Chiang's "demoralized and starving Chinese Nationalist forces" were left to defend the city, and they offered "little resistance" against the advancing Japanese 11th Army.[1]

Now it was mid-1945, and part of the Chinese offensive plan was to retake Kweilin. The 43rd Division—to which Phil was attached—was one of the units assigned to this mission. Phil described it as "our first big offensive in 15 months." For him and his unit, it began with a long, physically demanding march in a southerly direction toward Kweilin:

> We have certainly had more than our share of excitement of late. Ye Gads. I just finished 5 of the hardest days in my life. We had to walk 90 miles in 4 days with one day's rest. Damn near killed us all, but I think we arrived to do a little good nevertheless. Heat was terrible and water is almost impossible to get.
>
> * * *
>
> The first day of our 90 mile march my feet hurt like the devil, but after that things started to get oiled up so I didn't have too much trouble. This country is all like the Linden Beach Hill so you see what 90 miles in this damn place means. I am sure I couldn't do it again. Could write a whole book on what we saw and had to do, but no time now.[2]

Army records indicate this "90-mile march" started in the Wukang area (where elements of the 43rd Division had been located since mid-May) and stopped in Lungsheng, a village approximately 40 miles north and a little west of Kweilin.[3]

Phil's letter describing this phase of the offensive added that it "seems awful good to be on the winning side for a change," and "you won't hear anything about us in the news, but wherever the Chinese armies go—we are right there on the spot."[4]

On July 12, Phil provided a detailed account of the campaign's progress up to that time:

We are 8 hard days off the road so it's all walking or pack in these parts.

Never have I lived through such terrible days as we have had lately. The heat is a hell of a lot worse than anything else. We got the Japs running like the devil, but the next week or two will be the tough ones as we get close to their home base. We eat breakfast at 5 in the morning—no dinner, then sometimes supper usually around 8 or 9 at night, and in places the Japs have pulled out of all there is left is a little rice now and then. Coolies are almost impossible to get so we have had to throw away just about everything, and all I have with me now is one blanket and one small pack with a few odds and ends in it. Wish you could see the pills we have to take each day—One pill for malaria, one for the heat, one food concentrated pill, and some other damn things that nobody seems to know what they are for.

We get into the last phase of our campaign in a few days and we are all praying that things go well. The courage and guts of these poor, sick, dirty, hungry Chinese soldiers is something wonderful. Wish some of those fat hogs back in Washington could see what these poor devils go through. If they are wounded or get sick the chances of recovery for them is about 2%, yet they will keep going night and day until they are told to stop. It's just impossible to describe what I've seen in the last few weeks, one minute you see mankind at its worst and the next at its best.

Haven't received any mail for 2 weeks now and probably won't for another two, but then this is war.

I hope those people in the States eating ice cream, drinking cold water, and riding around in nice cars will appreciate their comforts just a little.

* * *

If you don't hear from me for a while now—don't worry—just no way of getting mail out.⁵

Three days later, Phil wrote this update:

We still are on the move. Last few days it's been more Jap opposition and less walking however.

Yesterday morning we started to climb a mountain at 6:30—we reach[ed] the top at 10:30—so you can get some idea of the tremendous difficulties in this type of country. We were completely wet by the time we reached the top, and then it started to rain and the fog came in so things went from bad to worse. On the low ground the heat almost kills us and then a couple hours later on the top of some darn mountain the cold almost gets us. No justice: How these Chinese soldiers can take this stuff is more than we can understand.⁶

In mid-July, the Army officially recognized Phil's active participation in combat. It did so by awarding him the Combat Infantryman's Badge (CIB) with an effective date of July 16, 1945. This award

> was established by the War Department on 27 October 1943. Lieutenant General Lesley J. McNair, then the Army Ground Forces commanding general, was instrumental in its creation. He originally recommended that it be called the "fighter badge." The CIB was designed to enhance morale and the prestige of the "Queen of Battle." Then Secretary of War Henry Stimson said, "It is high time we recognize in a personal way the skill and heroism of the American infantry."

The badge was "presented to those officers, warrant officers and enlisted soldiers, in the grade of Colonel and below, who participate[d] in active ground combat[.]" The 1943 War Department circular that established the award

> required infantrymen to demonstrate "satisfactory performance of duty in action against the enemy." The operative words "in action" connoted actual combat. A War Department determination in October 1944 specified that "action against the enemy" for purposes of award of the CIB was to be interpreted as "ground combat against enemy ground forces."[7]

The Headquarters for the Chinese Combat Command issued Phil's CIB in General Order Number 48. That document provided in relevant part:

> Pursuant to authority contained in Letter, Rear Echelon Headquarters, USF, CT, Subject: "Combat Infantryman's Badge', File 200.6, dtd 2 April 1945, and WD Circular 408, 1944, as amended by WD Circular 450, 1944, the Combat Infantryman's Badge is awarded to the following named Officers and Enlisted Men effective dates as indicated for satisfactory conduct in action against the enemy... Major PHIL W. SAUNDERS 0 446 777 Inf 16 Jul 45.[8]

Phil's next letter, written to his mother on July 19, began with comments about the mail:

> Will write now, but God only knows when I'll get to send this letter.
>
> Last night we certainly had a swell surprise. One of our medical officers came up from Army Hqs. and brought the mail

along. I did all right—several from you—one from Corinne and a couple from Leola. Your last letter was dated 22 June so considering how far out we are that's not bad.

He went on to describe other updates regarding the Kweilin offensive:

We have been more or less in one spot now for the past days because of heavy Jap opposition, but I suppose by the end of this week we will [be] on the move again. It's still awful hot—Lots of rain and very little food.

I had a rather interesting day on the 18th. Went up to the Regt. O.P. [Regimental Observation Post] and looked at the fighting from there. In fact things looked so good we went forward to the Bn. [Battalion] and then to the companies. (against W. D. [War Department] regulations). We could see the Japs getting ready to make one of their counter attacks, so just to satisfy ourselves we borrow[ed] a couple American rifles from the Chinese and took a few shots at them. I am rather sure they were out of rifle range, but it did help us pay them back for at least a few of the darn mountains we had to climb. I am glad we left when we did as the General told me this morning the Japs took back that particular ground.

Phil also responded to inquiries he had regarding the possibility of a medical discharge:

In the letters I get people keep asking if I am going to get a medical discharge because of my sickness last winter. Ye gads no.—Really it was nothing worse than a bad cold. I feel that anybody who can walk about 25 miles a day over some of the highest mountains in the world, with only a little rice and a few K rations to eat is in fairly good shape. Don't you? I feel wonderful and with some decent food for a couple of weeks I'll be like new[.]

Finally, he speculated a bit about his future in the Army:

Don't have enough points to get out under the W.D. point system, but if I get rotated back to the States I'll end up with an Am. Bn. [American Battalion] and I have forgotten too much for that job—like everybody else over here. So looks like I will take the 30 day leave in the States late this fall, and then come back here and starve and walk, and get no place for another year.

Have a good chance now for another promotion soon, but I guess my age is a little against me. Sometimes it would be much easier if I were just a little older. Most of the Colonels over here are rather ancient.[9]

The Kweilin offensive ended on or about August 1. Its last week was succinctly described in *Time Runs Out in CBI*:

By 26 July more Chinese from General Tang's army were up to the battle area, and an attack on Kweilin was possible. [General Tang En-po was the III Army Group Commander who directed Central Command troops.] The CCC did not think that the Japanese would make a stand for Kweilin. Two Japanese divisions plus two brigades were believed to have cleared the area by the 26th. Next day, I-ning fell and shortly after, Yung-fu, thirty miles south of Kweilin. Three days later the Chinese had taken Yung-fu, had covered the thirty miles, and were in Kweilin's southern suburbs. Soon after, the Japanese rear guards were pushed out of Kweilin, and as August began, the city was Chinese again.[10]

From Phil's vantage point, the last phase of the offensive turned out to be less difficult than he had anticipated:

> We finished our present campaign a few days ago. Our main objective wasn't so tough as was expected. Our biggest trouble was artillery fire, but all in all it wasn't so bad. The last two days we have done nothing but sleep—it's rained most of the time so that sorta added to the relaxation. These Chinese soldiers are really all pooped out[.]

He also described what the area was like now that the Japanese are gone:

> The Chinese civilians are really most cordial to all of us. The Japs I guess treated them rather rough when they were around. Most of the Chinese evacuated into the hills when the nips took over and as we came in most of them started coming back to their old homes,—good many of them carry their household effects in one basket and three or four kids in the other.
>
> All the important towns and cities have been completely destroyed—so all in all most of them don't have much to come back to.
>
> So darn many mosquitoes in this part of the country thought I would get malaria sure as the devil, but not as yet[.]

* * *

> We hope the truck road up to our present location will be completed soon—probably be in this general area for about a month—When our rear echelon gets up with us we will have some good old American rations, but until then I guess we will continue to eat this damn dry rice and like it.[11]

As noted above, Phil was awarded the Bronze Star Medal for his service during the Kweilin offensive. This award was given to ground troops who displayed "heroic or meritorious achievement on the field of battle." General George C. Marshall recommended that President Roosevelt authorize the medal to "boost morale amongst the ranks of long-suffering infantrymen." Roosevelt did so by signing Executive Order 9419 on February 4, 1944, and the award was made retroactive to the beginning of the war.[12]

Phil was given this award in CCC Headquarters General Order Number 67. The citation accompanying that order stated:

> Major PHIL W. SAUNDERS, 0-446777, Infantry, Army of the United States, is awarded the Bronze Star Medal for meritorious service during the period 1 July 1945 to 1 August 1945. Major SAUNDERS served as Executive Officer with the 43rd Division Liaison Team assigned to the 94th Army. During the KWEILIN offensive of July 1945, he assisted materially in expediting the movement of supplies, ammunition, and rations for both the Chinese and Americans. His outstanding work aided materially in the success of the Campaign. During the midst of the Campaign he assumed the duties of combat liaison with one of the Regiments of the Division pressing the attack upon the city of KWEILIN. His sound tactical advice, his enthusiastic and aggressive support, and his frank and open dealings effected liaison that was effective and vital to the swift conclusion of that offensive. His outstanding work during this period reflects great credit on himself and the Armed Forces of the United States.[13]

The end of the Kweilin offensive also marked the end of Phil's active involvement in combat. But he would face significant health challenges before finally being able to leave China.

CHAPTER 11

It's Over

On August 6 the atomic bomb was dropped on Hiroshima. On August 7 the Russians entered the war. On August 9 a second bomb was dropped on Nagasaki.... An unanticipated result of the bomb was to provide Japan with a face-saving reason for quick surrender and that development now followed more precipitately than foreseen. After an intense struggle over the status of the Emperor, ending in American agreement to his retention, Japan surrendered on August 14.

Barbara W. Tuchman

During the afternoon on August 9, Phil made a quick visit to Kweilin. He found it to be a sad, desolate place:

> The Japs completely destroyed the whole darn city. Not a building left standing. Wish you could see the civilians as they come back to their homes. About all they have left is what they carry with them, but most of them ... really can't comprehend just how bad off they are and I guess it's better that way.

Regarding the condition of American troops, Phil noted that "we are still hard up for food. American rations are supposed to be on the way up by pack mules, but something [has] gone haywire. These Chinamen just can't cook worth a darn."[1]

On the other hand, Phil was encouraged by recent developments in the war:

> Certainly lots of good war news the last few days—With the Russians now in things should speed up somewhat, but I hate to think of the complicated political question that's coming up. The Chinese of course are scared to death of Uncle Joe [Stalin]. Who isn't?
>
> We are all anxious to hear more details on this new super dooper bomb they seem to be now fooling around with. Sounds like it's rather a dangerous sort of a thing.

On a more personal note, Phil reported that an affliction he would expect to suffer in the United States had not occurred in his current location. "This is the time of the year for my hay fever to act up, but over here I am not affected with it. Guess in the years to come I'll have to spend the month of August in China.[2]

In an August 15 letter to his mother, Phil gave his initial reaction to the news that Japan had finally surrendered:

> Well this morning came the word that President Truman had officially announced the Jap surrender. Of course we are all more than happy about the whole thing.
>
> It's hard to say how soon they will get us out of here. It's been raining so much lately all the roads are out.
>
> We are all anxious to see how the Japs in China react to the surrender. Certainly hope they obey the orders.
>
> I'll bet the people in the States are having a big time today. It's just impossible for us to believe it's over.
>
> Lot of talk of us flying out from Kweilin to Manila, but would like a boat ride back.

We start this afternoon to turn our equipment in. . . . See you in Sept.—I hope—I hope—I hope.[3]

Four days later, Phil wrote to Lois that he "just can't believe it—I'll probably wake up one of these fine days and learn that it's just a wonderful dream." He asked her how she celebrated the war's end, and noted that, when it came to celebrating with his fellow Americans, "we are still so darn far away from civilization that about all we can do is just sit and stare at one another."[4]

Phil was unclear as to what his immediate post-war assignment would be:

> At one time we expected to be called back to Kunming, but the Chinese have the job of collecting all the thousands of Japs in China, and I guess we have to wait around and see that things turn out right. I fully expect them to get everything all mixed up like they do usually.

He also told Lois about his post-war plans after he returned to the United States:

> I was hoping at one time to get back to the States in time for school this fall, but that is out of the question now. Just as well I guess.

* * *

> I'll be so damn glad to get something to eat again, sleep in a real soft bed, and even a hot bath now and then—(about every five minutes).
>
> After a little over 3 years of short haircuts, I am now going to let the things grow. God only knows what it will look like, but at least it will be something new & different.

* * *

I certainly hope they start turning out cars in a hurry—Would like to get one just as soon as I get back. If I never walk another step in my life I'll be satisfied.[5]

The next day, Phil and his American group were "still waiting for developments. Have been receiving messages from just about everyone, including General Marshall, on what a good job we have done, but the message we are really looking for hasn't arrived as yet." While waiting, Phil found a new way to pass the time:

The last few days while we have had nothing to do but wait—I have taken up bridge. No question about it being a wonderful game. I can see now why people can play it day after day. Our medical officer is supposed to be an expert so of course he is the teacher. Almost made a small slam yesterday.[6]

With respect to his post-war Army career, Phil stated:

Think we will get a 30 day leave when we get back to the States—Then we probably will have to report again somewhere to be discharged or take some sort of administrative job for a few months. We will have a chance to stay in the regular army also. It's going to be hard to let go of a good job for a life time.—It would probably be the sensible thing to do to stay in, but I am willing to start all over again and with a little help from the Dear Father and a few good breaks here and there I probably won't starve to death.

He also expected to be in good financial shape when he returned home:

Haven't got paid in the last 4 months now, so one of these days the money will really roll in. Should have at least $7,000 in the bank by the time this thing is over, and with free schooling under the G. I. bill things don't look too bad. In fact they look damn good and believe you me it's about time.

And despite everything, Phil clearly regarded his wartime experience as a positive one:

> I have certainly been more than fortunate in this war. Been in several real hot places, but have come through without a single scratch, my general health is much better than when I entered, and the experiences I have had and the friends I have made are worth more than money can buy. I am completely satisfied with the whole thing.[7]

On August 22, Phil's American group "started on a long trip back to the States. Didn't do so good, however, only were able to make 8 miles because of the terrible heat and mountains, but from now on I hope to get jeeps and airplanes." (underlining in original). The first day's journey ended at the 94th Army Headquarters in Kweilin, which he described as "really a mad house. Just like grade school kids on the last day of the school year." While there, Phil's group spent "most of our spare time going to Chinese parties & celebrations, but they are awful hard on the system." He also had success at the bridge table when he and his partner "bid a grand slam last night and made the darn thing—redoubled, around 3,000 points. Wonderful game that bridge."[8]

After spending a few days at headquarters, Phil traveled to Liuchow, a city located about 90 miles southwest of Kweilin. This trip was "rather rugged," and he "had to stop every ten minutes while some damn [Chinese] fool made a speech." He noted that Luichow was "not a bad place—good food—saw a movie last night, but the heat is the worst thing I've ever run into. The damn sun is just like fire." It was still unclear what would happen next.

> The General said this morning that a few of us would be <u>selected</u> (He is under the impression that it would be a great honor) to fly to Shanghai with the Chinese occupation armies. I guess it's going to be one of the hot international places in Asia. Don't believe we will have to stay there long, but of course things change every 5 minutes so can't say one way or another.

(underlining in original).[9]

In late August, Phil began a letter to Lois on a romantic note:

> Wish you could see this moon tonight sweet—It's really beautiful even in China. Would give a million dollars if you could be here right now. We have a nice cool little stream running by and lots of swell music over these Sig[nal] Corps radios. Well maybe there will come a day.

He then told her that

> the situation over here is certainly changing rapidly. . . . It looks like I'll be going to Shanghai now for at least a few weeks or so. I guess the political set-up is such that we have to at least keep a finger in it. Think it will be nice to see how the other half of China lives, however.[10]

The next day, Phil reported that he had "been tearing around all day to get all this equipment we have turned over to the . . . Chinese lined up." He added that "out at the air field this afternoon I saw a white girl. We all damn near fell out of the jeep. I haven't talked to an honest to goodness American woman in about 2 years. You suppose I'll be speechless?—I didn't think you would." This letter ended with a joke:

Suppose you have heard this one. A guest in a Cairo hotel, hearing a scream in the corridor, discovered a nice young thing in a negligee being pursued by a gentleman who was, to put it bluntly, nude. Later it developed that the impetuous Romeo was an English major, who was promptly court martialed. His lawyer won him an acquittal, however, by virtue of the following paragraph in the army manual—"It is not compulsory for an officer to wear a uniform at all times, as long as he is suitably garbed for the sport in which he is engaged!"[11]

On September 1, Phil noted that "at the present time transportation is the big tie up over here. All these Chinese troops have to be hauled all over." He was staying in a tent that was either "too dusty or too wet," and "it will seem awful strange to live in a house again." And Phil's original optimism about coming home soon had faded: "It seems like we have a lot more to do now than when the darn war was going on. We were all excited at one time thinking we would get home in short order, but it's not looking so good now."

That night, he contracted amebic dysentery and was admitted to an Army field hospital in Liuchow:

> I have been right on the edge of amebic dysentery for about six months now—I finally came down with it . . . so now I am writing from our field hospital. It seems like everybody in China gets it either sooner or later, been a wonder I haven't had it before this. Only bad thing about it is that they have to give you injections right in the <u>ass</u>. Seems to me a better place could be selected, but the Doc says it is the only suitable location. The cure is complete and it only takes about 10 days.

(underlining in original). Despite this development, Phil still was "rather certain that better days are here to stay, but I'll be damned if I know when they are going to start operating."[12]

Five days later, he was "still in the hospital, but feeling swell—be out of here in a few more days—rather hate to leave. The people here are wonderful and the food gets better all the time. Had chicken last night." He also played bridge "but got the hell beat out of us." The soldier in the bed next to him was in far worse shape:

> Wish you could see this Captain that has got the bed next to me. For two days now he has done absolutely nothing but sit on the bed pan. As we say he has got amebic dysentery—M-2; & that's bad. To top it off he received a letter from his wife saying that she had purchased 4 new hats at $12 each. Needless to say his condition is much worse today.

Phil was still uncertain about his future assignment. Although "General Wedemeyer came out with the statement the other day saying that all American troops in China would be in the States for Xmas," Phil still had "no official dope yet as to . . . [his] final disposition." As far as he knew, he was "still going to Shanghai, but something new & different might show up."[13]

Three days later, Phil received the "official dope" on his next assignment. Rather than being sent to Shanghai with other elements of the 94th Army, he and 39 other American officers in Liuchow were relieved from further duty with the III Army Group Command, CCC (Prov) and transferred to the China Theater Replacement Service in the Services of Supply.[14] This assignment was only temporary. Shortly after it was made, he learned that he would soon be going home.

Phil got out of the hospital on September 11. The next day, he flew to Kunming, and he compared this journey to his previous one from Kunming to Liuchow: "Took me about 4 months with miles of walking to get from Kunming to Liuchow and then the return trip took just 3 hours. I do believe these airplanes are here to stay."[15] He described the situation in Kunming as follows:

> Wish you could see this mad house here. They stuck up a tent camp and darn near everyone in China is here waiting to go. Nobody tells you anything—just muddle around and get in every line you happen to see, but somehow it all works out. I have been getting all my property turned in today and also fixing up the various funds they sling at you from time to time. So far I don't owe the Govt. anything.[16]

In addition to turning in government property, Phil was reunited with his foot locker while in Kunming. He was not happy with the condition of his uniform:

> Finally got my foot locker. First time I had seen it in 18 months. My blouse & pinks I believe are ruined, the jug heads down at S. O. S. let them get wet about a dozen times. I can put a claim in and get my money back, but I'll have to get a new uniform soon as I get back.[17]

He had not received any mail for about a month. This did not surprise him, "as the poor people in the Post Office have gone completely nuts trying to keep track of everybody."[18] To illustrate this point, Phil recounted that "a lot of . . . [mail] came in the other day, but they sent most of it to Liuchow."[19]

Phil expected to leave Kunming "in the next few days," fly to Karachi, India, then take a boat to the United States, and arrive in New York City "sometime in the middle of Oct."[20] But like most of his experiences in the Army, the trip home took longer than anticipated.

CHAPTER 12

From Kunming to Milbank

Major Phil Saunders, who has been through some rugged events in China for about two years, is on his way home.

The *Grant County Review*

On September 15, Phil flew from Kunming to Chaba, India. (Chaba is located in northwestern India. It is about 1,900 miles from Kunming.) He enjoyed the trip: "We had a beautiful ride over the hump yesterday. Flew most of the time at 20,000 [feet] in order to get over the Himalaya Mountains. Rather high aren't they?—Had to use oxygen most of the way." Upon arriving in Chaba, he noted that "all of these various camps are full of soldiers headed for home so it's quite a mix up all over the place." He expected to be there for "about 4 days & if real lucky should catch a boat from Karachi or Calcutta sometime around the end of this month."[1]

Six days later, Phil was "still waiting at Chaba for these darn airplanes to start flying. Weather has been bad the last couple of days so nothing has been moving. Should be in Karachi, however, within the next 3 days." He had established a daily routine in Chaba that was quite enjoyable. Aside from being "terrible hot," the

> life around here is certainly wonderful. We get up about seven—play kittenball [another name for softball] & tennis in the morning, bridge in the afternoon, and a movie at night. Food is marvelous. Yesterday we even had ice cream—just nothing like civilization.

* * *

We play bridge for a fifth of a cent a point. So far I've picked up $16, needless to say I've got a darn good partner.

He "was hoping to run into old Nelson someplace along the line, but they tell me he passed through these parts several days ago."[2]

On September 26, Phil "finally got to Karachi." (Karachi is approximately 340 miles west, southwest of Chaba and is on the Arabian Sea.)[3] It was "a swell trip all the way once things got under way. Flew most of the way at night so the heat wasn't too bad." When their airplane landed, he and his fellow American soldiers found themselves to be in a much different condition than those who were already at the air base:

> We almost killed ourselves laughing at the airport yesterday morning. Everybody around the air base had on clean pressed clothes—shaved, their shoes polished & Wacs were tearing around the place acting like they really had something to do. Everything just so so—when out of the sky drops the beat up people from China. In we come with all our typical China appearances. Uniforms almost ready to fall off, combat boots for shoes, caps and hats of all descriptions. One of the boys thought he would improve his looks a little so he started to roll down his sleeves, but as he rolled the poor old cloth just peeled away into almost thin air. Before we got [out] of there I thought sure we would all end up in the M. P. station. The people in these rear echelons certainly have fought a tough war.[4]

After they arrived, the men were sent into "the desert at Camp Milar where the British 8th Army trained just before the African campaign. Wonderful place, the darn sand blows so much I haven't even been able to see the guy that sleeps next to me." According to the latest "hot dope," Phil understood that "we will sail from here to the

States sometime before the 20th of Oct. & they say it takes about 20 days to make the trip by the way of the Med. Sea."[5]

At this juncture, the Army presented Phil with further awards. He was authorized to wear a second bronze service star on his Asiatic-Pacific Campaign Ribbon. This was done to recognize his participation in the "Chinese Offensive" campaign during May to September, 1945. He was also issued a Commendation for his service with the Chinese Combat Command. That document stated: "This is to certify that Major Phil W. Saunders 0-446777 Infantry is commended for outstanding and meritorious service and attention to duty while serving with the Chinese Combat Command in China from January 1945 to September 1945." It was signed by both Ho Ying-chin, General C A, Supreme Commander, and Robert B. Mc Clure, Major General U S A, Commanding. Finally, he was awarded the "World War II Victory Ribbon," and was "authorized to wear 4 overseas service bars."[6]

As of October 2, Phil was "still waiting," but "there is a chance I might get out of here on a boat that leaves around the 10th; at least I am working on it." Meanwhile, he

> was looking over a few of the records at Hqs. this morning and I'll be damned if they didn't end up with about 400,000 Am. troops in the C. B. I. God only knows what they were doing. We also lost 2,030 airplanes flying supplies over the hump to China. It will be a strange story when they get everything all added up.

He also found time to play what had now become a familiar game: "My partner and I played bridge with a couple beat up old nurses yesterday. Well they weren't too bad, but they did beat us rather badly. Imagine getting $12 a day for such things—poor taxpayers."[7]

On October 11, Phil finally received word that he would be sailing "for the good old U. S. A." the next day, and it "takes about 25 days someone said just now." He expected to land in New York or

Hampton Roads, Virginia, and then "report to Camp McCoy Wis. either for separation or a short reassignment." On his last day in India, he packed his things, wrote a letter to Lois, and played softball. In that game he "was feeling so good I hit a home run & a triple, & that's really something for me."[8]

In the morning of October 12, Phil and over 4,000 American soldiers boarded the USS General G. O. Squier (AP-130) at Karachi and set sail for the United States. This transport ship, built by Kaiser Company, Inc. in Richmond, California, was originally launched on November 11, 1942. It was named after George Owen Squier, who served in the U. S. Army from 1887 to 1924 and retired as a Major General. The General Squier was 522 feet, 10 inches long and propelled by a steam turbine. Navy captain Robert Threshie was its commanding officer, and he was assisted by about 350 naval personnel. The ship was designed to transport 270 officers and 3,595 enlisted men.[9]

During the first week of the voyage, the ship sailed west on the Arabian Sea, and it continued west through the Gulf of Aden. It then went north on the Red Sea, passed through the Suez Canal, and reached Port Said, Egypt. At this point, Phil wrote a letter to "Dear All" that described his experience at sea:

> We are really having a wonderful trip. The sea has been very calm and it probably will be until we get in the Atlantic. Not a bad old tub this ship—about 4,000 men & 400 officers on board so it is a little tight fitting in places, but not bad. The food is certainly wonderful compared to that stuff we got in China. We get two meals a day so in between times we visit the P. X. [Post Exchange]—I go up on the gun deck each morning and night to take in the sights. The sea is really beautiful when the sun and moon hit it at just the right angle.
>
> Spend most of the day playing bridge and looking after my boys in compartment C-2. I've got about 450 of them in a

place not much larger than our living room—no kidding—Four bunks high and about four inches between them, nice and friendly like.

He also summarized the remaining portion of the voyage: "From here we will go through the Mediterranean into the Atlantic for the home lap. We get to see Malta, Southern Italy & Gibraltar—Nice trip don't you think?"[10]

On November 3, the USS General G. O. Squier arrived at New York City. Sailing from Karachi had taken 23 days, and it had been 50 days since Phil left Kunming. He disembarked and immediately took a train to the Army Separation Center at Camp McCoy, Wisconsin. After arriving there and filling out many forms, it was determined that his "date of relief from active duty" would be February 2, 1946. In the meantime, he was put on paid leave.[11]

Next, Phil travelled from Camp McCoy to Minneapolis, where he visited his sister Leola. He spent a day or two with her before taking the 180-mile bus ride to Milbank. When he arrived there during the second week of November, his mother was visiting her older daughter and granddaughter in Arlington, Virginia, so his reunion with them would not occur until later in the month. But he did see several family members and friends in his hometown.[12] He also had an interview with Phyllis Dolan, the undisclosed author of the "Ain't It Awful!" column in the *Grant County Review*. The resulting article indicated Phil's willingness to describe some aspects of his China experience but a reluctance to answer some of Miss Dolan's questions:

> Major Phil Saunders, just back from China, won't talk about the decoration the Chinese government presented him, turning off questions about it with claims that "they give them away in the PX" or "I got it for leading a retreat." He was stationed in the interior of China, for a long time along the Indo China northern border. The country he describes as beautiful, but

the ignorance of the Chinese as appalling. Chinese military officials openly admitted that casualties meant little to them—a shocking attitude to American army personnel. In the present civil war, Phil is convinced that we should back "the Generalissimo" to the limit. He is disgusted with the inaccurate, incomplete picture of the Chinese situation which the American press has carried during the last year or two.

The hospitality of the villagers Phil remembers with pleasure. It's a Chinese custom that the whole town should turn out for a welcoming celebration when an American army official shows up. It's also a custom that the officer visit the school and give a talk. Since every little area in China has a language of its own, our soldiers didn't attempt to learn Chinese. Phil used to talk through an interpreter. Comic that he is, he tells how it got to be such a regular event that he'd just say to the interpreter, "Slip them speech No. 13."

Language is a terrible handicap to the Chinese. When a press story is sent out saying that "Today Generalissimo Chiang Kai Shek spoke to the nation," it means, literally, Phil explains, that he talked to about 2,000 people in the capital. If the language were a national one, there are so few radios in China that it wouldn't help the situation much.[13]

On November 16, Phil took a bus across South Dakota to visit Lois in Hot Springs. It is a long trip, since Milbank is in the northeast corner of the state and Hot Springs is in the southwest corner. After traversing the state, he arrived in Lois's home town and spent the "happiest 3 days of my life" with her.[14] Allen Wilson had returned to Hot Springs from Europe during the previous month, so Phil was also able to see him, his wife Barbara, and their two-year-old daughter Suzan while he was in town.

He then returned to Milbank in time to enjoy Thanksgiving dinner with his sister Leola, aunt and uncle Alma and Arvid Johnson, cousin Hilfrid Johnson, and two couples who were old family friends. The following Sunday, Phil drove back to Minneapolis with Leola and Hilfrid. From there he took a train to Washington, D. C. to visit his mother, his sister Corinne, niece Nancy, and brother-in-law Jim.[15]

And so, as of late November 1945, Phil had returned to the United States and reunited with the people who meant the most to him. He was now more than ready to resume civilian life and pursue his goals that had been interrupted and long-delayed by World War II. That is what he did.

Epilogue

As previously mentioned, Phil's official "date of separation" from active duty in the U. S. Army was February 2, 1946. Shortly before that date arrived, he was promoted to lieutenant colonel.[1] In late June, the Army's Adjutant General (Major General Edward F. Witsell) informed him by telegram that he had been nominated to become a permanent officer in the Regular Army. Phil was one of 48 officers from South Dakota who were offered this position. The *Grant County Review* gave this description of the process:

> President Truman nominated 9,800 "top cream" veterans of World war II, as permanent officers. They were selected by the war department from an original list of 108,000 applications. The nominations will bring the officer corps of the regular army to its authorized strength of 25,000.
>
> The war department said it employed a new screening process in the selections designed to find "the best leaders in the world today."[2]

But, as he indicated he would do in a letter to his mother written shortly after the war ended, Phil declined the nomination in favor of pursuing a legal career. That pursuit began in the fall of 1946, when he enrolled in the Northwestern University Law School in Chicago. As he had predicted, it took some time to get back into the studying routine after being away from school for several years, but Phil made the adjustment.

In late December, the National Government, Republic of China awarded Phil the "Special Breast Order of Yun Hui with Ribbon." This award was given for "meritorious services achieved" and signed by Chiang Kai-shek. It was one of three authorized decorations China gave to American soldiers, and such "decorations were only rarely awarded to very senior U. S. officers during World War II."[3]

After completing his first year of law school, Phil and Lois were married on June 1, 1947. The wedding was held at the United Churches Church in Hot Springs, conveniently located next door to the Wilson home. The bride's brother (and groom's fraternity brother) Allen was the best man, and the bride's younger sister (and sorority sister) Dorothy served as maid of honor. Don Mueller and Paul Miller were the ushers, and Barbara Wilson "was in charge of the guest book." The bride and groom "exchanged vows in a single ring ceremony, with Rev. E. Paul Hovey, assisted by the Rev. H. L. Case of Mankato, Minn., grandfather of the bride, officiating." Jesse Thomas sang 'The Lord's Prayer' during the ceremony. A reception immediately followed, and then "Mr. and Mrs. Saunders left . . . on a two weeks' wedding trip in the Black Hills."[4]

Shortly after their wedding, the couple received a letter from H. W. Frankenfeld—the University of South Dakota Registrar who had suggested to Lois that she write to Phil while he was serving in China. "Frankie's" letter stated:

> Well, this is one match that I almost feel like taking some credit for, and it had better work out all right, too, or I will feel like a failure.
>
> Isn't that a bright introduction to a letter of congratulation? I certainly do wish you kids the very best of everything. All the Frankenfeld family is very happy over this combination of Wilson and Saunders. We will make due note of the event in the next issue of the alumni bulletin.
>
> And one more thing—you kids are to keep in touch with me because I'll be very much interested in what you are doing.[5]

Phil continued to serve in the Army's active reserve. From August 21 to September 4, 1948, he completed the basic course in "Military Rock Climbing and Summer Mountaineering" given at Camp Carson, Colorado.[6] He then returned to law school. In late September, son Phillip was born. Things were quite cozy for the three Saunders in their one-room apartment, and Phil often wound up studying in the bathroom. But he finished law school in February 1949, and in June he went into private practice with an experienced attorney in Fargo, North Dakota.[7]

That fall, Phil continued to fulfill requirements imposed on him as a reserve officer assigned to the North Dakota Administrative Service Group. He did so by attending "unit drills" on "Radiological Defense," "Map Reading, Aerial Photo & Photograph," "Operation Orders," and "Principles of Offense."[8]

By late fall, Phil and Lois decided they wanted to return to South Dakota, and Phil wanted to apply his legal training to a job in the public sector. He therefore accepted a position as an Assistant Attorney General in the South Dakota Attorney General's office, and the family moved to Pierre (the state's capital city) on January 1, 1950.[9]

Soon after their arrival, Phil began giving speeches in various venues. In April, he spoke to the Lincoln Club (a Republican group of state-house employees) in Pierre on "The Federal Administration's Blunders in China." The next month, he appeared at a Republican rally in Midland along with candidates for governor and the U. S. Congress. Described in the local newspaper as "an expert on China," Phil "related the blunders of our State Department in handling the China situation and quoted from the official state department records to illustrate his points." His speech "was short but very impressive."[10]

That June, Lieutenant Colonel Saunders fulfilled his reserve-officer military duties by completing a course in "Amphibious Communications." This course was taught by the United States Navy's Amphibious Training Unit at the Naval Amphibious Base in Coronado, California (located across the bay from San Diego). The training lasted two weeks and ended on June 16. It was an enjoyable, although brief, assignment.[11]

Debra was born in August, giving Phil and Lois their first daughter. In September and October, Phil resumed appearances at Republican rallies held in Sioux Falls, Madison, and Brookings. He continued to speak about China and voiced his support for Republican candidates who were either seeking re-election or first-time election in the fall.[12]

Sigurd Anderson, the Attorney General when Phil joined that office, was elected Governor on November 7, 1950. On December 30, he announced that Phil would become his executive secretary. Three days later, Phil helped his new boss move books and other items from the Attorney General's office to the Governor's suite in the capitol building. While the 1951 legislature was in session, the two spent several weeks "burning the midnight oil" as they reviewed every bill "offered for the chief executive's signature." Governor Anderson also sent his executive secretary to various public-interest events in the state as the representative of the Governor's office.[13]

On August 9, Phil announced he was a candidate for chairman of the South Dakota Young Republicans League, and he would seek the office when that group held its annual convention in Huron later in the month. Howard Wood, Republican from Sioux Falls, currently held the position and indicated he would seek re-election. A few days before the convention began, Phil resigned his position as executive secretary because the Governor "'indicated recently that the state chairmanship and the duties of executive secretary may conflict with each other.'"[14]

About 300 young-Republican delegates attended the convention. On August 25, they selected Phil for the chairmanship. Mr. Wood "fought hard to retain the key chair position," but when he realized that Phil had a substantial lead in the early balloting, he "brought the vote tabulation to a close by moving that the convention cast a unanimous ballot for his opponent."[15]

In early September, Phil returned to the Attorney General's office. That fall, in addition to representing the state in various legal matters, he continued to speak at both public and private events. His address to the American Legion Post #287 at Mission, given at its Armistice Day program, was described as "one of the best ever to be presented on such an occasion in Todd County."[16]

Daughter Jane was born in April 1952. Now the Saunders family had five members. That spring Phil continued to travel throughout the state and help form Young Republican groups in towns that did not have them. In July, he attended the Republican National Convention held in Chicago. While there, he shook General Eisenhower's hand when Ike arrived at the train depot. He and other Young Republican League members also convinced the convention site committee to hold the 1953 Young Republican National Convention in Rapid City—"within the shadow of the Shrine of Democracy on Mount Rushmore."[17] Later in the summer, Phil attended and spoke at both the State Republican Convention in Pierre and the Young GOP Convention in Aberdeen. At the latter event, he was re-elected chairman without opposition.[18]

That fall, Phil actively campaigned for Republican candidates running for state and national office. On October 1, he gave a talk at a Republican rally held at St. Lawrence High School. The speech lasted "for 1 solid hour and no one moved a muscle." After it was completed, the party chairman "got up with tears in his eyes to compliment Phil." Lois attended the speech and "wish[ed] Eisenhower could have heard him."[19]

The next week Phil made evening campaign appearances in Lake Andes, Yankton, Parker, and Salem.[20] This hectic pace continued until Election Day on November 4, when the GOP candidates were overwhelmingly successful. In South Dakota, all eight Republican candidates for statewide, constitutional offices (Governor, Lieutenant Governor, Attorney General, Secretary of State, State Auditor, State Treasurer, Commissioner of Schools and Public Lands, and Public Utilities Commissioner) won their elections by wide margins.

Incumbent Governor Sigurd Anderson was re-elected with slightly over 70% of the vote. In the U. S. presidential race, Dwight Eisenhower received over 69% of the popular vote in South Dakota. The state thereafter contributed four electoral votes to his electoral-college total of 442. South Dakota's two Republican candidates for seats in the U.S. House of Representatives (Harold O. Lovre and E. Y. Berry) also scored easy victories.[21]

On March 17, 1953, Phil, the four members of the South Dakota congressional delegation (Senators Karl Mundt and Francis Case, and Representatives Lovre and Berry), and others met with President Eisenhower in his office at the White House. The purpose of their visit was "to ask the president to come to the Black Hills of South Dakota on June 11, 12 and 13 to address the National Young Republican convention to be held in Rapid City." During this meeting, the South Dakotans gave Ike a large, framed photograph of Mount Rushmore, an "enlarged duplicate of 'South Dakota non-resident fishing license number one,'" and a "solid, 14-karat gold panel with an engraved invitation to enjoy Black Hills fishing."[22]

Phil thought the trip to the White House had gone well:

> We had a very nice meeting with the President this morning. He seemed to have plenty of time so we were in there about ½ hour. Several pictures were taken & they should be out in a day or so. Looks to me like he will come out. He is very informal & was even relaxed in '<u>my</u>' presence.

(underlining and single quotation marks in original).[23] Shortly after the meeting, the president sent Phil a thank-you note. It read: "Thank you once again for your kindness in bringing to me the gold panel invitation to excellent trout fishing in the Black Hills. Your assurances are very tempting indeed! It was nice to meet you this morning."[24]

Ike did accept the invitation, and the plans for his visit were finalized in May during a conference in Washington among Governor

Anderson, the South Dakota congressional delegation, and White House staff members.[25]

On May 30, Phil gave the Memorial Day Address during a program at the Gregory School Auditorium at 9:00 a.m. He then drove 26 miles west to Winner, where he presented the address during that town's 10:30 a.m. Memorial Day Program at the Legion Hall.[26]

The National Young Republican Federation Convention held its opening session in the Rapid City High School auditorium during the morning on June 11. That afternoon, the delegates travelled 22 miles to Mount Rushmore, where President Eisenhower gave the keynote address. He told the group that "his administration has made a 'good beginning' toward a regime serving 'the interests and needs of all our citizens.'"[27] After making his speech, Ike and his entourage went to the nearby State Game Lodge in Custer State Park, where they would stay for two nights. This facility was built in 1921. President Calvin Coolidge, his wife Grace, and the president's staff stayed there for three months in 1927. Coolidge called the lodge and its surrounding cabins his "Summer White House."[28]

Within ten minutes of their arrival, Ike changed his clothes, assembled his equipment, and went fishing on French Creek. He fished for two hours before dinner, caught five trout, and kept the two largest ones. After dinner and another clothes change, he went down the road to the Calvin Coolidge Inn and gave an informal talk to about 500 South Dakota Republican leaders.[29]

The next day, Ike was back on the stream again before 8:00 a.m. This time he fished in French Creek Canyon (now known as the French Creek Natural Area or French Creek Gorge)—located about 21 miles from the Game Lodge. This area features towering ponderosa pine trees and sheer granite walls that rise up to 200 feet above the creek. Using dry flies and later a Colorado spinner, he caught five trout by early afternoon. (He had also thrown back several smaller ones.) Ike described this second fishing venture as a "'whale of a good time.'" His "South Dakota non-resident fishing license number one" had clearly been put to good use.[30]

Meanwhile, the Young Republican conventioneers took further tours of the northern Black Hills, went to a trout fish fry at the Spearfish City Park, and attended a college night western jamboree in Rapid City. The convention also held further sessions and panel discussions at the Rapid City High School. One panel discussion—"Electing Republicans in 1954"—featured Senator Everett Dirksen from Illinois and other U. S. Senators and Representatives. Mrs. Ivy Priest, Treasurer of the United States, addressed the group on June 12. Its final session was held the next day, during which future officers were elected.[31]

Phil decided not to seek a third term as State Young Republican League chairman. The league held its annual convention in Mitchell on August 16 and 17. It elected James Abdnor as chairman.[32] That fall, Phil continued to give speeches to various groups. He delivered a "fine, inspiring address" to the South Dakota Federation of Women's Clubs' Sixth District Convention at Mobridge in late September.[33] In November, he gave an "outstanding address" at the Armistice Day program held in Pierre.[34]

In late December, Phil's status with the U. S. military changed. He was reassigned from the Headquarters & Headquarters Company, 5260 USAR Engineer Combined Group (Reinforcement Training) to the 5111 USAR Control Group. And he was transferred from "the Active Reserve to the Inactive Status List of the Standby Reserve."[35]

On February 16, 1954, Phil announced he would seek the Republican nomination for Attorney General at the party's upcoming July convention. Two months later, son John was born. The Saunders family was now "evened up" and complete. Shortly thereafter, Phil hit the campaign trail. Before the Republican convention was held, he travelled over 10,000 miles and visited all but four counties in the state to bolster his bid for Attorney General. Meanwhile, in the June gubernatorial primary, Joe T. Foss easily won the nomination over two rivals. In a much closer race, the Democrats nominated Ed C. Martin to run against Foss.[36]

The Republican state convention was held in Pierre on July 26. Phil's opponent withdrew before the convention began, and he was nominated for Attorney General by acclamation. The *Milbank Herald Advance* "believed it was the first time that the nomination for that office was made for a first term without a contest." The *Advance* also noted that "Saunders has gained popular recognition throughout the state, and there is already talk that he is a coming governor[.]"[37] In contrast, the nomination for Lieutenant Governor was hotly contested, and it took three separate ballots to select Roy Houck over five rivals.[38]

After he got the nomination, Phil resumed what had now become a familiar routine for him—barnstorming around the state to rally support for the Republican ticket. He, along with other candidates for statewide office, spoke at the Young Republican convention at Huron in September. That month, he also conducted "instruction schools" for Republican workers and met with party operatives in the eastern and central parts of the state.[39]

On October 4, Phil and Joe Foss both appeared at a Republican rally in the Milbank city auditorium. Foss told the group that "a sharp increase in South Dakota highway construction is necessary next year to prevent an abnormal lag between funds available and projects put to contract," and Phil "promised continued cooperation with county officials in explaining laws, assisting in prosecutions and in giving aid in disaster situations."[40]

After the Monday night rally in Milbank, Phil spent the remainder of that week making campaign appearances in Winner, White River, Kadoka, and Okaton. The last two weeks in October found him visiting Sioux Falls, Colton, Elk Point, Vermillion, Yankton, Virgil, Belle Fourche, Custer (with Foss), Hermosa, Fairburn, Buffalo Gap, Hot Springs (again with Foss), Oral, Edgemont, Oelrichs, Woonsocket, Watertown, and Henry.[41]

The Republican candidates did very well in the 1954 election. All eight candidates for statewide office won. Joe Foss received 56.7% of the vote, and Phil got 55.4%. On the national level, incumbent Karl

Mundt was returned to his Senate seat by a comfortable margin. U.S. Representatives Lovre and Berry were also re-elected. Phil received numerous congratulatory letters and telegrams. As the year ended, he and Lois began construction on a new home in Pierre, and they looked forward to 1955.[42]

That year began with the inauguration of the newly-elected governor and remaining seven constitutional officers. Shortly after noon on January 4, all were sworn into office before a joint session of the legislature. Outgoing governor Anderson then gave his farewell address, and new governor Foss delivered his inaugural message.[43]

The governor's reception began that evening at 6:30 p. m. in the state capitol's rotunda. Phil and Lois were among those greeting the public. The local paper gave this description of Lois's gown: "Mrs. Phil Saunders, wife of the attorney general, wore a gown of muted aqua net over taffeta. The diagonal interest of the one wide strap of the bodice was continued in the taffeta folds forming a hip bow. With the gown, Mrs. Saunders wore rhinestones." It was estimated that 4,500 people "jammed the capitol" to shake hands with those in the reception line; but "hundreds of people who lined up to meet their elected officials gave up, discouraged by the numbers ahead of them."[44]

The reception was followed by the inaugural ball held at the municipal auditorium. "Among the notables at the ball were Casey Tibbs, world champion rodeo performer, and Korczak Ziolkowski, sculptor of the Crazy Horse monument. While tuxedoes were common at the inaugural, Ziolkowski was the only visitor with a silk top hat and a cape." Lois described the reception and ball as "one of the highlights of our life, I'm sure."[45]

Phil quickly got down to work as Attorney General. Having previously served in that office for more than four years, he was already familiar with its operation. There were nine Assistant Attorneys General in the state's "Legal Department," so he had plenty of help.[46] Phil's position, described as the "State's chief lawyer and law enforcement officer," had several responsibilities. They included representing the state in the South Dakota Supreme Court in all actions in which the state had a civil or criminal interest; defending the state's Constitution and its laws; serving as legal advisor to the Governor, the six other constitutional officers, and many of the state's boards and agencies; consulting with and advising the State's Attorneys (who represented the state at the trial court level); issuing legal opinions to the Governor, Legislature, and other state and local officials upon request; and investigating and prosecuting major felonies.[47] Phil liked the job and the assistants who worked with him.

His military career continued to be dormant in 1955. In the spring, he was returned to the Inactive Status List of the Standby Reserve for another year.[48] Then on August 10, 1956, Phil was "honorably discharged from . . . [his] appointment as a Reserve commissioned officer of the Army.[49] His association with the U. S. Army was now formally at an end. It had begun when he became a cadet in the ROTC Basic course in 1938 and had continued for almost 18 years.

That fall, Phil was re-elected as Attorney General. All eight Republicans running for statewide office won their elections. Phil received the highest voter percentage of any state constitutional officer—55%. Joe Foss did almost as well, garnering 54.4% of the vote.[50]

On the national level, a few chinks appeared in the Republican electoral-success armor. President Eisenhower again carried the state, but his popular vote margin slipped by almost 11 points to 58.4% (as compared to 69.3% in 1952). Nationwide, Ike's 1956 election results went the other way. His popular vote percentage was more than two points higher than it was in 1952 (57.4% versus 55.2%), and his electoral-college vote increased to 457 (from 442 in 1952). Francis Case was re-elected as U. S. Senator, but this vote was much closer than his first election to that office in 1950. He received 50.8% of the vote in the 1956 election, as opposed to 63.9% in 1950. Finally, Republican candidate Harold Lovre lost his First District congressional seat to Democrat George McGovern, although E. Y.

Berry was re-elected in the Second District by a comfortable margin.[51]

Phil undertook his second term as Attorney General with the same nine Assistant Attorneys General that had served during his first term. They continued to perform the duties described above. In addition, Phil organized the state's first Juvenile Law Enforcement Committee in 1957. Its purpose was to study the current laws applicable to juveniles and make suggestions as to how those laws could be revised and improved. That year he also became an instructor in several local police schools, where he explained to his policemen-students how various state laws related to their work.[52]

In early December 1957, Phil announced what many had long expected—that he was a candidate for governor.[53] From that point up to the June 1958 primary, he once again campaigned hard throughout the state. When the primary results were tabulated, Phil "won a brilliant victory," "crushed his two opponents for the Republican nomination," and "carried all but four counties in the state." But "the Republican turnout was surprisingly light in view of the intense campaigns waged by his opponents, Roy Houck and Charles Lacy."[54] Republican Party leaders enthusiastically predicted "that 100,000 would go to the polls," but only 80,751 did so. Phil received 61.6% of this vote. Houck got 26.8% and Lacy 11.6%.[55] Governor Foss "called for complete party harmony as the smoke clear[ed] from the primary battlefields"—a call the *Rapid City Journal* editor and state GOP chairman Glen Rhodes believed was "very necessary." On the Democratic side, Ralph Herseth won the gubernatorial nomination without opposition. He had previously served in the state legislature and made an unsuccessful run for governor against Foss in 1956. Herseth was described as a "seasoned campaigner."[56]

The fall general election did not go well for Phil or many of his fellow Republican candidates in South Dakota and elsewhere. He lost the governor's race—receiving 48.6% of the vote to Herseth's 51.4%. The Republicans also lost four of the seven remaining state-wide officer elections (for Lieutenant Governor, Attorney General,

Secretary of State, and State Auditor) to the Democrats. They did manage to hold on to the remaining three state offices (State Treasurer, Commissioner of Schools and Public Lands, and Public Utilities Commissioner) by narrow margins.[57]

In the South Dakota elections for U. S. Congress, Joe Foss lost his bid to unseat George McGovern as Representative for the First District, although E. Y. Berry was re-elected in the Second District.[58]

Nationwide, the Republicans "suffered a stinging defeat in the [1958] midterm elections." The scope of that defeat was historic:

> Though the Democrats went into the 1958 election already controlling Congress, they won a historically unprecedented fifteen seats in the Senate (including two in a special election upon Alaska's statehood) as well as forty-nine additional seats in the House of Representatives. When the newly elected Eighty-Sixth Congress started its first session in 1959, the Democrats enjoyed a thirty-seat majority in the Senate and a 130-seat majority in the House. Republicans also lost thirteen of twenty-one gubernatorial elections.
>
> At the time, analysts attributed the outcome to several factors, including a recession, intra-Republican divisions and the Soviet Union's successful Sputnik satellite launch, which Democrats used to attack President Dwight Eisenhower. But the GOP's message also had clearly fallen short. After the election, the political scientist Frank Jonas, an expert on the western states, pointed to the superficiality of Republican candidates' "glittering generalities" and appeals to "faith and freedom" when voters were more interested in "their stomachs and their pocketbooks." Rather than "recognizing and meeting issues which arise from the needs and desires of the people," he wrote, "gimmicks were invented and straw men set up."[59]

For the first time in his adult life, Phil was without a job. He spent the last part of 1958 and first part of 1959 exploring employment opportunities. In January, he took a Civil Service examination in Washington, D. C. for a position with the National Labor Relations Board (NLRB or Board). He passed the exam and was interviewed in Washington for a Trial Examiner position with the Board. Shortly after the interview, Phil was offered the job, and he accepted. The position had a GS-15 rating and paid $12,775 a year.[60]

* * * *

In 1935, Congress passed the National Labor Relations Act (also known as the Wagner Act). This law

> gave employees the right . . . to form and join unions, and it obligated employers to bargain collectively with unions selected by a majority of the employees in an appropriate bargaining unit. The measure endorsed the principles of exclusive representation and majority rule and covered most workers in industries whose operations affected interstate commerce."[61]

The statute also "created the NLRB as the primary mechanism for enforcing its provisions." It "was subsequently amended several times, notably through the Taft-Hartley Act of 1947, thus altering the NLRB's jurisdiction and functions over time."[62]

One of the NLRB's principal functions was "preventing and remedying unfair labor practices by employers and labor organizations or their agents." As a Trial Examiner, it was Phil's job to "conduct hearings in unfair labor practice cases, make findings of fact and conclusions of law, and recommend remedies for violations found." His decisions could be appealed to the five-member NLRB for a "final agency determination," and "the Board's decisions are subject to review in the U.S. courts of appeals."[63]

Epilogue

Examples of unfair labor practices by employers included "firing workers for unionizing; threatening to cut compensation or benefits if an employee joins a union; singling out employees involved with union activities for unusual penalties . . . ; offering incentives to employees expressly for not joining a union; [and] screening out employees with union sympathies." Union unfair labor practices included "threatening that employees will lose their jobs if they don't support the union; discriminating against union members because they don't support the union leadership; [and] requiring employees to pay union dues after they have been expelled from the union."[64]

In the fall of 1959, Congress passed the Labor-Management Reporting and Disclosure Act (more commonly known as the Landrum-Griffin Act). That law "address[ed] gaps in both the Wagner Act and the Taft-Hartley Act." It basically "protected employees' union membership rights from unfair practices by unions."[65]

* * * *

Phil became a Trial Examiner on April 15, 1959 at the Washington, D. C. office. When he went to work for the NLRB, the Trial Examiners were located in either their main office in D. C. or in a smaller "west coast" office in San Francisco, California. Two years before he began this job, there were 45 Trial Examiners located in the two offices, with the vast majority assigned to Washington. Phil was one of nine examiners hired for this office during 1959.[66]

The D. C. Trial Examiners heard cases all over the eastern and central parts of the country, and Phil was required to travel a lot. His air travel time was reduced somewhat because the Boeing 707 jet was introduced in the United States a few months before he began work.[67]

The family joined Phil after the school year ended in Pierre. They lived for a short time in Wheaton, Maryland, before buying a permanent home in Chevy Chase, Maryland. This home was located inside the Beltway (the 64-mile interstate highway that surrounds Washington, D. C.), so Phil's commute to his downtown office was not too onerous.

Phil enjoyed being a Trial Examiner. In the late 1960s, he gave a succinct description of his job: "At work I am always looking out for the little guy."[68] As the Board's jurisdiction expanded, his work became more varied. In 1971, the Board became responsible for deciding "unfair labor practice charges and representation elections affecting U. S. Postal Service employees." Three years after that, NLRB jurisdiction was expanded again, when the Wagner Act was amended to cover "all privately operated health care institutions."[69]

Phil's job title also changed during the 1970s. In 1972, a U. S. Civil Service regulation replaced "Trial Examiner" with "Administrative Law Judge (ALJ). Six years later, Congress passed a statute that made this title change permanent.[70]

In addition to doing his work at the NLRB, Phil and Lois became international travelers in the 1970s. They took three tours overseas during the latter half of that decade. Their first one, a 15-day excursion that began in September 1975, included visits to England, Holland, Germany, Switzerland, Lichtenstein, Austria, Italy, and France. Two years later, they teamed up with Barbara and Allen Wilson for a 17-day trip to Norway, Sweden, Finland, Russia, Latvia, and Denmark. They enjoyed touring with these more experienced travelers. After the trip, Phil advised his friends "that if you go traveling overseas and want marvelous company—get Allen and Barbara to go with you—they are both tremendous travelers and besides that they can travel anytime to anyplace on anything."[71]

Following his own advice, Phil and Lois took another trip abroad with the Wilsons in October 1979. One more couple accompanied them on this excursion—Suzan Wilson Spates (the Wilsons' oldest daughter) and her husband Ken. These six spent 15 days on a tour that visited Greece, several Greek Islands (including Mykonos, Patmos, Santorini, Crete, and Rhodes) and Egypt. Suzan recalls that "the Pyramids, the Parthenon, the Oracle of Delphi—all were enhanced by Uncle Phil's hilarious comments. I remember the laughter."[72]

Toward the latter part of his NLRB career, Phil's job-related travel was reduced because two additional offices for Board ALJs had opened, and the overall number of Judges had increased. The two new offices were in New York City (opened in 1979) and in Atlanta, Georgia (opened in 1980). By March 1981, 61 Judges were located in the Washington, D. C. office, 28 in the San Francisco office, 13 in the New York City office, and 9 in the Atlanta office.[73] The total number of Judges had therefore more than doubled since Phil came to Washington in 1959.

After serving as an NLRB Trial Examiner/Administrative Law Judge for almost 27 years, Phil retired on April 4, 1986.[74] Lois and he had enjoyed their time in the Washington area. Their four children grew up there and all graduated from Bethesda/Chevy Chase High School. Lois had a part-time job with a nearby insurance agency named Insurance Associates, where she worked two or three days a week and was able to walk to the office. The Saunders often socialized with many South Dakotans who had migrated to the D. C. area.[75]

When he was not working or traveling, Phil and the family would frequently visit a small cottage they owned on Cobb Island in Maryland or go water skiing on the Occoquan River in northern Virginia. They also attended Washington Redskins football games. Phil continued to enjoy playing bridge, cribbage, and chess. Lois and he were enthusiastic bowlers and would often take the family to their favorite bowling alley in Wheaton.[76]

Charades was one of his favorite games to play with family, relatives, and friends. In the Saunders version of this game, the players divided into two teams, and each team member wrote the name of a book, movie, song, or play on a separate piece of paper. Each member of the opposing team was given one of these paper slips, and it was her or his task to convey, within a one-minute time limit, the written word or phrase to her or his teammates by gestures and pantomime. No words or sounds were allowed.

Phil was famous for giving somewhat obscure clues to his teammates and then wondering in wide-eyed amazement how they could not come up with the right answer. Two examples illustrate this point. In an attempt to solicit the answer to the movie *Poseidon Adventure* (1972 film in which passengers struggled to survive and escape after their ocean liner capsized), Phil lay down on the carpet on his back for about 30 seconds and then suddenly flipped over. In another instance, he tried to convey the book and movie *The Invisible Man* (1933 film based on novel about a chemist who discovered how to make himself invisible and became an insane murderer) by simply leaving the room. On this occasion, the best his exasperated teammates could come up with was *Gone with the Wind*.

Shortly after he retired, Lois and Phil moved to Rapid City. There they readjusted to life in South Dakota and reacquainted themselves with old friends who had stayed in the state. They also participated in two family reunions. The first such gathering was held in Rapid City in the summer of 1987. The Saunders' four children, their children's spouses, and five grandchildren attended. Three years (and two additional grandchildren) later, the group met again in Sun River, Oregon, to celebrate Phil's 70th birthday.

Phil's interest in politics and public affairs continued in retirement. He frequently watched the Cable-Satellite Public Affairs Network (better known as C-SPAN) and enjoyed critiquing the televised proceedings that took place in the U. S. Congress. In November 1990, on the eve of the first Gulf War, Phil wrote a letter to President George Bush urging restraint. That letter, with "Dear Mr. President" as its salutation, stated:

> I hope we have learned something from the Vietnam and Korean Wars and this is the fact that ground troops must always be used to actually secure and hold enemy territory. In order to confront Iraq, it appears again that ground troops will be vital to any successful effort, and in so doing military people are estimating casualties of 20,000 to 30,000 and very likely even a higher figure. This, in turn, will lead to TV pictures

each night in our living rooms showing countless front line fighting and killings with the "body bags" holding dead American soldiers. It appears to me that under these horrible circumstances the support for such a conflict will be short-lived to say the least, and serious questions will soon be asked by most all Americans as to why we have to defend the oil billionaires who can probably "buy off" Hussein if we give them enough time to do so.

Let us give our U. N. sanctions, mediations, and <u>embargo</u> a sufficient and real chance to work before we do any shooting.

Why alienate for decades to come, most if not all of the Arab world when we have at least some chance to starve this monster to his knees, and in all likelihood he will lose support and allies faster than we will. Let's "cool it" for now.

(underlining in original). The letter was signed "Sincerely, Phil Saunders, Infantry Lt. Colonel, Chinese Combat Command, World War II."[77] It is not known whether he received a response.

* * * *

Lois died on April 6, 1996 at Rapid City Regional Hospital. Her obituary noted that "she spread love around her world with joy and generosity, and was loved and admired by all those she touched. She had a wonderful zest for life, a great sense of humor and was a ton of fun." And

> her idea of a perfect day was listening to music, taking a walk, visiting with family and friends, enjoying nature's beauty, and shopping at a nearby Hallmark card store. She never forgot a birthday. She loved the Black Hills and South Dakota history, but mostly she cherished family and friends.[78]

Less than a year later, Phil died at his West Hills Village home in Rapid City (on March 15, 1997). His death notice summarized his educational, military, political, and federal government careers. It then added:

> Phil was known for his incredible sense of humor and hilarious stories. He was a superlative public speaker and a great entertainer. When Phil was in the room, there was always laughter. He loved discussing politics and sports, in particular, baseball. He enjoyed many games of cards and charades with his family and friends.[79]

Rushmore VFW Post 1273 presented military honors at Phil's life celebration.[80]

A few months after his death, Phil's surviving sister Leola made a contribution to help build the World War II Memorial in Washington, D. C. By doing so, she became a Charter Member of the World War II Memorial Society. She also had Phil's name entered "into the World War II Registry of Remembrances." There he was honored "for participating in World War II and helping to win our nation's greatest military victory in history."[81]

Photos, Maps, and Other Illustrations

The Saunders children. Left to right, Corinne, Phil, and Leola, circa 1932.

Milbank High School graduate, 1938.

Corinne and Jim's wedding day in Milbank, September 9, 1940. Left to right: Jean, Jim Mackle, Corinne, Phil, and Leola.

Seniors

PHIL SAUNDERS, successful, conscientious student president, worked hard with the student senate "towards student betterment," sharpened campus interest in the potentialities of student self-government. Soft-spoken, but determined, Saunders merits the praise-word, "outstanding," applied to his work. By no means a one-field man, law-destined Saunders found time to work as a Stroller and serve as president of his fraternity.

Excerpt from '42 Coyote Yearbook describing Phil as one of the University's six Outstanding Seniors.

Soldiers receiving weapons training at Fort Benning, Georgia. (Reproduced from Booklet titled *Fort Benning, Georgia* (San Antonio, TX: Universal Press in cooperation with the Fort Benning Public Relations Office, publication date unknown) (hereinafter noted as *Fort Benning Booklet*). Booklet obtained from Wartime Press's World War II Archives. *See* www.wartimepress.com).

On the firing range at Fort Benning. (Reproduced from *Fort Benning Booklet* obtained from Wartime Press's World War II Archives. *See* www.wartimepress.com).

Physical training at Fort Benning. (Reproduced from *Fort Benning Booklet* obtained from Wartime Press's World War II Archives. *See* www.wartimepress.com).

Bayonet assault training at Camp Wheeler, Georgia. (Reproduced from Booklet: *Infantry Replacement Training Center, Camp Wheeler, Ga.* (Albert Love Enterprises, 1945) (hereinafter noted as *Camp Wheeler Booklet*). Booklet obtained from Wartime Press's World War II Archives. *See* www.wartimepress.com).

Trainee confronts pop-up target on Close Combat Course at Camp Wheeler. (Reproduced from *Camp Wheeler Booklet* obtained from Wartime Press's World War II Archives. *See* www.wartimepress.com).

Soldiers negotiate Infiltration Course at Camp Wheeler. (Reproduced from *Camp Wheeler Booklet* obtained from Wartime Press's World War II Archives. *See* www.wartimepress.com).

Leola and Phil in Milbank before Phil left for China.

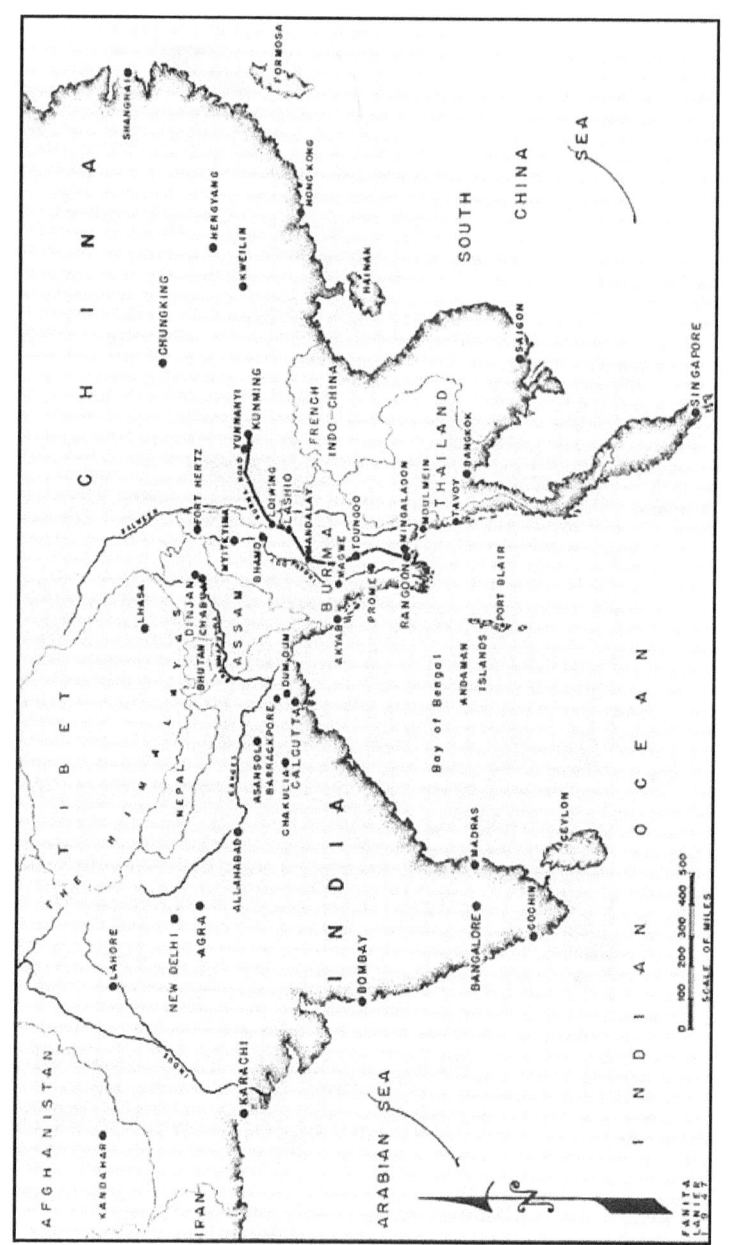

India, Burma, and China. (Reproduced from Carl W. Weidenburner (compiler), "World War II China-Burma-India Theater Maps," accessed March 26, 2015, cbi-theater-1.home.comcast.net/~cbi-theater-1/maps/_Map_Main.html (hereinafter noted as *World War II CBI Maps*).

American transport plane flying over the Hump to China. (Reproduced from Charles F. Romanus and Riley Sunderland, *Stilwell's Mission to China* (Washington, D.C.: Office of the Chief of Military History, United States Army, 166 (hereinafter noted as *Stilwell's Mission*)).

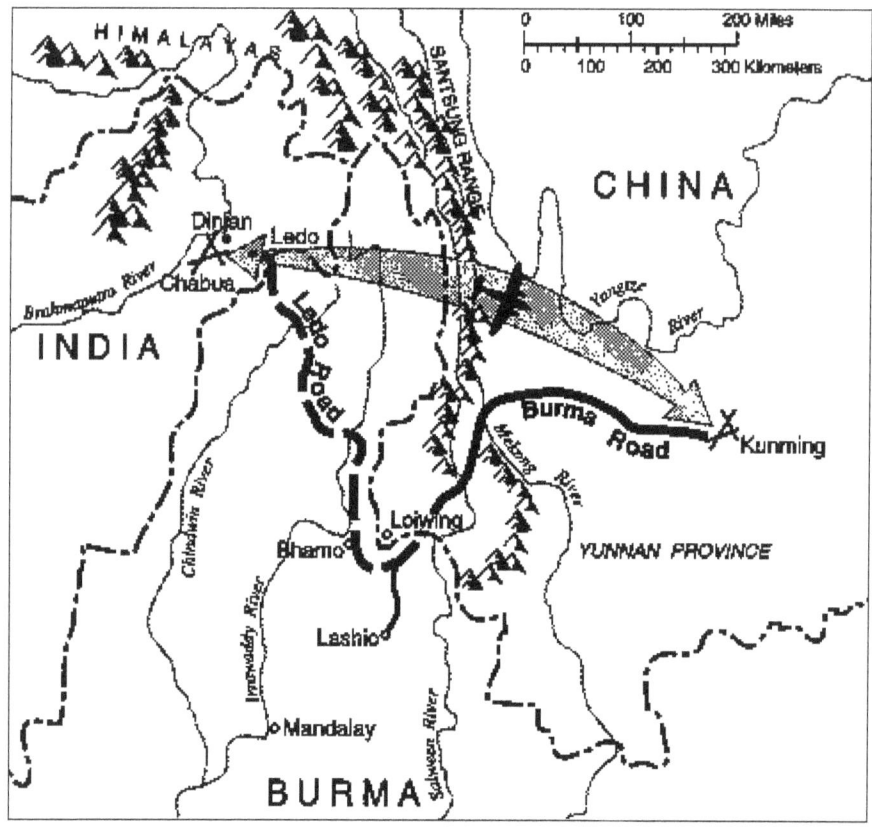

Route from India to southern China over the Hump. (Reproduced from *WWII CBI Maps*).

Photos, Maps, and Other Illustrations 187

Airfield at Kunming, China. (Reproduced from Charles
F. Romanus and Riley Sunderland, *Time Runs Out in CBI*
(Washington, D.C.: Office of Military History, Department of
the Army, 1959), 24 (hereinafter noted as *Time Runs Out*)).

Area around Kunming.
(Reproduced from *Time Runs Out*, 11).

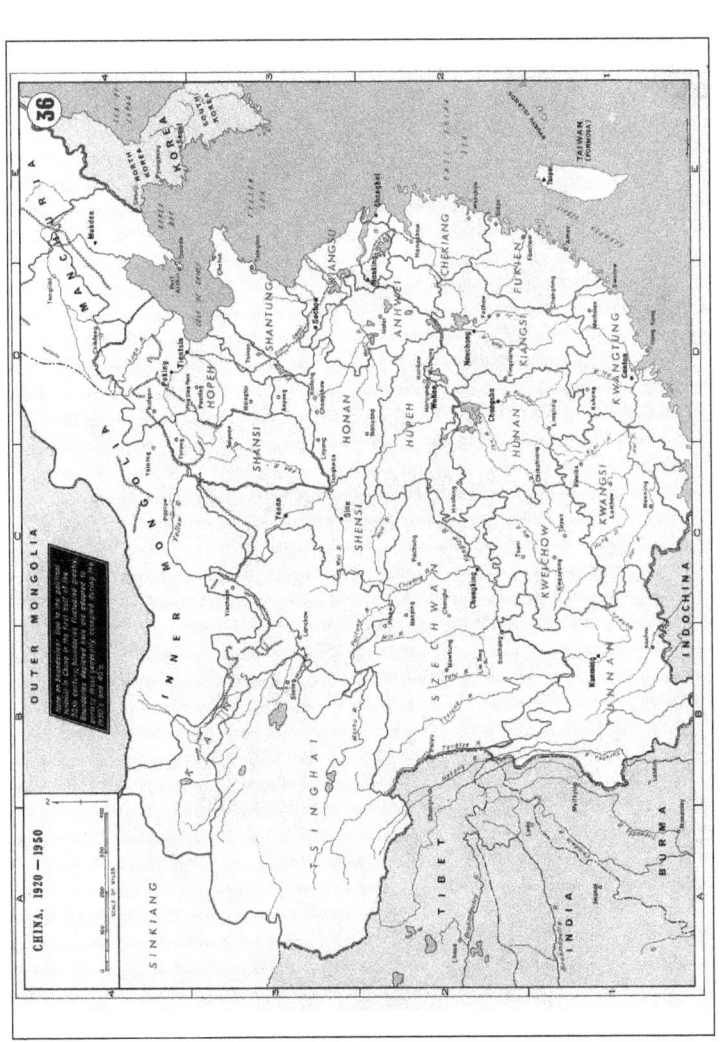

China map showing provinces and major cities. (Reproduced from "China, 1920-1950," United States Military Academy West Point, accessed March 26, 2015, www.westpoint.edu/history/SitePages/WWII%20Asian%20Pacific%20Theater.aspx. Maps courtesy of The Department of History, United States Military Academy at West Point).

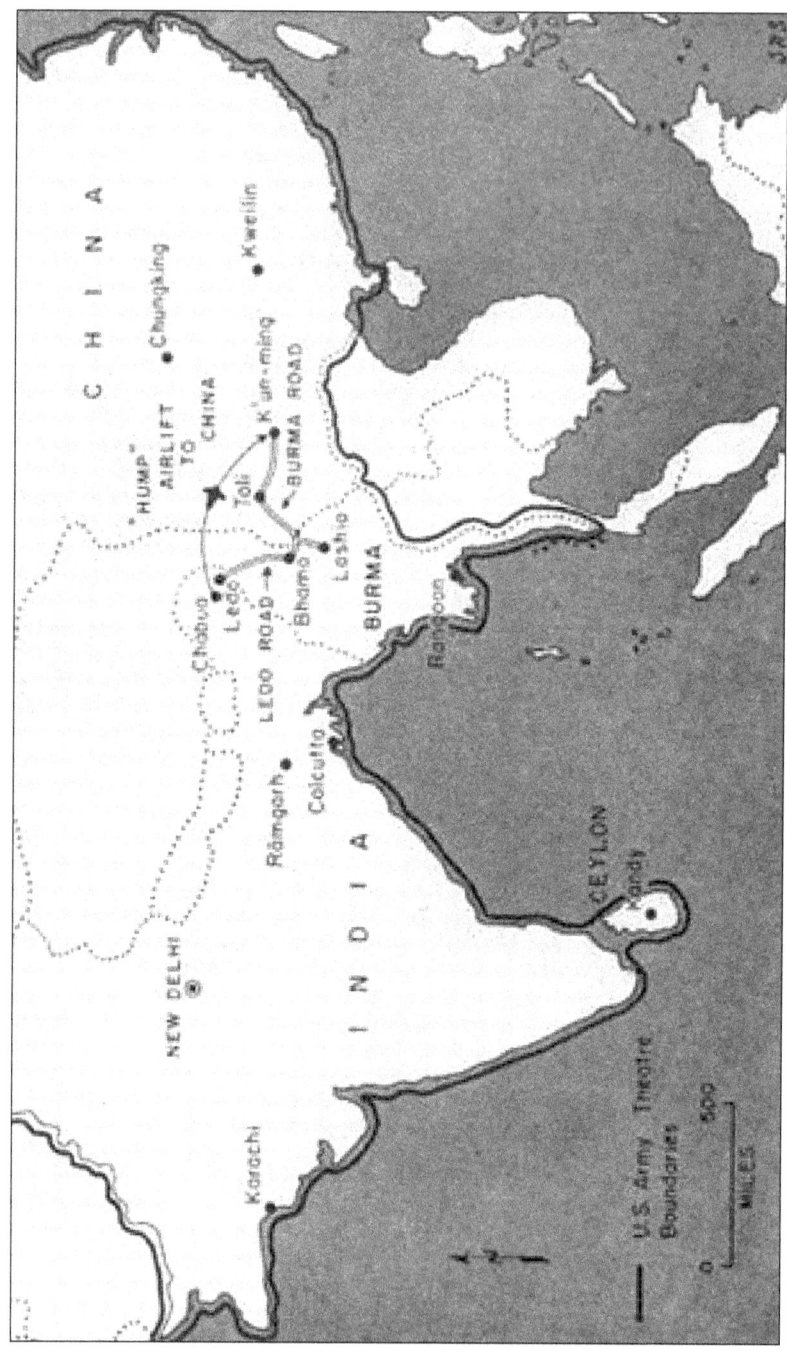

China-India-Burma theater boundaries. (Reproduced from *WW II CBI Maps*).

Generalissimo Chiang Kai-shek, November 1943. Reproduced (and modified) from Charles F. Romanus and Riley Sunderland, *Stilwell's Command Problems* (Washington, D. C.: Office of the Chief of Military History, Department of the Army, 1956), 60 (hereinafter noted as *Stilwell's Command Problems*)).

Members of Traveling Instructional Group No. 4. Left to right: unidentified, Irwin (Mow 'Em Down) Nelson, Ben Ward, and Phil.

General Stilwell (left) and Vice Admiral Lord Louis Mountbatten, March 1944. (Reproduced from *Stilwell's Mission*, 365).

Chinese women doing the laundry in a river with American soldier (possibly Phil) in background. Describing the clothes-washing process, Phil noted that "they just beat the hell out of them."

Chinese senior officers.
(Reproduced from *Time Runs Out*, 234).

Phil (lower left) with three unidentified members of his "signal team."

Map showing areas in CBI under Japanese control, March 1944. (Reproduced from *Stilwell's Command Problems*, 307).

Chinese general and staff officers observe result of
artillery fire on enemy positions, 1944.
(Reproduced from *Stilwell's Command Problems*, 334).

Chinese water buffalo "taking mud cure."

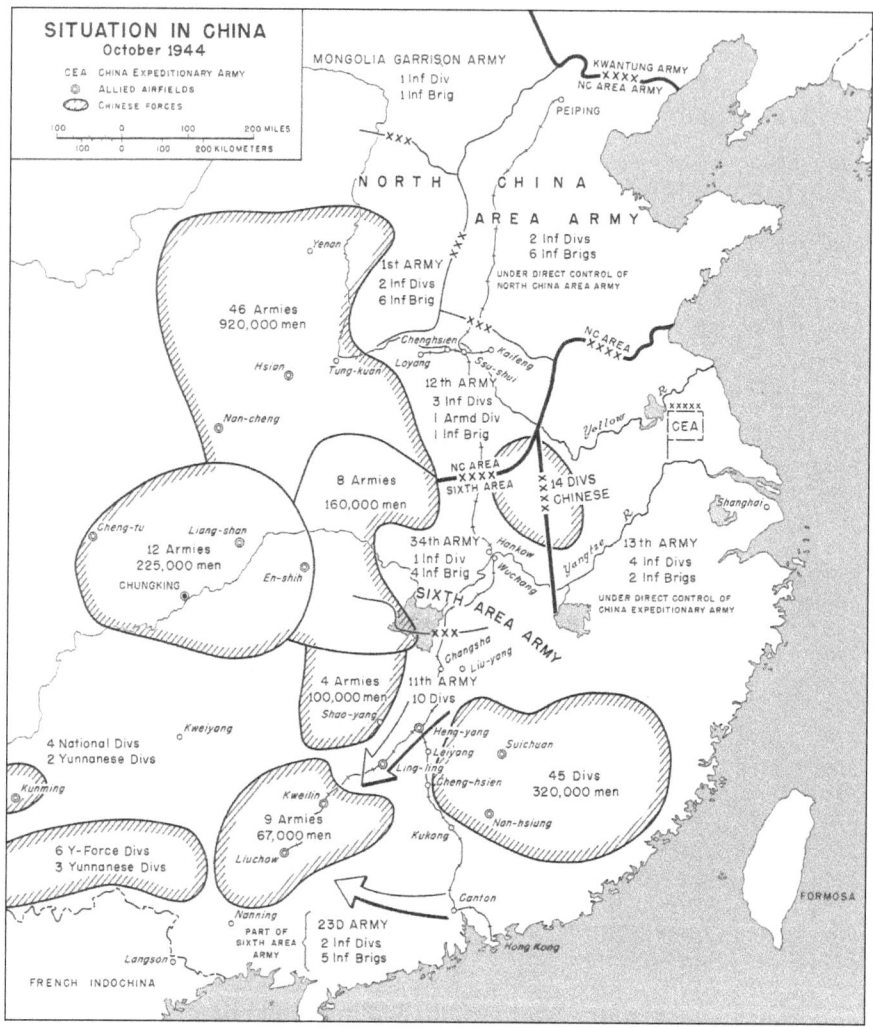

The "Situation in China," October, 1944.
(Reproduced from *Time Runs Out*, 48).

General Claire Chennault (left) welcomes General Albert Wedemeyer to China, October 1944. (Reproduced from *Time Runs Out*, 22).

> A Letter from a primary school girl
>
> Dear Brave American Soldiers:
> 勇敢的盟軍:
> You are fighting on the front. To resist the Axis powers
> 你們在前方打仗抵抗軸心國家,
> We thank you very much. Recently you come to China
> 我們非常感謝你們. 最近你們來中國
> to fight for us and supply us with a lot of ammunition
> 幫中國打仗, 並且供給我們許多軍火, 這樣
> In this way we cooperate to fight against the Axis. We will
> 我們互助合作攻打軸心國家 不久就要
> win before long.
> 勝利了.
> Frequently, the teachers tell us that how hard and
> 我們常常聽到老師說你們多麼辛苦
> bravely you American soldiers fight. We are touched very
> 多麼勇敢的打仗, 我們聽了非常感動這
> much while hearing of it. Thus after the victory is obtained
> 樣等到抗戰勝利以後我們便一齊來維
> we'll go together to maintain the peace of the world.
> 持世界之和平. 祝你們 wishing you
> victory
> 勝利
> Your Chinese little friend Cheng Hsin
> 你們的中國小朋友張嫻 Hsin
> girl 8 years old class
> 女 八歲 三年級
>
> 通信處重慶沙坪壩中大附小
> Address: Primary school, Central University
> Sa Pen Pa Chungking.

Letter to "Dear Brave American Soldiers" from eight-year-old Chinese school girl, (undated but believed to be written in fall 1944).

Phil and the Chinese Commanding General (in front row, left), and several other Chinese and American officers, fall 1944.

Phil (in back row, partially obscured), another unidentified American advisor, and "the [Chinese] boys we work with at the present. The big lug in the middle is supposed to be one of the Generalissimo's right hand men." In a January 1, 1945 letter to Leola that enclosed this photograph (taken in fall 1944), Phil asked her if she thought his picture "would be darn good if I would have moved just a little more to the left."

Phil and his engineer officer at a U. S. Forces Rest Camp, December 1944.

Chinese troops waiting to board Tenth Air Force plane for return flight over the Hump to China, December 1944. (Reproduced from *Time Runs Out*, 149).

Photos, Maps, and Other Illustrations 207

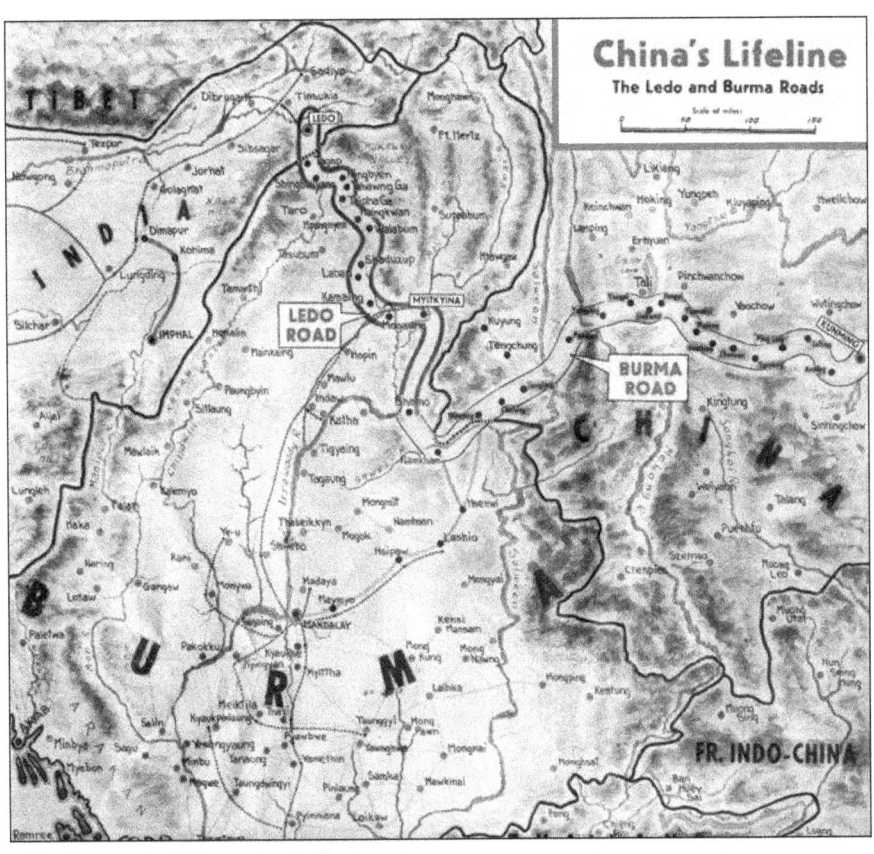

The Ledo and Burma Roads—connected in late 1944. (Reproduced from *WWII CBI Maps*).

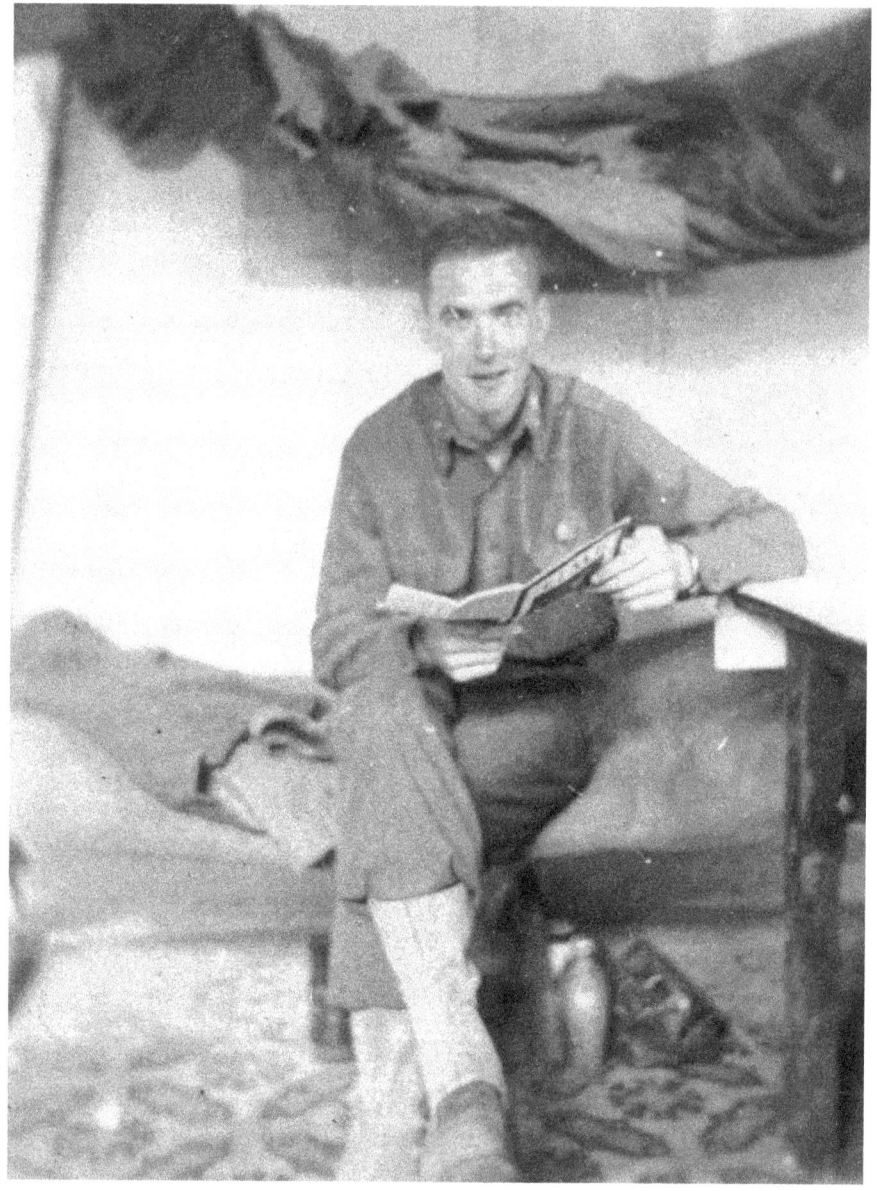

Phil reading *Time* magazine, early 1945.

Chinese soldiers wait to be rehabilitated at a field hospital before they replace troops on the battlefield, May 1945. (Reproduced from *Time Runs Out*, 370).

Three generations back home. Left to right: Nancy Mackle, Corinne Mackle, and Jean Saunders.

Refugees wait at Kweilin railroad station to evacuate the city, fall 1944. (Reproduced from *Stilwell's Command Problems*, 373).

New Chinese soldiers, August 1945.
(Reproduced from *Time Runs Out*, 371).

This photograph was taken from a dead Japanese soldier during the Kweilin offensive. On the back, Phil wrote: "Japs that defended their main strong point on our route of advance.—The Chinese say all were killed, but that I doubt."

Chinese returning to Liuchow, July 1945.
(Reproduced from *Time Runs Out*, 389).

USS General G. O. Squier (AP-130)—the ship Phil took from Karachi, India, to New York City in October-November, 1945. (Reproduced from *NavSource Online: Service Ship Photo Archive*, accessed July 20, 2015, www.navsource.org/archives/09/22/22130.htm; U. S. Navy photo contributed by Stan Svec).

Lois and Phil leaving the church after their wedding held on June 1, 1947. Also pictured are Reverend H. L. Case (far left), who performed part of the wedding ceremony, and unidentified woman behind him.

Lieutenant Colonel Phil W. Saunders, circa 1950.

HEAR
Phil Saunders

CHAIRMAN OF THE SOUTH DAKOTA YOUNG REPUBLICAN LEAGUE

AT

St. Lawrence High School

Wed. Oct. 1

8:00 P. M.

PHIL IS AN OUTSTANDING YOUNG SPEAKER WITH A
VITAL AND INTERESTING MESSAGE FOR BOTH YOUNG AND OLD

HE SERVED IN CHINA DURING WORLD WAR II
AND HE KNOWS THE HORRORS OF WAR
AND
HE IS VERY WELL VERSED IN STATE AND NATIONAL AFFAIRS

NO ONE IN HAND COUNTY 21 YEARS OR OVER SHOULD MISS THIS TALK

ESPECIALLY THOSE OF EITHER OR NO PARTY WHO WILL CAST THEIR FIRST BALLOT ON NOV. 4

YOU WILL BE SORRY IF YOU MISS IT
PHIL WILL WELCOME QUESTIONS AFTER HIS ADDRESS

Entertainment by the "Alley Cats" prior to the address   Lunch

Everything Free   Come and Bring Your Friends

Flyer announcing Phil's upcoming speech at St. Lawrence High School on October 1, 1952.

At a White House meeting held March 17, 1953, President Eisenhower is presented with a framed photograph of Mount Rushmore and a case containing South Dakota's No. 1 non-resident fishing license. Pictured left to right are Phil, the President, Mrs. Carol Arth and Representative Herbert Warburton (R-Del). (Photo by F. Clyde Wilkinson, 3030 North Quincy Street, Arlington 7, Virginia).

> THE WHITE HOUSE
> WASHINGTON
>
> March 17, 1953.
>
> Dear Mr. Saunders:
>
> Thank you once again for your kindness in bringing to me the gold panel invitation to excellent trout fishing in the Black Hills. Your assurances are very tempting indeed!
>
> It was nice to meet you this morning.
>
> Sincerely,
>
> *[signature]*
>
> Mr. Phil Saunders,
> South Dakota
>   Young Republican League,
> Rapid City,
> South Dakota.

Ike's March 17, 1953, note to Phil that thanked him for the invitation to go trout fishing in the Black Hills.

Republican candidates nominated for state offices at Republican state convention held July 26, 1954. Seated in front row are Larry Mayes for state auditor (on left) and Bernard Linn for land commissioner. In back row, left to right, are Phil Saunders for attorney general, Roy Houck for lieutenant governor, Joe Foss for governor, and Geraldine Ostroot for secretary of state. Not pictured are Fred Lindekugel for public utilities commissioner and Ed Elkins for state treasurer. All eight candidates were elected to their respective offices that fall.

REPUBLICAN RALLY

JOE FOSS
Candidate for Governor

AND

PHIL SAUNDERS
Candidate for Attorney General

Monday Evening, Oct. 4th
8 o'clock P. M.

Milbank City Auditorium

Flyer announcing candidates Joe Foss and Phil Saunders will appear at the Milbank City Auditorium on October 4, 1954.

THE SAUNDERS FAMILY

- Phil is married to the former Lois Wilson of Hot Springs and they have four children — Phillip, 9; Debra, 7; Jane, 5; and Johnny, 3.

- Phil's mother, an early Grant County pioneer, still resides in Milbank. She was left a widow with three small children in 1926. She now spends her winters visiting with each of her three children (Corinne, Leola, and Phil) and their families.

Excerpt from *Saunders for Governor* brochure.

Outside the Saunders' new home in Chevy Chase, Maryland, 1960. From left to right: Phillip, Debra, Jane, John, and Phil.

Saunders-Wilson travel team in Leningrad, Russia, September 1977. Left to right: Barbara, Allen, Phil, and Lois.

Saunders family reunion in Rapid City, South Dakota, summer 1987. Front row (seated), left to right: Carl Saunders, Carina Saunders, Phillip Saunders, Emilie Saunders (on Phillip's lap), John Saunders (seated on lawn), Phil, Lois, Jane Saunders Mauss, Jessica Mauss (on Jane's lap), and Trevor Mauss. Back row (standing), left to right: Kevin Saunders, Gordon Smith, Debra Saunders Smith and Steve Mauss. (Copyright 1987 by Newnum Photography. Courtesy of Steve Newnum.)

Lois and Phil with their seven grandchildren. Photo taken during Phil's 70th birthday celebration at Sun River, Oregon, in September 1990. Front row, left to right: Kevin Saunders, Carl Saunders, Trevor Mauss, Emilie Saunders, Jessica Mauss, and Cristy Smith. Back row, left to right: Lois, Shelley Mauss (in Lois's arms), and Phil.

Acknowledgments

My dad Allen Wilson and uncle Phil Saunders were fraternity brothers in college, World War II veterans, and lifelong friends. In 2006, I first published a memoir about my parents' war experience. After reading that book, Phil's four children—Phillip, Debra, Jane, and John—encouraged me to do a similar work regarding their dad's wartime years spent in China. That encouragement, along with input and help from them and many others, resulted in this book.

I am grateful to several people who provided assistance and useful guidance during the book's research phase. Thanks to Debbie Hemmer, former office manager, reporter, and co-owner of the *Grant County Review* in Milbank, South Dakota, for giving me background information regarding that paper's publication during the war years and steering me toward the Grant County Library, where the *Review*'s 1941-1945 editions are available on microfilm. At that library, I received valuable assistance from Mary Lee, the Acting Librarian, and Jody Carlson, who showed me how to operate the library's modern microfilm reader. Staff members Libby Brantner and Tammy Wollschlager were also helpful during my three-day visit to their library.

At the National Archives in College Park, Maryland, thanks to Shane Walsh, Amy Morgan, Amy Schmidt, and Martin A. Gedra for explaining how the Archives operates and helping me locate the records relied on in this book. I also thank taxi driver Michael Sun, who made sure I arrived at the Archives when the doors opened in the morning. And special thanks to Eric Van Slander, Archivist and China consultant at the facility, who located critical documents and made arrangements to have more records ready and waiting when I made a follow-up visit.

At the South Dakota State Archives in Pierre, South Dakota, I gratefully acknowledge Ken Stewart for coordinating, and Carol A. Jennings for performing, additional research on several issues that needed more attention and clarification.

During the writing and publishing phase of this project, I am indebted to my wife Kris for helping me choose the book's title, proofreading and editing the manuscript and interior layout, and thereby improving the final product. Both Kris and our son Matt provided valuable input to the book's cover design. And Matt, son Todd, and daughter Sarah also displayed admirable patience in showing their technologically-challenged dad how to navigate the word-processing program used to produce the manuscript.

Thanks to my former professor Nancy Hoy McCahren, mother Barbara Wilson, sister Suzan Spates, and brother-in-law Ken Spates for respectively providing information about Rube Hoy and his children; the 1977 trip to Scandinavia, Finland, Russia, and Latvia; and the 1979 trip to Greece and Egypt.

The knowledgeable and dedicated people at Mill City Press were responsible for publishing this book's first edition. Thanks to Lois Stanfield, Kate Ankofski, Tim Schaeppi, and Biz Cook for their work on various stages of this project. And extra thanks to Ali McManamon, who acted as liaison between publisher and author from start to finish.

Thanks to David Wogahn, Kerri Esten, and Manon Wogahn at AuthorImprints for revising and republishing this second edition, creating an ebook version, and establishing accounts for the book's distribution.

Lastly, my four "Saunders cousins" played a huge role in the production of this book. All provided useful information regarding Phil's wartime recollections and their memories after the family moved to the Washington, D. C., area in 1959. In addition, Phillip located a commendation from the Chinese Combat Command that did not surface in other military records, and he suggested doing follow-up research on grandfather Saunders's untimely death. Debra supplied early family photos, several wartime and post-war letters, and Lois's *Blue*

Scrapbook and travel diaries. Jane provided her parents' college yearbooks and additional wartime letters, did research on the Saunders family history, and gathered photos and other information from her own sources and from Corinne Mackle's and Leola Keeler's family members. And John got the whole process rolling in 2011 by preparing and signing the Request Pertaining to Military Records sent to the National Personnel Records Center in St. Louis, Missouri. He also provided the photograph of Lieutenant Colonel Phil W. Saunders. Thanks to all of them for giving me this information and materials—and for readily responding to my frequent requests for more information and materials.

This book is dedicated to Phillip, Debra, Jane and John—and to Lois and Phil.

Notes

Much of the information and content for this book came from letters Phil wrote to his mother Jean Saunders (with "Dear Ma" as the salutation); to his older sister Corinne and her husband Jim Mackle (and after their daughter was born, to Corinne, Jim, and Nancy); to his younger Leola Saunders; and to Lois Wilson. Unless otherwise stated, these letters are noted as "Letter to (first name(s)) dated _____." Letters Phil wrote to other people are noted as "Letter to (first and last name(s) dated _____." Portions of his letters are quoted verbatim throughout the book. In some instances, minor spelling errors have been corrected, and words have been added or completed—in brackets—for clarification.

PROLOGUE

1 Letter to Jean (undated).

2 *Ibid.*

3 Grant County Historical Society, *100 Years in Grant County South Dakota 1878—1978* (Pierre, SD: State Publishing Co., 1979), 466; "Grant County, South Dakota," *Genealogy, Inc.,* accessed June 25, 2014, www.genealogyinc.com/southdakota/grant-county/.

4 "Phil C. Saunders Victim of Auto Accident: Prominent Banker and Highly Esteemed Citizen Meets Tragic Death on Highway Early Saturday Morning. Milbank and Vicinity Deeply Grieved. Funeral Services Tuesday," *Grant County Review* (Milbank, SD), August 5, 1926 (hereinafter noted as *Saunders Victim of Auto Accident*).

5 *Ibid.*

6 "Jennie Johnson in the 1900 United States Federal Census," *Ancestry.com*, accessed July 14, 2015; Emails between Jane Saunders Mauss and author sent May-June, 2015.

7 Mark D. Sherry, "China Defensive 1942-1945," *U.S. Army Center of Military History*, accessed January 18, 2012, http://www.history.army.mil/

brochures/72-38/72-38.HTM (hereinafter noted as *China Defensive 1942-1945*).

8 Charles F. Romanus and Riley Sunderland, *Stilwell's Command Problems* (Washington, D.C.: Office of the Chief of Military History, Department of the Army, 1956), 336-37 (hereinafter noted as *Stilwell's Command Problems*).

9 Barbara W. Tuchman, *Stilwell and the American Experience in China, 1911-45* (New York: Grove Press, 1985), 363 (hereinafter noted as Tuchman).

10 *Ibid.*, 278.

11 Charles F. Romanus and Riley Sunderland, *Stilwell's Mission to China* (Washington, D.C.: Office of the Chief of Military History, United States Army, 1987), 267 (hereinafter noted as *Stilwell's Mission*). In addition to the 96-member ground force as of December 31, 1942, American troop strength in China consisted of 812 in the Air Force, 152 in Services of Supply, and 195 in the Air Transport Command. *Ibid.*

12 Charles F. Romanus and Riley Sunderland, *Time Runs Out in CBI* (Washington, D.C.: Office of the Chief of Military History, Department of the Army, 1959), 258 (hereinafter noted as *Time Runs Out*). As of August 15, 1945, the United States also had 34,726 in the "Air forces" and 5,492 designated as "Other" stationed in China. *Ibid.*

CHAPTER 1. COMMISSIONED OFFICER AND COLLEGE MAN

The quotation at the beginning of the chapter is from I. D. Weeks, who served as the University of South Dakota's president from 1935 to 1966. It is taken from a portion of a letter "From President to Student" that appeared in the University's 1942 yearbook. See Cedric Cummins, *The University of South Dakota 1862-1966* (Vermillion, SD: Dakota Press, 1975), 209, 309 (hereinafter noted as Cummins); Mac McEachron, editor, *Coyote of '42* (Vermillion, SD: University of South Dakota students, 1942), 6 (hereinafter noted as *'42 Coyote Yearbook*).

1 Cummins, 214; *'42 Coyote Yearbook*, 86-87.

2 *'42 Coyote Yearbook*, 83.

3 *Ibid.*, 86.

4 *Ibid.*, 82.

5 *Ibid.*, 9.

6 Ibid., 117, 129.

7 *Ibid.*, 156.

8 Letter to Lois dated March 11, 1945. Phil and Joe Foss were fraternity brothers and were roommates at the University for two years. Foss went on to have an outstanding career as a fighter pilot in the Marine Corps. On May 18, 1943, President Roosevelt awarded Captain Foss the Medal of Honor for his actions in aerial combat while he served at Guadalcanal in the South Pacific from October 9, 1942 to January 23, 1943. And as discussed in the Epilogue below, Foss became Governor of South Dakota in the 1950s. See "Ain't It Awful!," *Grant County Review* (Milbank, SD), Aug. 26, 1943; "Joseph Jacob Foss, Medal of Honor," *Geni*, accessed December 12, 2014, www.geni.com/people/Joseph-Foss/6000000017957009184; Walter Simmons, *Joe Foss, Flying Marine* (New York: American Book-Stratford Press, Inc., 1943), 157-59.

9 *'42 Coyote Yearbook*, 157.

10 *Ibid.*, 69, 103, 129, 144.

CHAPTER 2. STATESIDE DUTY

The quotation at the beginning of the chapter is from page 40 in a booklet titled *Infantry Replacement Training Center, Camp Wheeler, Ga.* A citation to this booklet is provided in note 19 below. General George S. Patton, Jr. has been described as "audacious and profane," and "one of the ablest and most controversial U. S. commanders in World War II." He once said that "Compared to war, all other forms of human endeavor shrink to insignificance." In 1942-1943, Patton successfully led campaigns in North Africa and Sicily. As commander of the American Third Army in 1944, he crossed France and later fought in the Battle of the Bulge near Bastogne, Belgium. While Germany collapsed in 1945, Patton's troops drove across that country and into Czechoslovakia and Austria. After the German surrender in May, he commanded the occupation troops in the American zone. But General Eisenhower relieved Patton from his Third Army command because he criticized the Allied denazification policy. In December 1945, Patton died in Germany from injuries sustained in a car accident. *See* "Biography: George S. Patton Jr.," *American Experience: TV's most-watched history series.*, accessed July 18, 2015, www.pbs.org/wgbh/americanexperience/features/biography/bulge-patton/; James L. Stokesbury, "Patton, George Smith, Jr.," *The World*

Book Encyclopedia, Volume 15 (Chicago: World Book, Inc., 1992), 199. The term "doughboy" refers to an American infantryman, especially in World War I. The origin of the word is unclear. Two plausible but unsubstantiated explanations are that it originated in the 1860s and referred to the globular brass buttons on the soldier's uniform that were likened to the pastry known as a doughboy; or that the "dough" portion of the word referred to a type of clay the soldier used to clean his white uniform belt. *See* "Doughboy," *Dictionary.com*, accessed July 18, 2015, www.dictionary.reference.com/browse/doughboy.

1 "Local Mention," *Grant County Review* (Milbank, SD), June 4, 1942; Officer's and Warrant Officer's Qualification Card for Saunders, Phil Walter, W.D. A.G.O. Form No. 66-1, February 1, 1942 (hereinafter noted as *Officer's Qualification Card*).

2 Immunization Register for Saunders, Phil W., U.S.A.F.-I.B.C. (hereinafter noted as *Immunization Register*); "Fort Benning," accessed July 21, 2015, www.fortwiki.com/Fort_Benning; Booklet: *Fort Benning, Georgia* (San Antonio, TX: Universal Press in cooperation with the Fort Benning Public Relations Office, publication date unknown), 1.

3 Robert R. Palmer, Bell I. Wiley and William R. Keast, *The Procurement and Training of Ground Combat Groups* (Washington, D.C.: Center of Military History, United States Army, 1991), 250 (hereinafter noted as *Procurement and Training*).

4 *Officer's Qualification Card*; *Procurement and Training*, 289.

5 *Officer's Qualification Card*.

6 *Procurement and Training*, 263.

7 *Ibid.*, 299.

8 *Ibid.*, 300.

9 *Ibid.*, 289.

10 *Ibid.*, 289-290.

11 *Ibid.*, 290.

12 "With Our Boys Serving Uncle Sam," *Grant County Review*, July 23, 1942.

13 *FM 7-10, Infantry Field Manual, Rifle Company, Rifle Regiment* (Washington, D.C.: United States Government Printing Office, 1942), 2-4 (hereinafter noted as *FM 7-10*); *FM 7-15, Infantry Field Manual, Heavy Weap-*

ons Company, Rifle Regiment (Washington, D.C.: United States Government Printing Office, 1942), 2-6 (hereinafter noted as *FM 7-15*).

14 *FM 7-10*, 14-92; *FM 7-15*, 26-87; *Procurement and Training*, 293.

15 *Procurement and Training*, 338.

16 *Officer's Qualification Card*; "Camp Wheeler Historical Marker," *GeorgiaInfo*, accessed July 21, 2015, http://georgiainfo.galileo.usg.edu/topics/historical_markers/county/bibb/camp-wheeler. (hereinafter noted as *GeorgiaInfo*).

17 *GeorgiaInfo*; "Other IRTCs," *Camp Croft, South Carolina: U S Army Infantry Replacement Training Center*, accessed June 12, 2014, www.schistory.net/campcroft/irtcs.html. The other three centers operating in 1941 were located at Camp Roberts, California; Camp Wolters, Texas; and Camp Croft, South Carolina. *Ibid*.

18 *Procurement and Training*, 381.

19 *Ibid*., 375-76; Booklet: *Infantry Replacement Training Center, Camp Wheeler, Ga.* (Atlanta, GA: Albert Love Enterprises, 1945) 43 (hereinafter noted as *Camp Wheeler Booklet*).

20 *Camp Wheeler Booklet*, 43; "Ambrose Robert Emery, Brigadier General, United States Army," *Arlington National Cemetery Website*, accessed June 14, 2014, www.arlingtoncemetery.net/aremery.htm.

21 *Officer's Qualification Card*; *Procurement and Training*, 377-79.

22 *Procurement and Training*, 444-45.

23 *Camp Wheeler Booklet*, 13. Ernie Pyle was a widely-read and well-respected World War II war correspondent. He wrote feature columns—primarily for Scripps-Howard newspapers— during the war, and he won a Pulitzer Prize in 1944 "for his stories about ordinary soldiers." On April 18, 1945—when he was 44 years old—Pyle was killed by a Japanese machine gunner on a small island near Okinawa. See "Ernie Pyle," *Indiana University Journalism*, accessed July 31, 2015, www.mediaschool.indiana.edu/erniepyle/; "Welcome to the online home of the Ernie Pyle World War II Museum," *The Ernie Pyle WW II Museum*, accessed July 31, 2015, www.erniepyle.org.

24 *Ibid*., 12.

25 *Procurement and Training*, 386, 445; *Camp Wheeler Booklet*, 8, 12-15.

26 *Procurement and Training*, 445.

27 *Ibid.*, 388.

28 "Ain't It Awful!," *Grant County Review* (Milbank, SD), December 24, 1942.

29 *Procurement and Training*, 181.

30 *Ibid.*, 387.

31 *Ibid.*, 388.

32 *Ibid.*

33 *Camp Wheeler Booklet*, 27; Sgt. Walter Bernstein, "Fighting Through Villages is Part of the Training at Camp Wheeler," *Yank, the Army Weekly*, July 13, 1945, *UNZ.org-Periodicals, Books, and Authors*, accessed July 21, 2015, www.unz.org/Pub/Yank-1945jul13-00016.

34 *Procurement and Training*, 387.

35 *Camp Wheeler Booklet*, 25.

36 *Officer's Qualification Card*; Separation Qualification Record for Saunders, Phil W., WD AGO Form 100, July 1, 1945 (hereinafter noted as *Separation Qualification Record*).

37 *Procurement and Training*, 390.

38 "Buzzell, Reginald William," *Generals from USA*, accessed June 12, 2014, www.generals.dk/general/Buzzell/Reginald_William/USA.html; Training Cycle Memorandum Number 5 from Headquarters Infantry Replacement Training Center, Camp Wheeler, Georgia (IRTC), March 5, 1943; General Correspondence, 1942-48; Ground Adj Gen Section; HQ Army Ground Forces, Record Group (RG) 337, Entry No. 55, Box No. 728; National Archives at College Park, MD (NACP).

39 "Local Mention," *Grant County Review* (Milbank, SD), March 18, 1943. The exact nature of Phil's injury is unclear, as his children recall him telling them that he was stabbed in the leg during a bayonet drill at Camp Wheeler. In any event, no evidence suggests the injury caused any long-lasting or permanent damage.

40 *Officer's Qualification Card*.

41 *Ibid.*

42 Message to Commanding General, IRTC from Headquarters Army Ground

Forces, AWC, Washington, D.C., June 5, 1943; General Correspondence, 1942-48; Ground Adj Gen Section; HQ Army Ground Forces, RG 337, Entry No. 55, Box No. 728; NACP.

43 *Procurement and Training*, 384, 391.

44 "With Our Boys Serving Uncle Sam," *Grant County Review* (Milbank, SD), July 1, 1943.

45 *Separation Qualification Record*; "American Theater Campaign Ribbon," *Military Vets PX.com*, accessed March 28, 2015, www.militaryvetspx.com/amthcari.html.

46 Training Memorandum Number 48 from IRTC, June 1, 1943; General Correspondence, 1942-48; Ground Adj Gen Section; HQ Army Ground Forces, RG 337, Entry No. 55, Box. No. 728; NACP.

47 *Procurement and Training*, 389.

CHAPTER 3. FROM MILBANK TO KUNMING

The quotation at the beginning of the chapter is from a letter Phil wrote to his mother dated September 20, 1943.

1 "Local Mention," *Grant County Review* (Milbank, SD), August 12, August 19, and August 26, 1943.

2 *Immunization Register*.

3 Military Record and Report of Separation Certificate of Service for Saunders, Phil W., WD AGO Form 53-98, November 1, 1944 (hereinafter noted as *Report of Separation*).

4 Letter to Jean dated September 14, 1943.

5 Letter to Jean dated September 20, 1943.

6 Letter to Jean dated September 26, 1943.

7 *Ibid.*

8 Letter to Jean dated September 30, 1943.

9 *Ibid.*

10 Joseph Lazzaro, "Bengal Famine of 1943—A Man-Made Holocaust," *International Business Times*, February 22, 2013, accessed August 2, 2014, www.ibtimes.com/bengal-famine-1943-man-made-holocaust-1100525.

11 "Taj Mahal," *Savion Travel Services Pvt. Ltd*, accessed July 31, 2014, www.tajmahal.org.uk/index.html.

12 Letter to Jean and Leola dated October 4, 1943.

13 *Ibid.*

14 *Ibid.*

15 Tuchman, 247, 302; *Stilwell's Mission*, 77.

16 Letter to Corinne, Jim, and Nancy dated July 10, 1944.

17 *Time Runs Out*, Map 1.

18 Tuchman, 198, 223.

19 Letter to Jean and Leola dated October 14, 1943.

20 *Stilwell's Mission*, 202, 207.

21 E. R. Johnson, "World War II: Fourteenth Air Force—Heir to the Flying Tigers," *HistoryNet*, accessed July 22, 2015, www.historynet.com/world-war-ii-fourteenth-air-force-heir-to-the-flying-tigers.htm.

22 *Time Runs Out*, Map 1; *Stilwell's Mission*, 6, 193. Throughout this book, Chinese places and names are provided in the Wade-Giles system of romanization that was in effect during World War II. In mainland China, this system has since been replaced by the clearer Pinyin romanization system. Under the latter, "Chungking" is now transcribed as "Chongqing." *See* "Wade-Giles romanization," *Encyclopaedia Britannica*, accessed July 16, 2015, www.britannica.com/topic/Wade-Giles-romanization.

23 "When You are Overseas: These Facts Are Vital," *War Department Pamphlet No. 21-1, 29 July 1943* (Washington, D.C.: U. S. Government Printing Office, 1943).

24 Letter to Jean and Leola dated October 9, 1943. When he compares Chinese drivers to "old man Lockhart," Phil appears to be referring to Judge S. S. Lockhart, who was an honorary pall bearer at Phil's father's funeral. *See Saunders Victim of Auto Accident.*

CHAPTER 4. JOINING TRAVELING INSTRUCTIONAL GROUP NO. 4

The quotation at the beginning of the chapter is from an October 11, 1943, Memorandum to all Chiefs of Instructional Groups from Colonel Frank Dorn, who headed the American Y Force Operations Staff. The memorandum's record citation is provided in note 18 below.

1 Historical Report for 1943 to the Adjutant General, Washington, D.C. from Commanding General, United States Army Forces, China-Burma-India (CG, CBI), July 10, 1944, 1; General Correspondence, 1943-45; U.S. Forces in CBI Theaters of Operations, RG 0493, Entry No. UD-UP 513, Container No. 10; NACP (hereinafter noted as *Historical Report for 1943*).

2 *Order of Battle of the United States Army Ground Forces in World War II, Pacific Theater of Operations, United States Army Forces, China, Burma and India (USAF CBI)* (Washington, D.C.: Office of the Chief of Military History, Department of the Army, 1959), 25 (hereinafter noted as *Order of Battle*).

3 General Orders No. 19 from Headquarters, U.S. Army Forces, China, Burma and India (HQ USAF CBI), June 13, 1943; General Correspondence, 1943-45; U.S. Forces in CBI Theaters of Operations, RG 0493, Entry No. UD-UP 513, Container No. 10; NACP.

4 *Historical Report for 1943*, 3.

5 *Ibid.*, 9; Memorandum from Headquarters, Y-Force Operations Staff, United States Army Forces, China Burma India (HQ, YFOS, USAF, CBI), October 1, 1943; General Correspondence, 1943-45; U.S. Forces in CBI Theaters of Operations, RG 0493, Entry No. UD-UP 513, Container No. 18: NACP (hereinafter noted as *October 1, 1943 Memorandum*).

6 Enclosure 2 to Memorandum to CG, CBI from HQ, YFOS, USAF, CBI, January 11, 1944, 3; General Correspondence, 1943-45; U.S. Forces in CBI Theaters of Operations, RG 0493, Entry No. UD-UP 513, Container No. 18; NACP (hereinafter noted as *January 11, 1944 Memorandum*).

7 *Stilwell's Command Problems*, 7; *October 1, 1943 Memorandum*.

8 Special Orders Number 84 from HQ, YFOS, USAF, CBI, October 11, 1943; Special Orders, 1943-44; U.S. Forces in CBI Theaters of Operations, RG 0493, Entry No. UD-UP 523, Container 36; NACP.

9 Memorandum Re Troops In Yunnan from HQ, YFOS, USAF, CBI, October 25, 1943; General Correspondence, 1943-45; U.S. Forces in CBI Theaters of Operations, RG 0493, Entry No. UD-UP 513, Container No. 27; NACP; *Time Runs Out*, Map 1. It is not known how many Chinese troops

were in the divisions comprising the 52nd and 8th Armies when Phil was ordered to report to Colonel Enslow in October, 1943. As of January 31, 1944, YFOS estimated the strength of each division was 6,500 men. *See* Memorandum re Strength Report and Status of Replacements for January 1944 to CG, CBI from HQ, YFOS, USAF, CBI, February 8, 1944; General Correspondence, 1943-45; U.S. Forces in CBI Theaters of Operations, RG 0493, Entry No. UD-UP 513, Container No. 28; NACP.

10 Letter to Jean and Leola dated October 17, 1943.

11 Tuchman, 125.

12 *Ibid.*, 4.

13 *Ibid.*

14 *Stilwell's Mission*, 357-60, 364; Donovan Webster, *The Burma Road: The Epic Story of the China-Burma-India Theater in World War II* (New York: Perennial, an imprint of HarperCollins Publishers, Inc., 2004), 108 (hereinafter noted as Webster).

15 Letter to Jean and Leola dated October 21, 1943.

16 *Ibid.*

17 *Ibid.*

18 Memorandum to all Chiefs of Instructional Groups from HQ, YFOS, USAF, CBI, October 11, 1943; General Correspondence, 1943-45; U.S. Forces in CBI Theaters of Operations, RG 0493, Entry No. UD-UP 513, Container No. 18; NACP.

19 Enclosure 2 to *January 11, 1944 Memorandum*, 3.

20 *Ibid.*

21 *October 1, 1943 Memorandum*; Traveling Instructional Groups, undated; General Correspondence, 1943-45; U.S. Forces in CBI Theaters of Operations, RG 0493, Entry No. UD-UP 513, Container No. 18; NACP.

22 Enclosure 2 to *January 11, 1944 Memorandum* , 3-4

23 *Ibid.*, 4.

24 Letter to "Grandmother and Aunty" [Jean and Leola] dated October 28, 1943.

25 *Ibid.*

26 *Ibid.* Phil's sister Corinne married Jim Mackle on September 9, 1940. She met Jim while the two were working for the Federal Bureau of Investigation in Washington, D. C. Jim served in U.S. Navy during the war, and he apparently was stationed in the D. C. area during the 1943-45 time period. He was honorably discharged as a Seaman First Class on February 28, 1946. *See* emails to Jane Saunders Mauss from Nancy Mackle sent June 4, 2015; interview with Jane on August 31, 2014.

27 *Ibid.*

28 Letter to Jean and Leola dated October 30, 1943.

29 Letter to "Grandmother and Aunty" [Jean and Leola] dated November 1, 1943.

30 Letter to Jean and Leola dated November 10, 1943.

31 *Ibid.*

32 Letter to Jean and Leola dated November 12, 1943.

33 Letter to Jean and Leola dated November 15, 1943.

34 *Ibid.*

35 Letter to Jean and Leola dated November 19, 1943.

36 Letter to Jean and Leola dated November 22, 1943.

37 Letter to Jean and Leola dated November 26, 1943.

38 *Ibid.*

39 *Ibid.*

40 *Ibid.*

41 Letter to Corinne and Jim dated December 3, 1943.

42 Letter to Leola dated December 4, 1943.

43 Letter to Phyllis Dolan dated December 4, 1943.

44 Letter to Phil from Chan Gurney dated December 18, 1943.

45 Letter to Jean and Leola dated December 19, 1943.

46 *Ibid.*

47 Training Memorandum Number 8 from HQ, YFOS, USAF, CBI, Decem-

ber 19, 1943; General Correspondence, 1943-45; U.S. Forces in CBI Theaters of Operations, RG 0493, Entry No. UD-UP 513, Container No. 12; NACP.

48 Letter to Corinne dated December 20, 1943.

49 Letter to Leola and Jean dated December 29, 1943.

CHAPTER 5. A CHALLENGING ASSIGNMENT

The quotation at the beginning of the chapter is from a March 24, 1944, Memorandum for all Yoke Personnel from now-promoted Brigadier General Dorn at YFOS Headquarters. The memorandum's record citation is provided in note 37 below.

1 Letter to Corinne and Jim dated January 2, 1944.

2 Memorandum re Y-Force Training Activities from HQ, YFOS, USAF, CBI, January 11, 1944; General Correspondence, 1943-45; U.S. Forces in

CBI Theaters of Operations, RG 0493, Entry No. UD-UP 513, Container No. 28; NACP.

3 Letter to Corinne and Jim dated January 2, 1944.

4 Letter to Leola dated January 7, 1944.

5 Letter to Jean and Leola dated January 13 and 14, 1944.

6 "With Our Boys Serving Uncle Sam," *Grant County Review* (Milbank, SD), March 2, 1944.

7 Letter to Jean and Leola dated January 13 and 14, 1944.

8 *Ibid*.

9 Letter to Corinne and Jim dated January 23, 1944.

10 Memorandum re Battle Order, Chinese Units in Yunnan Province to Chief of Staff, United States Army, Washington, D.C. from HQ, YFOS, USAF, CBI, February 7, 1944; General Correspondence, 1943-45; U.S. Forces in CBI Theaters of Operations, RG 0493, Entry No. UD-UP 513, Container No. 18; NACP (hereinafter noted as *February 7, 1944 Memorandum*); Letter to Leola dated January 26, 1944.

11 Letter to Leola dated January 26, 1944.

12 *February 7, 1944 Memorandum*.

13 Liaison Memorandum Number 2 for Chief of Staff, Y-Force from HQ, YFOS, USAF, CBI, February 5, 1944, 5; General Correspondence, 1943-45; U.S. Forces in CBI Theaters of Operations, RG 0493, Entry No. UD-UP 513, Container No. 32; NACP (hereinafter noted as *February 5, 1944 Memorandum*).

14 Liaison Memorandum Number 1 for Chief of Staff, Y-Force from HQ YFOS, USAF, CBI, November 1, 1943, 4-5; General Correspondence, 1943-45; U.S. Forces in CBI Theaters of Operations, RG 0493, Entry No. UD-UP 513, Container No. 32; NACP.

15 *February 5, 1944 Memorandum*, 5.

16 Letter to Jean and Leola dated February 7, 1944.

17 Letter to Corinne and Jim dated February 11. 1944.

18 Letter to Corinne and Jim dated February 21, 1944.

19 *China Defensive, 1942-1945*, 3, 5; Webster, 62, 80.

20 Journal Entry from Headquarters, Reserve Command, Chinese Combat Command (Prov), United States Forces, China Theater, May 18, 1945; The Chinese Combat Command General Staff, Records of G-3; U.S Forces in CBI Theaters of Operations, RG 0493, Entry No. UD-UP 539, Container No. 65; NACP; Letter to Jean and Leola dated October 4, 1943.

21 Memorandum to Commanding General, CBI from Headquarters, TIG #4, February 24, 1944; General Correspondence, 1943-45; U.S. Forces in CBI Theaters of Operations, RG 0493, Entry No. UD-UP 513, Container No. 28; NACP.

22 Memorandum to the Commanding Officer, TIG No. 4, IX Group Army (CO, TIG 4, IX GA) from HQ, YFOS, USAF, CBI, February 28, 1944; General Correspondence, 1943-45; U.S. Forces in CBI Theaters of Operations, RG 0493, Entry No. UD-UP 513, Container No. 28; NACP.

23 Letter to Corinne and Jim dated February 21, 1944.

24 *Ibid*.; Letter to Jean and Leola dated February 28, 1944.

25 Letter to Jean and Leola dated February 28, 1944.

26 Memorandum to CO, TIG 4, IX GA from HQ, YFOS, USAF, CBI, March 11, 1944; General Correspondence, 1943-45; U.S. Forces in CBI The-

aters of Operations, RG 0493, Entry No. UD-UP 513, Container No. 28; NACP.

27   Letter to Jean and Leola dated March 1, 1944.

28   *'42 Coyote Yearbook*, 8.

29   Letter to Lois dated March 4, 1944. In his autobiography, Rube Hoy explained the extensive correspondence he conducted with former students during the war:

> Boys who had played for me, or who were just good friends, began writing to get some information and a little warmth from the old campus. I determined to answer every letter in full on the same day it arrived, and before long I was keeping a secretary busy with the one job of typing those letters. The word got out among the boys some way that if they would write to Rube, he would tell them what was going on.
>
> The initiative came from them, and they wrote from the battlefields of Europe, the South Pacific, and army camps all over the United States. I found myself in correspondence with over 300 boys, sometimes writing a dozen letters in one day. All their letters were placed on file alphabetically, so that when a former student dropped in on leave and asked about Frank, John Tom, or Jake, we just got out the file. The boys copied the addresses and soon messages would be on the way to their friends. A few times I was able to be of more immediate help. South Dakota soldiers and sailors who found themselves sighting down the wrong gun barrel sometimes wrote me; I passed their problem on to Senator Chan Gurney, he usually secured the needed remedy.

See Carl B. Hoy, *According to Hoy* (Vermillion, SD: State University of South Dakota, 1960), 76-77.

30   Letter to Lois dated March 4, 1944.

31   Memorandum to All Personnel of Yoke Force from HQ, YFOS, USAR, CBI, March 2, 1944, 2-3; General Correspondence, 1943-45; U.S. Forces in CBI Theaters of Operations, RG 0493, Entry No. UD-UP 513, Container No. 32; NACP.

32   Letter to Corinne and Jim dated March 4, 1944.

33   Letter to Jean and Leola dated March 6, 1944.

34   Letter to Leola and Jean dated March 8, 1944.

35 Bulletin No. 10 from HQ, YFOS, USAF, CBI, March 8, 1944, 1-2; General Correspondence 1943-45; U.S. Forces in CBI Theaters of Operations, RG 0493, Entry No. UD-UP 513, Container No. 31; NACP.

36 Letter to Corinne and Jim dated January 17, 1944; Letter to Jean and Leola dated February 28, 1944; Letter to Corinne and Jim dated March 4, 1944.

37 Memorandum re Attitude of Yoke Personnel from HQ, YFOS, USAF, CBI, March 24, 1944; General Correspondence 1943-45; U.S. Forces in CBI Theaters of Operations, RG 0493, Entry No. UD-UP 513, Container No. 34; NACP.

38 *Ibid.*

39 Letter to Jean and Leola dated April 1, 1944.

40 Letter to Jean and Leola dated April 4, 1944.

41 Letter to Corinne and Jim dated April 13, 1944.

42 Letter to Jean and Leola dated April 13, 1944.

43 Letter to Corinne and Jim dated April 17, 1944.

44 *Ibid.*

45 *Ibid.*

46 Letter to Jean dated April 23, 1944.

47 Letter to Leola and Jean dated April 29, 1944.

48 "Ain't It Awful!," *Grant County Review*, June 1, 1944.

49 Letter to Corinne and Jim dated May 1, 1944.

50 Letter to Jean and Leola dated May 6, 1944.

51 *Ibid.*

52 Letter to Corinne and Jim dated May 14, 1944.

53 Letter to Corinne and Jim dated May 19, 1944.

54 *Ibid.*

55 Letter to Jean and Leola dated June 8, 1944.

56 *Ibid.*

57 *Ibid.*

58 Letter to Jean, Leola, & "Reader" dated June 18, 1944.

59 *Ibid.*

60 Letter to Jean and Leola dated June 29 and July 1, 1944.

61 Letter to Jean and Leola dated June 18, 1944.

62 *Officer's Qualification Card*; Isaac Cubillos, "What's the difference between a Bronze Star and a Bronze Service Star?", *MilitaryReporter.net*, accessed July 20, 2015, www.militaryreporter.net/what's-the-difference-between-a-bronze-star-and-a-bronze-service-star/; "Asiatic-Pacific Campaign Medal," *Clothing and Heraldry PSID*, accessed March 28, 2015, www.veteranmedals.army.mil/awardg&d.nsf (hereinafter noted as *Asiatic-Pacific Campaign Medal*); *Separation Qualification Record*.

63 Letter to Corinne, Jim, and Nancy dated June 28, 1944.

64 *Ibid.*

CHAPTER 6. THE CHINESE ARMY AND ITS AMERICAN ADVISORS HANG ON

The quotation at the beginning of the chapter is in a letter to Jean from Phil dated July 28, 1944.

1 G-1 Periodic Report No. 6, Inclosure No. 1, Station List, July 2, 1944; Reports and Correspondence, 1944-45; U.S. Forces in CBI Theaters of Operations, RG 0493, Entry No. UD-UP 535, Container No. 61; NACP; Memorandum re Strength Report and Status of Replacements for July,

1944 to CG, Forward Echelon Headquarters, USAF, CBI from HQ, YFOS, USAF, CBI, July 5, 1944, 2; General Correspondence, 1943-45; U.S. Forces in CBI Theaters of Operations, RG 0493, Entry No. UD-UP 513, Container No. 29; NACP.

2 Letter to Corinne, Jim, and Nancy dated July 10, 1944.

3 Letter to Jean and Leola dated July 31, 1944.

4 Letter to Leola dated July 23, 1944.

5 Letter to Jean dated July 28, 1944.

6 Letter to Jean and Leola dated August 3, 1944.

7 Letter to Jean dated August 9, 1944.

8 *Ibid*.

9 Letter to Leola dated August 9, 1944.

10 Letter to Jean dated August 20, 1944.

11 Interview with Nancy Hoy McCahren on April 27, 2015.

12 Letter to Lois dated August 24, 1944.

13 Letter to Jean dated August 29, 1944.

14 "Capt. Phil Saunders Is Instructor Of Chinese Troops Under Stilwell," *Grant County Review* (Milbank, SD), August 31, 1944.

15 Letter to Allen Wilson dated September 2, 1944.

16 Memorandum re Strength Report and Status of Replacements for August, 1944 to CG, Forward Echelon Headquarters, USAF, CBI from HQ, YFOS, USAF, CBI, September 4, 1944, 2; General Correspondence, 1943-45; U.S. Forces in CBI Theaters of Operations, RG 0493, Entry No. UD-UP 513, Container No. 29; NACP.

17 Letter to Corinne, Jim, and Nancy dated September 4, 1944.

18 Letter to Jean and Leola dated September 5, 1944.

19 Letter to Leola dated September 7, 1944

20 Letter to Corinne, Jim, and Nancy dated September 4, 1944.

21 Letter to Jean dated September 11, 1944.

22 Letter to Jean dated September 16, 1944.

23 Letter to Jean dated September 11, 1944.

24 Letter to Lois dated September 16, 1944.

25 G-1 Periodic Report No. 18, Inclosure No. 1, Station List, September 24, 1944; Reports and Correspondence, 1944-45; U.S. Forces in CBI Theaters of Operations, RG 0493, Entry No. UD-UP 535, Container No. 61; NACP.

26 G-1 Periodic Report No. 19, Inclosure No. 1, Station List, October 1, 1944; Reports and Correspondence, 1944-45; U.S. Forces in CBI Theaters of Operations, RG 0493, Entry No. UD-DP 535, Container No. 61; NACP.

27 Bulletin No. 30, Section IV, Soldier Voting from HQ, YFOS, USAF, CBI, July 26, 1944, 2-3; Bulletins, January-November, 1944; U.S. Forces in CBI Theaters of Operations, RG 0493, Entry No. UD-UP 518, Container No. 31; NACP.

28 Letter to Jean dated September 21, 1944.

29 Memorandum re Morale in CBI Theater to CG, Services of Supply, USAF, CBI and others from HQ USAF, CBI, September 23, 1944; General Correspondence, 1943-45; U.S. Forces in CBI Theaters of Operations, RG 0493, Entry No. UD-UP 513, Container No. 7, NACP.

30 *Ibid.*

31 Letter to Corinne, Jim, and Nancy dated October 2, 1944.

CHAPTER 7. CHANGE IN AMERICAN LEADERSHIP

The quotation at the beginning of the chapter is from Rana Mitter's book on China's war with Japan from 1937 to 1945. *See* Rana Mitter, *Forgotten Ally: China's World War II, 1937-1945* (Boston/New York: Houghton Mifflin Harcourt, 2013), 343.

1 Letter to Jean and Leola dated October 14, 1944.

2 Letter to Jean dated October 23, 1944.

3 *Stilwell's Mission*, 318.

4 Webster, 146.

5 *Ibid.*, 286.

6 *Ibid.*, 286-87.

7 *Ibid.*, 237.

8 *Ibid.*, 289.

9 *Ibid.*, 290-91.

10 *Ibid.*, 289.

11 *Ibid.*; *Time Runs Out*, 6.

12 Webster, 294.

13 *Ibid.*, 289.

14 Letter to Lois dated November 3, 1944.

15 Letter to Leola dated November 8, 1944.

16 Letter to Corinne, Jim, and Nancy dated November 7, 1944.

17 Letter to Leola dated November 8, 1944.

18 Letter to Jean dated November 15, 1944.

19 *Time Runs Out*, 157.

20 *Order of Battle*, 23.

21 Letter to Leola dated December 1, 1944.

22 Letter to Jean, Corinne, Jim, and Nancy dated December 1, 1944.

23 Letter to Jean, Corinne, Jim, and Nancy dated December 5, 1944.

24 Letter to Leola dated December 12, 1944.

25 Letter to Lois dated December 18, 1944.

26 Letter to "Hello" dated December 15, 1944.

27 Letter to "How Bo How, (That's hello in Chinese)" dated December 20, 1944.

28 Letter to Lois dated December 18, 1944.

29 Letter to "Folks" dated December 25, 1944.

30 Memorandum re Per Diem Allowance for CT & CC Personnel to CG, Rear Echelon Headquarters, USF, China Theater from Headquarters (HQ), Chinese Training & Combat Command (CT & CC), United States Forces (USF), China Theater (CT), dated December 20, 1944; General Correspondence, 1943-45; U.S. Forces in CBI Theaters of Operations, RG 0493, Entry No. UD-UP 513, Container No. 30; NACP.

31 Letter to Leola dated December 26, 1944.

32 Letter to "All" dated January 1, 1945.

CHAPTER 8. NEW LEADERSHIP—MIXED RESULTS

The quotation at the beginning of the chapter is included in a February 18, 1945, Letter of Instruction to All U. S. Officers Concerned from Lieutenant General A. C. Wedemeyer. Note 12 below provides the record citation for this document.

1 Letter to Corinne and Jim dated January 6, 1945.

2 *Ibid.*

3 *Order of Battle*, 23.

4 *Officer's Qualification Card*.

5 *Order of Battle*, 44.

6 *Ibid.*

7 *Time Runs Out*, 236.

8 *Order of Battle*, 44.

9 *Officer's Qualification Card*.

10 *Time Runs Out*, 264.

11 Letter to Lois dated February 11, 1945. In December 1942, Americans began constructing the Ledo Road at Ledo (located in India's Assam province) under General Stilwell's direct supervision. About two years later, this road had been extended far enough to connect to the Burma Road at Mong Yu, Burma. Linking these two roads established a 1,079-mile highway stretching from Assam, India to Kunming, China. The first convoy, consisting of 113 vehicles, left Ledo on January 12, 1945, and reached Kunming on February 4. Shortly after the Ledo Road was opened, Chiang Kai-shek suggested it be renamed the Stilwell Road. This suggestion was approved. The Ledo (Stilwell) Road extends 465 miles from Ledo to Mong Yu. Cost estimates to build it range from $137,000,000 to $148,000.000. See "Stilwell Road," *A Profile of Changlang District*, accessed November 1, 2014, www.changlang.nic.in/stilwell.html; *Time Runs Out*, 136-41.

12 Letter of Instruction to All U. S. Officers Concerned from HQ, USF, CT, February 18, 1945, 1-2; General Correspondence, 1944-45; U. S. Forces in CBI Theaters of Operations, RG 0493, Entry No. UD-UP 541, Container No. 172; NACP.

13 *Ibid.*, 3.

14 Letter to "All" dated February 23, 1945.

15 Letter to "Hello" dated March 2, 1945.

16 Memorandum re Training Program to Commanding General, Fourteenth Air Force, APO 627 and others from Rear Echelon, HQ USF, CT, March

20, 1945, 1; General Correspondence, 1944-45; U. S. Forces in CBI Theaters of Operations, RG 0493, Entry No. UD-UP 541, Container No. 172; NACP.

17 Letter to "Hello" dated March 2, 1945.

18 Letter to Leola dated March 7, 1945.

19 Letter to "All" dated March 19, 1945.

20 *'42 Coyote Yearbook*, 69, 130; "Terrence C. McCay," accessed May 21, 2015, www.vetaffairs.sd.gov/sdwwiimemorial/SubPages/profiles/Display.asp?P=1252.

21 "Cpt. Arlo L. Olson Monument Dedication," accessed October 30, 2014, www.vetaffairs.sd.gov/resources/Medal%20of%20Honor/Olson.pdf.

22 "Grant County Honor Roll," *Grant County Review* (Milbank, SD), February 22, 1945.

23 "Grant County Honor Roll," *Grant County Review* (Milbank, SD), April 5 and August 2, 1945.

24 Letter to Lois dated March 11, 1945.

25 Letter to "All" dated March 19, 1945.

26 Letter to "Folks" dated March 21, 1945.

27 Letter to Lois dated March 25, 1945.

28 Letter to "Folks" dated March 21, 1945.

29 *Ibid*.

30 Letter to Lois dated March 25, 1945.

31 "Lois Wilson Is Elected President," *Volante* (Vermillion, SD), April 18, 1944; Doris Lindroth, editor, *1945 Coyote* (Vermillion, SD: Student Board of Publications, 1945), 24 (hereinafter noted as *1945 Coyote Yearbook*).

32 *1945 Coyote Yearbook*, 70.

33 *Ibid*., 58, 88.

34 *Ibid*., 70, 97.

35 *'42 Coyote Yearbook*, 146, 149, 150; *1945 Coyote Yearbook*, 28, 34, 90, 91, 94, 96.

36 Letter to "All" dated March 26, 1945.

37 Letter to Jean dated April 1, 1945.

38 Letter to Jean dated April 4, 1945.

39 Letter to Lois dated April 8, 1945.

40 Letter to Jean dated April 14, 1945.

41 "Commander-in-Chief Stricken," *Grant County Review* (Milbank, SD), April 19, 1945. The full article reads:

> The colorful career of Franklin Delano Roosevelt, serving his fourth term as our president, deeply loved and admired by millions of Americans, while ardently hated by others, came to a sudden end at 4:35 o'clock last Thursday afternoon at Warm Springs, Georgia, where he had gone about two weeks previous for rest and recuperation.
>
> Apparently in normal health, Mr. Roosevelt was seated in a chair while an artist sketched him, at about 1:15 o'clock, when he suddenly raised his left hand to his head and said, "I have a terrific headache," and almost immediately sank into unconsciousness, in which he remained until death came, due to a cerebral hemorrhage.
>
> News of his passing shocked the nation. In this country as well as most of the world he had come to be regarded as the champion of the rights and liberties of the masses, and of world peace and liberty, the one man above all others upon whom millions based their greatest hope for establishment of a workable peace organization as the outcome of this war.
>
> The body was taken by special train to the White House in Washington, where funeral services were conducted Saturday afternoon, and then to his beloved home at Hyde Park, New York, where burial was made on Sunday morning, in the garden of his home in accord with his pre-arranged plans.
>
> Never in the history of this country has one of our citizens been accorded the acclaim and tribute the world over that was accorded him.
>
> Here in South Dakota, as in other states, Governor Sharpe issued a proclamation ordering that appropriate tribute be paid our fallen leader. Flags on public buildings will fly at half mast for a period of 30 days, and in Milbank, as in most towns and cities of the nation, flags were displayed at half mast and all business suspended Saturday afternoon during the funeral services at Washington.
>
> Harry S. Truman, vice president, was sworn in as president a few hours after the death of Mr. Roosevelt became known.

42 *Time Runs Out*, 356-57.

43 Letter to Lois dated April 15, 1945.

CHAPTER 9. ASSIGNED TO CENTRAL COMMAND

The quotation at the beginning of the chapter is from Special Orders Number 105 dated April 23, 1945. Its record citation is Special Orders No. 105 from HQ, CCC (Prov), USF, CT, April 23, 1945, 2; Special Orders, 1944-45, U. S. Forces in CBI Theaters of Operations, RG 0493, Entry No. UD-UP 549, Container No. 208; NACP. Translated from Army language into regular English, the order reads:

> The following named officers are assigned to Central Command, CCC (Prov) and will proceed via first available transportation from American Post Office 627 to such places in China as may be necessary for them to report to the Commanding General, Central Command for duty: Major PHIL W. SAUNDERS 044677 Infantry[.]
>
> Travel by government-owned motor vehicle, rail, animal, air transportation, or any other available means of transportation is authorized.

1 *Time Runs Out*, 231, 236, 237.

2 *Ibid.*, 264, Map 1.

3 *Officer's Qualification Card*.

4 Letter to Jean dated April 22, 1945.

5 Letter to Leola dated April 27, 1945.

6 Letter to Jean dated May 2, 1945.

7 Letter to Jean dated May 4, 1945.

8 Memorandum to Deputy Commander, CCC (Prov) from HQ, CCC (Prov), USF, CT, May 1, 1945, 3; General Correspondence, 1944-5; U.S. Forces in CBI Theaters of Operations, RG 0493, Entry No. UD-UP 541, Container No. 173; NACP; *Time Runs Out*, Map 1.

9 Letter to Jean dated May 4, 1945.

10 Letter to Leola dated May 6, 1945.

11 *Ibid.*

12 G-3 Periodic Report No. 18, May 16, 1945, 3; Reports, 1945; U.S.Forces in

CBI Theaters of Operations, RG 0493, Entry No. UD-UP 538, Container No, 64 (hereinafter noted as *G-3 Report No. 18*); NACP; *Time Runs Out*, Map 1.

13 *Officer's Qualification Card.*

14 *Time Runs Out*, 279, 285.

15 Theresa L. Kraus, "China Offensive: The U. S. Army Campaigns of World War II," accessed September 10, 2013, www.history.army.mil/brochures/chinoff/chinoff.htm.

16 *G-3 Report No. 18*, 7.

17 Letter to Jean dated May 13, 1945.

18 Letter to Marge Price and others dated May 15, 1945.

19 Letter to Lois dated May 22, 1945.

20 "With Our Boys Serving Uncle Sam," *Grant County Review* (Milbank, SD), June 28, 1945.

21 Letter to Leola dated May 27, 1945.

22 *Ibid*.

23 Letter to Jean dated May 27, 1945.

24 "World Battlefronts: Something New," *Time Magazine*, May 14, 1945, accessed September 27, 2013, http://content.time.com/time/magazine/article/0,9171,792086,00.html.

25 Letter to Jean dated June 1, 1945.

26 Letter to Leola dated June 9 and 10, 1945.

27 Letter to Jean dated June 11, 1945.

28 *Time Runs Out*, 90, 95.

29 Joseph B. Shupe, "Mars Task Force," *CBIVA Sound-off*, Winter 2002, *CBI Order of Battle Lineages and History*, accessed November 26, 2014, www.cbi-history.com/part_vi_mars2.html.

30 *Time Runs Out*, 230.

31 Letter to Leola dated June 15, 1945; Letter to Jean (undated).

32 *Time Runs Out*, 341-42.

33 Letter to Jean dated June 18 and June 20, 1945.

34 "China: The New Army," *Time Magazine*, June 4, 1945, accessed September 27, 2013, http://content.time.com/time/magazine/article/0,9171,775748,00.html.

35 Letter to Jean dated June 24, 1945.

CHAPTER 10. THE KWEILIN OFFENSIVE

The quotation at the beginning of the chapter is taken from Phil's Bronze Star Medal citation. The citation is attached to a memorandum described in note 13 below.

1 Webster, 294-95; *Time Runs Out*, 56, Map 1.

2 Letter to Jean dated July 2, 1945.

3 *G-3 Report No. 18*, 5; G-3 Periodic Report No. 26, July 10, 1945, 5; Reports, 1945; U. S. Forces in CBI Theaters of Operations, RG 0493, Entry No. UD-UP 538, Container No. 64; NACP; *Time Runs Out*, Map 1.

4 Letter to Jean dated July 2, 1945.

5 Letter to Jean dated July 12, 1945.

6 Letter to Jean dated July 15, 1945.

7 General Orders Number 48 from HQ, CCC (Prov), USF, CT dated September 17, 1945 (hereinafter noted as *General Orders No. 48*); "History of the Combat Infantryman's Badge," *Combat Infantryman's Association, Inc.*, accessed November 26, 2014, http://cibassoc.com/history-of-the-combat-infantryman-s-badge.

8 *General Orders No. 48*.

9 Letter to Jean dated July 19, 1945.

10 *Time Runs Out*, 353, 387-88.

11 Letter to Jean dated August 1, 1945.

12 "Q: Who are the Bronze Star recipients of WWII?," *Ask*, accessed November 28, 2014, www.ask.com/history/bronze-star-recipients-wwii-478473e40ecbfc4d; "Bronze Star Medal (BSM)," *ww2awards.com*, accessed November 27, 2014, www.ww2awards.com/award/245.

13 Memorandum re Award of Bronze Star Medal to Major Phil W. Saunders from HQ, CCC, USF, CT, November 5, 1945 (with enclosed Citation and General Order No. 67).

CHAPTER 11. IT'S OVER

The quotation at the beginning of the chapter appears at pages 520-21 of Barbara W. Tuchman's *Stilwell and the American Experience in China, 1911-45*.

1 Letter to Jean dated August 10, 1945.

2 *Ibid*.

3 Letter to Jean dated August 15, 1945.

4 Letter to Lois dated August 19, 1945.

5 *Ibid*.

6 Letter to Jean dated August 20, 1945.

7 *Ibid*.

8 Letter to Jean dated August 23, 1945.

9 Letter to Leola dated August 25 or 26, 1945.

10 Letter to Lois dated August 28 and 29, 1945.

11 *Ibid*.

12 Letter to Jean, Corinne, and Nancy dated September 1, 1945. Amebic (also spelled amoebic) dysentery is a gut infection. It is caused by an amoeba known as Entamoeba histolytica—a single-cell parasite. The disease is often contracted by eating contaminated food or drinking contaminated water. Its symptoms include "abdominal pain; fever and chills; nausea and vomiting; watery diarrhea, which can contain blood, mucus or pus; painful passing of stools; fatigue; [and] intermittent constipation." The infection is often treated "with a 10-day course of an antimicrobial medication [.]" *See* "Amoebic dysentery—symptoms, diagnosis, treatment, prevention," *Boots Web MD*, accessed January 10, 2015, http://www.webmd.boots.com/digestive-disorders/amoebic-dysentery; Christian Nordquist, "What is dysentery? What causes dysentery?", *MNT Knowledge Center*, accessed January 10, 2015, http://www.medicalnewstoday.com/articles/171193.php.

13 Letter to "All" dated September 6, 1945.

14 Special Orders Number 244 from HQ, CCC (Prov), USF, CT, September 9, 1945; Special Orders: 1944-45; U. S. Forces in CBI Theaters of Operations, RG 0493, Entry No. UD-UP 549, Container No. 209; NACP.

15 Letter to Lois dated September 13, 1945.

16 Letter to "One & All" dated September 13, 1945.

17 *Ibid.* Phil's comment that his "blouse & pinks . . . are ruined" refers to his winter officer's service uniform. The "blouse" is his officer's service coat. It was made from a wool elastique fabric and dyed in a dark shade of olive drab—sometimes referred to as "chocolate." The "pinks" are the uniform's trousers. They were also made from wool elastic but dyed in a lighter olive-drab shade. Because he was an officer, Phil was required to purchase this uniform. *See* "U.S. Army Regulation Winter Officer's Service Uniform," *WW II Impressions, Inc.*, accessed January 6, 2015, www.wwiiimpressions.com/newusarmyofficerwinteruniform.html.

18 *Ibid.*

19 Letter to Lois dated September 13, 1945.

20 *Ibid.*

CHAPTER 12. FROM KUNMING TO MILBANK

The quotation at the beginning of the chapter is from the *Grant County Review*'s "Local Mention" column—November 1, 1945 edition.

1 "Chaba Map—Satellite Images of Chaba," *maplandia.com*, accessed July 17, 2015, www.maplandia.com/india/himachal-pradesh/mandi/chaba; *The Hammond World Atlas Superior Edition* (Maplewood, NJ, Hammond, Inc., 1973), 16 (hereinafter noted as *Hammond World Atlas*); Letter to Jean dated September 16, 1945.

2 Letter to Jean dated September 20, 1945; Letter to Lois dated September 21, 1945.

3 *Time Runs Out*, Map 6.

4 Letter to Jean dated September 27, 1945.

5 *Ibid.*

6 *Asiatic-Pacific Campaign Medal*; *Officer's Qualification Card*; Commenda-

tion signed by General Ho Ying-chin and Major General Robert B. McClure; *Separation Qualification Record*.

7 Letter to "All" dated October 2, 1945.

8 Letter to Lois dated October 11, 1945.

9 Letter to "All" dated October 19, 1945; "USS General G. O. Squier (AP-130)," *NavSource Online: Service Ship Photo Archive*, accessed January 8, 1945, www.navsource.org/archives/09/22/22130.htm; "General G. O. Squier (AP-130)," *Naval History and Heritage Command*, accessed July 20, 2015, www.history.navy.mil/research/histories/ship-histories/danfs/g/general-g-o-squier-ap-130.html.

10 *Hammond World Atlas*, 17; Letter to "All" dated October 19, 1945.

11 "Local Mention," *Grant County Review* (Milbank, SD), November 8, 1945; *Separation Qualification Record*.

12 "Local Mention," *Grant County Review* (Milbank, SD), November 15, 1945.

13 "Ain't It Awful!," *Grant County Review* (Milbank, SD), November 22, 1945.

14 Letter to Lois dated November 21, 1945.

15 "Local Mention," *Grant County Review* (Milbank, SD), November 22 and November 29, 1945.

EPILOGUE

A significant amount of information for this portion of the book was obtained from a scrapbook Lois kept that generally covered the years 1946 to 1954. The book includes newspaper clippings, photographs, letters, and telegrams that Phil received from various people, and written comments from Lois. Its front and back covers are blue, and it is noted below as *Blue Scrapbook*.

1 Memorandum to Lt. Colonel Phil Walter Saunders from Army Service Forces, Sixth Service Command, Headquarters Camp McCoy and WDPC dated January 27, 1946.

2 Telegram to Lt Col Phil Saunders from Witsell, TAG dated June 28, 1946; "Saunders Declines Army Nomination as Permanent Officer," *Grant County Review* (Milbank, SD), July 4, 1946.

3 Certificate of Award to Major Phil W. Saunders from the National Government, Republic of China dated December 23, 1946; "Authorized foreign decorations of the U.S. Military," accessed December 3, 2015, https://en.wikipedia.org/wiki/Authorized_foreign_decorations_of_the_United_States_military.

4 "Wilson-Saunders Nuptials at United Church," *Hot Springs Weekly Star* (Hot Springs, SD), June 5, 1947.

5 Letter to Mr. and Mrs. Phil Saunders from H. W. Frankenfeld dated June 5, 1947.

6 Certificate O R C Training Detachment from Headquarters 38th Regimental Combat Team, Camp Carson, Colorado dated September 4, 1948.

7 *Blue Scrapbook*.

8 Certificates of Individual Performance of Reserve Duty from Unit Instructor, ORC, Fargo, North Dakota, dated October 5, 12, 19, and 25, 1949, and November 5 and 23, 1949.

9 *Blue Scrapbook*.

10 *Ibid*.; "GOP Rally at Midland Monday Night Well Attended," *Midland Mail* (Midland, SD), May 25, 1950.

11 "Brief History of the Naval Amphibious Base (NAB) Coronado," *The Power Hour*, accessed February 4, 2015, www.thepowerhour.com/news2/Coronado_history.htm; Certificate from Amphibious Training Command, United States Pacific Fleet, Naval Amphibious Training Unit dated June 16, 1950.

12 *Blue Scrapbook*.

13 *Ibid*.; "Legislative Briefs," *Daily Capital Journal* (Pierre, SD), February 22, 1951.

14 "Saunders Resigns Job as Secretary," *Rapid City Daily Journal* (Rapid City, SD), August 24, 1951.

15 "Phil Saunders, Milbank, Successful in Bid to Head State Young GOP's," *Huronite and the Daily Plainsman* (Huron, SD), August 26, 1951.

16 *Blue Scrapbook*; Letter to Phil Saunders from Thomas H. Pozarnsky dated November 14, 1951.

17 *Blue Scrapbook*; Fred C. Christopherson, "South Dakotans Share Convention City Bustle," *Daily Argus Leader* (Sioux Falls, SD), July 6, 1952.

18 E. J. Karringan, "Young GOP's Hear Ike Praise, Victory Tips," *Daily Argus Leader* (Sioux Falls, SD), August 16, 1952.

19 *Blue Scrapbook*.

20 *Ibid*.

21 South Dakota Secretary of State, *1952-1958 Election Returns*, 4-12, accessed February 12, 2015, http://sdsos.gov/elections-voting/assets/1952-1958.pdf (hereinafter noted as *South Dakota Election Returns*) (Page cites are to those utilized in the pdf format.); Dave Leip, "1952 Presidential General Election Results," *Atlas of U.S. Presidential Elections*, accessed February 12, 2015, www.uselectionatlas.org (hereinafter noted as *Dave Leip's Atlas*).

22 "South Dakotans Invite President to GOP Convention," *Daily Capital Journal* (Pierre, SD), March 18, 1953.

23 Letter to Lois dated March 17, 1953.

24 Note to Mr. Saunders from Dwight D. Eisenhower dated March 17, 1953.

25 "So. Dak. Hosts President, Young GOP," *South Dakota Republican News* (Pierre, SD), June 1, 1953.

26 *Blue Scrapbook*.

27 "Powerful Program Ready for Young GOP Convention," *South Dakota Republican News* (Pierre, SD), June 1, 1953; "Ike Attacks Demo Rule," *Post-Register* (Idaho Falls, ID), June 12, 1953.

28 T.D. Griffith, "Custer State Park is a Place of Boundless Beauty, Forests and Free-Roaming Wildlife," *Deadwood Magazine*, September 2006, accessed January 24, 2015, www.deadwoodmagazine.com/back_issues/article.php?read_id=136; "A Visit from the President," *Custer State Park Resort*, accessed January 24, 2015, custerresorts.com/about-custer-resorts/history/presidential-visits/.

29 Anthony Leviero, "President Finds Trout Fishing Good," *New York Times* (New York, NY), June 13, 1953; "Ike Attacks Demo Rule," *Post-Register* (Idaho Falls, ID), June 12, 1953.

30 Leviero, *Ibid*.; "President Reels Them in on Dakota Trout Stream," *Buffalo Courier-Express* (Buffalo, NY), June 13, 1953.

31 "Powerful Program Ready for Young GOP Convention," *South Dakota Republican News* (Pierre, SD), June 1, 1953.

32 *Blue Scrapbook*.

33 Letter to Mr. Phil Saunders from Mrs. Earl Kindred dated September 30, 1953.

34 Letter to Phil from Howard Anderson dated November 12, 1953.

35 Special Orders Number 253 from Headquarters, 5111th Area Service Unit, South Dakota Military District (HQ, 5111th ASU) dated December 22, 1953; Memorandum to Lt. Col. Phil W. Saunders from HQ, 5111th ASU dated December 24, 1953.

36 *Blue Scrapbook*; *South Dakota Election Returns*, 13.

37 "Phil Saunders Nominated for Attorney General," *Milbank Herald-Advance* (Milbank, SD), July 29, 1954.

38 "Republicans Nominate Veterans to '54 Slate," *Daily Capital Journal* (Pierre, SD), July 27, 1954.

39 Young GOP Convention Speakers Say State Must Push for New Industry; River Program Seen Boon to Area," *Daily Plainsman* (Huron, SD), September 19, 1954; *Blue Scrapbook*.

40 "Republicans Joe Foss and Phil Saunders to Speak Here Monday," *Milbank Herald Advance* (Milbank, SD), September 30, 1954; "Foss, Saunders Attract Big Crowd at GOP Rally," *Milbank Herald Advance* (Milbank, SD), October 7, 1954.

41 Memorandums from South Dakota Republican Central Committee re Schedule of Hon. Phil Saunders, Candidate for Attorney General dated September 27, October 12, and October 20, 1954.

42 *South Dakota Election Returns*, 15-20; *Blue Scrapbook*.

43 Warren Morrell, "Thru the Hills," *Rapid City Journal* (Rapid City, SD), December 7, 1954.

44 Officials' Wives Dress in High Fashion for Inaugural," *Daily Argus Leader* (Sioux Falls, SD), January 9, 1955; "4,500 Jam Capitol During Reception to Meet Governor," *Daily Capital Journal* (Pierre, SD), January 5, 1955.

45 *Ibid.*; *Blue Scrapbook*.

46 Morris G. Hallock and Catherine Pulles, *South Dakota Legislative Manual 1955* (Pierre, SD: State Publishing Co., 1955), 493.

47 "The Office," *South Dakota Office of the Attorney General*, accessed February 17, 2015, www.atg.sd.gov/TheOffice.aspx.

48 Memorandum to Lt Colonel Phil W Saunders from HQ from HQ, 5111th ASU dated May 5, 1955.

49 Memorandum to Phil W. Saunders from Headquarters Fifth Army (thru Chief, South Dakota Military District) dated August 10, 1956; Honorable Discharge Certificate dated August 10, 1956.

50 *South Dakota Election Returns*, 31-34.

51 Dave Leip, "1956 Presidential General Election Results-South Dakota," "1952 Presidential General Election Results-South Dakota," "1956 Presidential General Election Results," "1952 Presidential General Election Results," *Dave Leip's Atlas*; "Historical Election Data—1946-1950 Election Returns," *South Dakota Secretary of State*, accessed June 27, 2015, https://sdsos.gov/elections-voting/assets/1944-1950.pdf; *South Dakota Election Returns*, 29-30.

52 Morris G. Hallock and Catherine Pulles, *South Dakota Legislative Manual 1957* (Pierre, SD: State Publishing Co., 1957), 526; Biographical Sketch: Phil W. Saunders, 1920-1958, (undated); Brochure: *Saunders for Governor*, (undated).

53 "Phil Saunders to be Candidate for Governor Next Year," *Milbank Herald Advance* (Milbank, SD), December 5, 1957.

54 "S.D. Editors Forecast a Lively Campaign" and "Pleasant Moment," *Daily Argus Leader* (Sioux Falls, SD), June 7, 1958.

55 *Ibid.*; *South Dakota Election Returns*, 40.

56 "S.D. Editors Forecast a Lively Campaign," *Daily Argus Leader* (Sioux Falls, SD), June 7, 1958; "South Dakota Governor Ralph Herseth," *National Governors Association*, accessed June 28, 2015, www.nga.org/cms/home/governors/past-governors-bios/page_south_dakota/col2-content/main-content-list/title_herseth_ralph.html; *South Dakota Election Returns*, 31.

57 *South Dakota Election Returns*, 43-46.

58 *Ibid.*, 42.

59 Paul J. Saunders, "The GOP's Identity Crisis: Can the Republican Party reinvent itself?, " *The National Interest*, March-April 2014, accessed January 23, 2015, www. nationalinterest.org/article/the-gops-identity-crisis-9928.

60 "Saunders Takes Post with U.S. Labor Relations Board," *Sioux Falls Argus-Leader* (Sioux Falls, SD), April 8, 1959.

61 "The 1935 Passage of the Wagner Act," *National Labor Relations Board*, accessed June 28, 2015, www.nlrb.gov/who-we-are/our-history/1935-passage-wagner-act.

62 "National Labor Relations Board (NLRB)," *Reference for Business/ Encyclopedia of Business*, 2nd ed., accessed January 27, 2015, www.referenceforbusiness.com/encyclopedia/Mor-Off/National-Labor-Relations-Board-NLRB.html (hereinafter noted as *NLRB Reference for Business*).

63 "National Labor Relations Board," *U.S. Government Manual*, 607, accessed January 27, 2015, www.gpo.gov/fdsys/pkg/GOVMAN-1997-05-30/pdf/GOVMAN-1997-05-30-Pg607.pdf (hereinafter noted as *USG Manual*).

64 *NLRB Reference for Business.*

65 "1959 Landrum-Griffin Act," *National Labor Relations Board*, accessed June 28, 2015, www.nlrb.gov/who-we-are/our-history/1959-landrum-griffin-act.

66 Richard J. Linton, *A History of the NLRB Judges Division: With Special Emphasis on the Early Years* (2004), 61, 106, 209, accessed January 27, 2015, www.nlrb.gov/sites/default/files/attachments/basic-page/node-1532/judgesdivisionhistory.pdf (hereinafter noted as Linton). (Page cites are to those utilized in the pdf format.)

67 *Ibid.*, 16.

68 Interview with Debra Saunders Smith on February 12, 2015.

69 *USG Manual*, 607-08.

70 Linton, 16.

71 Lois Saunders, *European Travel Log* (1975); Lois Saunders, *Travel Diary* (1977); interview with Barbara Wilson on February 23, 2015; letter to Parties of the First Part from Phil Walter dated 1977.

72 Interviews with Barbara Wilson, Suzan Wilson Spates, and Ken Spates on

February 23 and July 26, 2015; Greece-Egypt trip brochure: "The Cleopatra," (undated).

73 Linton, 62, 135-37.

74 *Ibid.*, 189.

75 Interview with Jane Saunders Mauss on February 16, 2015.

76 *Ibid.*

77 Letter to George Bush from Phil Saunders dated November 9, 1990.

78 "Lois A. Saunders," *Rapid City Journal* (Rapid City, SD), April 8, 1996.

79 "Phil W. Saunders," *Rapid City Journal* (Rapid City, SD), March 17, 1997.

80 Bulletin: "Life Celebration for Phil W. Saunders," (undated).

81 Certificate of Appreciation to Mrs. M. Keeler from Gen. Fred F. Woerner, USA (Ret), Chairman, American Battle Monuments Commission and Peter Wheeler, Chairman, World War II Memorial Advisory Board dated June 16, 1997.

Sources

BOOKS

Cummins, Cedric. *The University of South Dakota 1862-1966*. Vermillion, SD: Dakota Press, 1975.

Grant County Historical Society. *100 Years in Grant County, South Dakota*. Pierre, SD: State Publishing Co., 1979.

Hallock, Morris G. and Catherine Pulles. *South Dakota Legislative Manual*. Pierre, SD: State Publishing Co., 1955.

_____. *South Dakota Legislative Manual*, Pierre, SD: State Publishing Co., 1957.

Hoy, Carl B. *According to Hoy*. Vermillion, SD: State University of South Dakota, 1960.

Lindroth, Doris, ed. *1945 Coyote*. Vermillion, SD: Student Board of Publications, 1945.

McEachron, Mac, ed. *Coyote of '42*. Vermillion, SD: University of South Dakota Students, 1942.

Mitter, Rana. *Forgotten Ally: China's World War II, 1937-1945*. Boston/New York: Houghton Mifflin Harcourt, 2013.

Palmer, Robert R., Bell I. Wiley and William R. Keast. *The Procurement and Training of Ground Combat Troops*. Washington, D.C.: Center of Military History, United States Army, 1991.

Romanus, Charles F. and Riley Sunderland. *Stilwell's Mission to China*. Washington, D.C.: Office of the Chief of Military History, United States Army, 1987. (first printed 1953).

_____. *Stilwell's Command Problems*. Washington, D.C.: Office of the Chief of Military History, Department of the Army, 1956.

_____. *Time Runs Out in CBI*. Washington, D.C.: Office of the Chief of Military History, Department of the Army, 1959.

Simmons, Walter. *Joe Foss, Flying Marine*. New York: American Book Stratford Press, Inc., 1943.

The World Book Encyclopedia, Volume 15. Chicago: World Book, Inc., 1992.

Tuchman, Barbara W. *Stilwell and the American Experience in China, 1911-45*. New York: Grove Press, 1985.

Webster, Donovan. *The Burma Road: The Epic Story of the China-Burma-India Theater in World War II*. New York: Perennial, an imprint of HarperCollins Publishers, Inc., 2004.

NEWSPAPERS

Buffalo Courier-Express (Buffalo, NY)

Daily Argus Leader (Sioux Falls, SD)

Daily Capital Journal (Pierre, SD)

Daily Plainsman (Huron, SD)

Grant County Review (Milbank, SD)

Hot Springs Weekly Star (Hot Springs, SD)

Huronite and the Daily Plainsman (Huron, SD)

Midland Mail (Midland, SD)

Milbank Herald-Advance (Milbank, SD)

New York Times (New York, NY)

Post-Register (Idaho Falls, ID)

Rapid City Daily Journal (Rapid City, SD)

Rapid City Journal (Rapid City, SD)

Sioux Falls Argus Leader (Sioux Falls, SD)

South Dakota Republican News (Pierre, SD)

Volante (Vermillion, SD)

ONLINE MATERIALS

"A Visit from the President." *Custer State Park Resort*. Accessed January 24, 2015. custerresorts.com/about-custer-resorts/history/presidential-visits/.

"Ambrose Robert Emery, Brigadier General, United States Army." *Arlington National Cemetery Website*. Accessed June 14, 2014. www.arlingtoncemetery.net/aremery.htm.

"American Theater Campaign Ribbon." *Military Vets PX.com*. Accessed March 28, 2015. www.militaryvetspx.com/amthcari.html.

"Amoebic dysentery—symptoms, diagnosis, treatment, prevention." *Boots Web MD*. Accessed January 10, 2015. http://www.webmd.boots.com/digestive-disorders/amoebic-dysentery.

"Asiatic-Pacific Campaign Medal," *Clothing and Heraldry PSID*. Accessed March 28, 2015. www.veteranmedals.army.mil/awardg&d.nsf.

"Authorized foreign decorations of the U.S. Military." Accessed December 3, 2015. https://en.wikipedia.org/wiki/Authorized_foreign_decorations_of_the_United_States_military.

Bernstein, Sgt. Walter. "Fighting Through Villages is Part of the Training at Camp Wheeler." *Yank, the Army Weekly. UNZ.org-Periodicals, Books, and Authors*. Accessed July 21, 2015. www.unz.org/Pub/Yank-1945jul13-00016.

"Biography: George S. Patton Jr." *American Experience: TV's most-watched history series*. Accessed July 18, 2015. www.pbs.org/wgbh/americanexperience/features/biography/bulge-patton/.

"Brief History of the Naval Amphibious Base (NAB) Coronado." *The Power Hour*. Accessed February 4, 2015. www.thepowerhour.com/news2/Coronado_history.htm.

"Bronze Star Medal (BSM)." Accessed November 27, 2014. *ww2awards.com*. www.ww2awards.com/award/245.

"Buzzell, Reginald William." *Generals from USA*. Accessed June 12, 2014. www.generals.dk/general/Buzzell/Reginald_William/USA.html.

"Camp Wheeler Historical Marker." *GeorgiaInfo*. Accessed July 21, 2015. http://georgiainfo.galileo.usg.edu/topics/historical_markers/county/bibb/camp-wheeler.

"Chaba Map—Satellite Images of Chaba," *maplandia.com*. Accessed July 17, 2015. www.maplandia.com/india/himachal-pradesh/mandi/chaba.

"China: The New Army," *Time Magazine*, June 4, 1945. Accessed September 27, 2013. http://content.time.com/time/magazine/article/0,9171,775748,00.html.

"China, 1920-1950." *United States Military Academy West Point*. Accessed March 26, 2015. www.westpoint.edu/history/SitePages/WWII%20Asian%20Pacific%20Theater.aspx.

"Cpt. Arlo L. Olson Monument Dedication." Accessed October 30, 2014. www.vetaffairs.sd.gov/resources/Medal%20of%20Honor/Olson.pdf.

Cubillos, Isaac. "What's the difference between a Bronze Star and a Bronze Service Star?" *MilitaryReporter,net*. Accessed July 20, 2015. www.militaryreporter.net/what's-the-difference-between-a-bronze-star-and-a-bronze-service-star/.

"Doughboy." *Dictionary.com*. Accessed July 18, 2015. www.dictionary.reference.com/browse/doughboy.

"Ernie Pyle." *Indiana University Journalism*. Accessed July 31, 2015. www.mediaschool.indiana.edu/erniepyle/.

"Fort Benning." Accessed July 21, 2015. www.fortwiki.com/Fort_Benning.

"General G. O. Squier (AP-130)." *Naval History and Heritage Command*. Accessed July 20, 2015. www.history.navy.mil/research/histories/ship-histories/danfs/g/general-g-o-squier-ap-130.html.

"Grant County, South Dakota." *Genealogy, Inc*. Accessed June 25, 2014. www.genealogyinc.com/southdakota/grant-county/.

Griffith, T. D. "Custer State Park is a Place of Boundless Beauty, Forests and Free-Roaming Wildlife," *Deadwood Magazine*, September 2006. Accessed January 24, 2015. www.deadwoodmagazine.com/back_issues/article.php?read_id=136.

"Historical Election Data—1946-1950 Election Returns." *South Dakota Secretary of State*. Accessed June 27, 2015. https://sdsos.gov/elections-voting/assets/1944-1950.pdf.

"History of the Combat Infantryman's Badge." *Combat Infantryman's Association, Inc.* Accessed November 26, 2014. http://cibassoc.com/history-of-the-combat-infantryman-s-badge.

"Jennie Johnson in the 1900 United States Federal Census." *Ancestry.com*. Accessed July 14, 2015.

Johnson, E. R. "World War II: Fourteenth Air Force—Heir to the Flying Tigers." *HistoryNet*. Accessed July 22, 2015. www.historynet.com/world-war-ii-fourteenth-air-force-heir-to-the-flying-tigers.htm.

Kraus, Theresa L. "China Offensive: The U.S. Army Campaigns of World War II." Accessed September 10, 2013. www.history.army.mil/brochures/chinoff/chinoff.htm.

Lazzaro, Joseph. "Bengal Famine of 1943—A Man-Made Holocaust." *International Business Times*, February 22, 2013. Accessed August 2, 2014. www.ibtimes.com/bengal-famine-1943-man-made-holocaust-1100525.

Leip, Dave. Various articles at *Atlas of U.S. Presidential Elections*. Accessed February 12, 2015. www.uselectionatlas.org.

Linton, Richard J. *A History of the NLRB Judges Division: With Special Emphasis on the Early Years*. 2004. Accessed January 27, 2015. www.nlrb.gov/sites/default/files/attachments/basic-page/node-1532/judgesdivisionhistory.pdf.

"National Labor Relations Board (NLRB)." *Reference for Business/Encyclopedia of Business*, 2nd ed. www.referenceforbusiness.com/encyclopedia/Mor-Off/National-Labor-Relations-Board-NLRB.html.

"National Labor Relations Board." *U.S. Government Manual*. Accessed January 27, 2015. www.gpo.gov/fdsys/pkg/GOVMAN-1997-05-30/pdf/GOVMAN-1997-05-30-Pg607.pdf.

Nordquist, Christian. "What is dysentery? What causes dysentery?" *MNT Knowledge Center*. Accessed January 10, 2015. http://www.medicalnewstoday.com/articles/171193.php.

"Other IRTC's." *Camp Croft, South Carolina: US Army Infantry Replacement Training Center*. Accessed June 12, 2014. www.schistory.net/campcroft/irtcs.html.

"Q: Who are the Bronze Star recipients of WWII?" *Ask*. Accessed November 27, 2014. www.ask.com/history/bronze-star-recipients-wwii-478473e40ecbfc4d.

Saunders, Paul J. "The GOP's Identity Crisis: Can the Republican Party Reinvent Itself?" *The National Interest*, March-April, 2014. Accessed January 23, 2015. www.nationalinterest.org/article/the-gops-identity-crisis-9928.

Sherry, Mark D. "China Defensive 1942-1945." *U. S. Army Center of Military History*. Accessed January 18, 2012. http://www.history.army.mil/brochures/72-38/72-38.HTM.

Shupe, Joseph B. "Mars Task Force." *CBIVA Sound-off*, Winter 2002. *CBI Order of Battle Lineages and History*. Accessed November 26, 2014. www.cbi-history.com/part_vi_mars2.html.

"South Dakota Governor Ralph Herseth." *National Governors Association*. Accessed June 28, 2015. www.nga.org/cms/home/governors/past-governors-bios/page_south_dakota/col2-content/main-content-list/title_herseth_ralph.html.

South Dakota Secretary of State. *1952-1958 Election Returns*. Accessed February 12, 2015. http://sdsos.gov/elections-voting/assets/1952-1958.pdf.

"Stilwell Road." *A Profile of Chanlang District*. Accessed November 1, 2014. www.changlang.nic.in/stilwell.html.

"Taj Mahal." *Savion Travel Services Pvt. Ltd*. Accessed July 31, 2014. www.tajmahal.org.uk/index.html.

"Terrence C. McCay." Accessed May 21, 2015. www.vetaffairs.sd.gov/sdwwiimemorial/SubPages/profiles/Display.asp?P=1252.

"The Office." *South Dakota Office of the Attorney General*. Accessed February 17, 2015. www.atg.sd.gov/TheOffice.aspx.

"The 1935 Passage of the Wagner Act." *National Labor Relations Board*. Accessed June 28, 2015. www.nlrb.gov/who-we-are/our-history/1935-passage-wagner-act.

"U. S. Army Regulation Winter Officer's Service Uniform." *WW II Impressions, Inc.* Accessed January 6, 2015. www.wwiiimpressions.com/newusarmyofficerwinteruniform.html.

"USS General G. O. Squier (AP-130)." *NavSource Online: Service Ship Photo Archive.* Accessed July 20, 2015. www.navsource.org/archives/09/22/22130.htm.

"Wade-Giles Romanization." *Encyclopaedia Britannica.* Accessed July 16, 2015. www.britannica.com/topic/Wade-Giles-romanization.

Weidenburner, Carl W. (compiler). "World War II China-Burma-India Theater Maps." Accessed March 26, 2015. cbi-theater-1.home.comcast.net/~cbi-theater-1/maps/_Map_Main.html.

"Welcome to the online home of the Ernie Pyle World War II Museum." *The Ernie Pyle World War II Museum.* Accessed July 31, 2015. www.erniepyle.org.

"World Battlefronts: Something New." *Time Magazine*, May 14, 1945. Accessed September 27, 2013. http://content.time.com/time/magazine/article/0,9171,792086,00.html.

"World War II Archives." *Wartime Press.* Accessed October 17 and December 28, 2013. www.wartimepress.com.

"1959 Landrum-Griffin Act." *National Labor Relations Board.* Accessed June 28, 2015. www.nlrb.gov/who-we-are/our-history/1959-landrum-griffin-act.

GOVERNMENT MANUALS, RECORDS, AND OTHER DOCUMENTS

FM 7-10, Infantry Field Manual, Rifle Company, Rifle Regiment. Washington, D.C.: United States Government Printing Office, 1942.

FM 7-15, Infantry Field Manual, Heavy Weapons Company, Rifle Regiment. Washington, D.C.: United States Government Printing Office, 1942.

Order of Battle of the United States Army Ground Forces in World War II, Pacific Theater of Operations, United States Army Forces, China, Burma and India (USAF CBI). Washington, D.C.: Office of the Chief of Military History, Department of the Army, 1959.

Records in the National Archives at College Park, College Park, MD. The record groups consulted are listed here. Descriptions of, and citations to, individual records are provided in the Notes section above.

--Bulletins, January-November, 1944; U. S. Forces in CBI Theaters of Operations, Record Group 0493, Entry No. UD-UP 518.

--General Correspondence, 1942-48; Ground Adj Gen Section; HQ Army Ground Forces, Record Group 337, Entry No. 55.

--General Correspondence, 1943-45; U. S. Forces in CBI Theaters of Operations, Record Group 0493, Entry No. UD-UP 513.

--General Correspondence, 1944-45; U. S. Forces in CBI Theaters of Operations, Record Group 0493, Entry No. UD-UP 541.

--Reports and Correspondence, 1944-45; U. S. Forces in CBI Theaters of Operations, Record Group 0493, Entry No. UD-UP 535.

--Reports, 1945; U. S. Forces in CBI Theaters of Operations, Record Group 0493, Entry No. UD-UP 538.

--Special Orders, 1943-44; U. S. Forces in CBI Theaters of Operations, Record Group 0493, Entry No. UD-UP 523.

--Special Orders, 1944-45; U. S. Forces in CBI Theaters of Operations, Record Group 0493, Entry No. UD-UP 549.

--The Chinese Combat Command General Staff, Records of G-3; U. S. Forces in CBI Theaters of Operations, Record Group 0493, Entry No. UD-UP 539.

"When You are Overseas: These Facts Are Vital." *War Department Pamphlet No. 21-1, 29 July 1943.* Washington, D.C.: Government Printing Office, 1943.

MISCELLANY

Biographical Sketch: Phil W. Saunders, 1920-1958, (undated).

Booklet: *Fort Benning, Georgia.* San Antonio, TX: Universal Press in cooperation with the Fort Benning Public Relations Office, (publication date unknown).

Booklet: *Infantry Replacement Training Center, Camp Wheeler, Ga.* Atlanta,

GA: Albert Love Enterprises, 1945.

Brochure: *Saunders for Governor*, (undated).

Bulletin: "Life Celebration for Phil W. Saunders," (undated).

Certificate of Appreciation to Mrs. M. Keeler from Gen. Fred F. Woerner, USA (Ret), Chairman, American Battle Monuments Commission and Peter Wheeler, Chairman, World War II Memorial Advisory Board dated June 16, 1997.

Certificate of Award to Major Phil W. Saunders from the National Government, Republic of China dated December 23, 1946.

Emails between Jane Saunders Mauss and author sent May-June, 2015.

Emails to Jane Saunders Mauss from Nancy Mackle sent June 4, 2015.

Family photographs provided by Jane Saunders Mauss, Debra Saunders Smith, and John Saunders.

Greece-Egypt trip brochure: "The Cleopatra," (undated).

Interviews with Jane Saunders Mauss, Nancy Hoy McCahren, John Saunders, Phillip Saunders, Debra Saunders Smith, Ken Spates, Suzan Wilson Spates, and Barbara Wilson conducted from April 2011 to July 2015.

Letter to George Bush from Phil Saunders dated March 9, 1990.

Letter to Phyllis Dolan from Phil dated December 4, 1943.

Letter to Lois from Phil dated March 17, 1953.

Letters to Corinne and Jim Mackle from Phil dated from December 1943 to May 1944 and January 6, 1945.

Letters to Corinne, Jim, and Nancy Mackle dated from June 1944 to October 1945.

Letter to Parties of the First Part from Phil Walter dated 1977.

Letter to Phil from Howard Anderson dated November 12, 1953.

Letter to Phil from Chan Gurney dated December 18, 1943.

Letter to Marge Price and others from Phil dated May 15, 1945.

Letters to Jean Saunders from Phil dated from September 1943 to October 1945.

Letters to Leola Saunders from Phil dated from October 1943 to October 1945.

Letter to Mr. and Mrs. Phil Saunders from H. W. Frankenfeld dated June 5, 1947.

Letter to Mr. Phil Saunders from Mrs. Earl Kindred dated September 30, 1953.

Letter to Phil Saunders from Thomas H. Pozarnsky dated November 14, 1951.

Letter to Allen Wilson from Phil dated September 2, 1944.

Letters to Lois Wilson from Phil dated from March 1944 to November 1945.

Memorandums from South Dakota Republican Central Committee re Schedule of Hon. Phil Saunders, Candidate for Attorney General dated September 27, October 12, and October 20, 1954.

"Military Papers" file. This file contains Phil's individual military records. It includes his Immunization Register, Officer's Qualification Card, Separation Qualification Record, Report of Separation, and orders, memorandums, letters and certificates from the U. S. Army. These military records are cited in more detail in the Notes section above.

Note to Mr. Saunders from Dwight D. Eisenhower dated March 17, 1953.

Note to My dear Saunders from Paul R. M. Miller dated May 2, 1944.

Saunders, Lois. *Blue Scrapbook*, 1946-1954.

Saunders, Lois. *European Travel Log*, 1975.

Saunders, Lois. *Travel Diary*, 1977.

Index

Page numbers in **bold** indicate photos, maps, or other illustrations.
Page numbers in *italics* refer to notes.

A

Abdnor, James, 160
Admiral Hotel, 18
Agra, 25, **184**
air travel, 24, 26, 109, 142, 146
airplanes, 57-58, 58-59, 74-75, 78, 147, **185, 206**
ALPHA force, 113
ambush, 1, 34
amebic dysentery, 4, 141-42, *258*
American air ground school, 77
American Theater Ribbon, 21
American troops
    conduct expected of, 61, 67-68, 83, 85, 103
    leadership change, 87-91
    MARS Task Force/5332d Brigade (Provisional), 121-22
    morale, 84-86
    paperwork demands, 109
    replacements, 15-22, 75, 102, 104, 110, 121
    troop strength, 5, 147
    workload of, 104
American Volunteer Group (AVG), 57-58
Anderson, Sigurd, 156, 158-59, 162
appendectomy incident, 55-57, 74
Arabian Sea, 146, 148
armies in Central Command, 113
Arlington, 149
Arms, Thomas S., 121
Army Infantry Replacement Training Centers, 15, 18, *237*
Army Schools (in China), 32-33, 38-40, 51, 54-55
Army Separation Center, 149
Army Services of Supply (SOS), 26, 142, 143
Arth, Carol, **219**
Asiatic-Pacific Service Ribbon, 75, 147
Atlanta, 147
Atlantic Ocean, 24, 148, 149
atomic bombs, 135
attack on unit, 79
attitude of Yoke personnel (American), 64-66

B

B-25 airplanes, 58-59
B-29 airplane forced down, 78
B-29 raid on Japan, 74-75
basic infantry officers' course, 11-15, **178, 179**
basketball game, 41
"battle inoculation" courses, 18-20
bayonet assault course, 17, **180**
Bengal famine, 25
Benning, Henry L., 11
Berry, E.Y., 158, 162, 164, 165
Black Hills, 154, 158, 160, 171, **220**
bowling, 169
Brazil, 23-24
bridge (card game), 138, 139, 142, 145-46, 147, 148, 169
Bronze Star ("campaign star"), 75, 147
Bronze Star Medal, 125, 133
Brown, Albert E., 21
Burma, 26, 59, 64, 70, 95, 121, **184, 186, 190, 197, 207**

Burma offensive, 49, 50, 64, 121
Burma Road, 1, 26, 30, 34, 102, 121, **186, 190, 207**, *252*
Bush, George, 170-71
Buzzell, William Reginald, 21

C

Cadre School, 16
Calvin Coolidge Inn, 159
Camouflage Demonstration Area, 22
campaigns and elections
  in 1950, 155-56, 163
  in 1952, 157-58
  in 1954, 160-62, 221, 222
  in 1956, 163-64
  in 1958, 164-65, 223
Camp Carson, 155
Camp McCoy, 148, 149
Camp Milar, 146
camp in northern India, 24, 25
Camp Wheeler, 3, 15-22, **180, 181, 182**
Case, Francis, 158, 163
Case, H.L., 154, **216**
casualties
  American, 34, 105-06, 119, 170-71
  Chinese, 3, 49, 66, 82, 115, 150
  Japanese, 34, 49, 119, 213
CBI. *See* China-Burma-India theater (CBI)
CCC. *See* Chinese Combat Command (Prov) (CCC) (Prov))
censorship (Chinese government), 42
censorship (American military), 27-29, 53, 62-64, 72, 79
Central Command, 101, 113, 114, 117, 122, 131
Chaba, 145
charades, 169-70
Chen Cheng, 33
Cheng Hein-Hein, 92
Chennault, Claire L., 57-58, 111, **201**
Chenyuan, 115
Chevy Chase, 167, 169, **224**
Chiang Kai-shek, 3, 4, 57-58, 87-90, 111, 123, 125, 150, 154, **191**, *252*
China, 3, 25, 59, 60, 65, 66, 73, 80, 91, 111, 112, 119, 123-24, 145, 146, 149, 155, 156, **184, 186, 189, 190, 197, 200**
China Air Task Force, 57
China-Burma-India theater (CBI), 3, 23, 32, 35, 40, 82-86, 89-90, **184, 190, 197**
"China Defensive" campaign, 75
"China Offensive" campaign, 147
China theater, 90, 92-93, 102, **200**
China Theater Replacement Service, 142
Chinese Army. *See* Nationalist Chinese Army
Chinese Army defense drills, 69
Chinese Army Service Medal, 75
Chinese Combat Command (Prov) (CCC) (Prov)), 101, 102-03, 109, 113-14, 129, 131, 142, 147. *See also* Central Command
Chinese Expeditionary Force, 31-32, 33, 38
Chinese Field Hospital, 107
Chinese girl, letter from, 91-92, **202**
Chinese government
  censorship, 42
  "Special Breast Order of Yun Hui with Ribbon," 153-54
Chinese Group Armies in Yunnan province, 32-33
Chinese language, 30, 60-62, 91, 100, 105, 119, 150
Chinese Service Bar, 48
Chinese Training and Combat Command (CT & CC), 33, 35, 92-93, 96, 99, 101
Chinese Training Command (Prov) (CTC) (Prov)), 101
ching ba juice, 48, 99-100
Chinghsien, 115
Christmas (1942), 18
Christmas (1943), 50, 53, 55
Christmas (1944), 94-97, 101
Chungking, 27, 90, 92, 113, 120, 189, **190, 197, 200**, *240*

Church, Joseph, 8
church service, 34
civilian volunteers (American), 57-58
civilians (Chinese), 35-36, 43, 69, 91, 97, 102, 125, 132, 135, 150, **194**, **211**, **214**
climate. *See* weather
close combat course, 18, 19, **181**
Cobb Island cottage, 169
collective bargaining, 166-67
Combat Infantryman's Badge (CIB), 105, 128-29
Coolidge, Calvin, 159
Coolidge, Grace, 159
Coolidge, John, 159
Crazy Horse monument, 162
Custer State Park, 159

D

D-Day, 73-74
dead Chinese soldiers along road, 115
deep-sea fishing trip, 1, 23
defense drills (Chinese), 69
Delhi, 87, 89
Dirksen, Everett, 160
Dixon, Albert, 8
Dolan, Phyllis, 45-46, 54, 149-50
Dorn, Frank, 31-33, 51, 80, 101, *240–41*, *244*
"doughboy," 11, 17, *236*

E

Easter (1945), 109
Eastern Command, 101, 113
Egypt, 24, 148, 168
8th Army, 34, *243*
Eisenhower, Dwight, 157, 158, 159, 163, 165, **219**, **220**
Emery, Ambrose Robert, 16, 21
Enslow, Philip H., 34, *242*
execution of Chinese soldiers, 66

F

family reunions, 170, **226**, **227**
Fargo, 155
field hospital, 25, 107, 141-42

field training at Camp Wheeler, 21
52nd Army, 34, 51, 52, 54, 77, *241–242*
52nd Chinese Army Service Medal, 75
fishing on French Creek, 159
fleas, 43, 68
"Flying Tigers," 57-58
food
  banquets for Americans with Chinese Army, 48, 51, 97, 99-101
  at Chaba, 145
  C rations, 81, 82, 101, 109
  on Christmas (1944), 96
  at CCC Headquarters, 109, 114
  dog as, 71
  in field hospital, 142
  at French hotel, 36
  on George Washington's birthday, 58
  in India, 24
  K rations, 66, 130
  in Kunming after initial arrival, 30
  lacking, 71, 81-82, 87-88, 135
  in Luichow, 139
  monotony of, 47
  on New Year's Day (1945), 97
  from relatives back home, 55, 88
  at Rest Camp, 93-94
  in small village, 70, 71
  on Thanksgiving (1943), 45
  on Thanksgiving (1944), 92
Fort Benning, 3, 11-15, **178**, **179**
43rd Division, 117, 125, 126
Foss, Joe, 9, 160-65, **221**, **222**, *235*
Fourteenth Air Force, 26, 52, 57, 58-59, 120, 125
Frankenfeld, Herman W. ("Frankie"), 59-60, 74, 154
French Creek Canyon, 159
French Indochina, 26, 34, 52-53, 101, **184**, **197**, **200**, **207**
French officers, 80, 105
Frenchman, rescue of, 53

G

Gallo, Major, 54

Gauss, Clarence, 89
George Washington's birthday, 58
Gibraltar, 149
gin ba juice, 48, 99-100
goat, 79
Goodridge, George L., 117
Gow, General, 50, 51
Grant County, 1, 2
"Grant County Honor Roll," 106
Grant County Review (newspaper), 13, 21, 46, 80, 81, 106, 111, 118, 145, 149, 153, *254, 259*
Grant, Ulysses S., 1
Gulf of Aden, 148
Gulf War, 170-71
Gurney, Chan, 42, 47, 53-54

H

Hanks, Sergeant, 53
Herseth, Ralph, 164
Himalayan mountains. *See* "the Hump"
Hiroshima, 135
Ho Ying-Chin, 113, 147
horses, 5, 43, 58-59, 66-67, 109
Hot Springs, 150, 154, 161
Houck, Roy, 161, 164, **221**
Hovey, E. Paul, 154
Hoy, Carl ("Rube"), 41, 53, 60, 80, 96, *246*
Hoy, Carleton, 80, 96
Hoy, Hazel, 80, 96
Hoy, Nancy, 80, 96
Hoy, Richard, 80, 96
"the Hump," 26, 57, 79, 145, 147, **185, 186, 190, 206**
Hunan province, 113, **189**

I

India, 24-26, 29, 65, 70, 78, 89, **184, 186, 190, 197,** *252*
India-Burma theater, 90
Indochina. *See* French Indochina
Infantry and Field Artillery Training Centers, 32
Infantry Replacement Training Center (IRTC), 3, 15, 17, *237*
infiltration course, 18, 19-20, **182**
I-ning, 131
International Harvester Company, 23
interpreters, 60-62, 91, 100, 105, 119, 150
IX Group Army, 34, 39, 40

J

Jacotel, Dr. and Mrs. J.A., 41
Japan, 57, 74, 89, 135, 136
Japanese troops
  ambushed by, 1, 34
  in Burma offensive, 49
  photo of, **213**
  as prisoners of war, 68, 117-18, 119
  second encounter with, 36
  subsequent encounters with, 44, 45, 52, 72, 79, 115, 128, 130, 133
  surrendered, 135, 136
  threat against Americans, 73
Johnson, Alma and Arvid, 151
Johnson, Emil, 44
Johnson, Hilfrid, 41, 53, 151
Johnson, Jean ("Jennie"). *See* Saunders, Jean ("Jennie")
Jonas, Frank, 165
Julian, J. Herndon, 53
Juvenile Law Enforcement Committee, 164

K

Karachi, 143, 145, 146, 148, **184, 190**
Keeler, Leola. *See* Saunders, Leola
Kialing River, 27, **189**
Kunming, 26, 32-34, 72, 93, 102, 113-15, 137, 142-43, 145, 149, **184, 186, 187, 188, 189, 190, 197, 200, 207,** *252*
Kwangsi Command, 101
Kwangsi province, 125, **189**
Kweichow province, 113, **189**
Kweilin, 125, 126, 131, 133, 135, 136, 139, **184, 190, 197, 200, 211**
Kweilin offensive, 126-33, **213**
Kweiyang, 113, 115, **189, 200**

L

Labor-Management Reporting and Disclosure Act (Landrum-Griffin Act), 167
Lacy, Charles, 164
Landrum-Griffin Act, 167
language, 30, 60-62, 91, 100, 105, 116, 150
Larkin, Major, 71
Lashio, 26, **186**, **189**
law school, 118, 153, 155
leadership change, 87-91
Ledo, 102, **186**, **190**, **207**, *252*
Ledo (Stilwell) Road, 95, 102, **186**, **190**, **207**, *252*
letter from Chinese girl, 91-92, **202**
letter of instruction from General Wedemeyer, 102-03
Linn, Bernard, **221**
Liu Lu Chang, 54, 77
Liuchow, 139, 141-43, **189**, **200**, **214**
living conditions in China
    of Chinese soldiers, 3, 37, 40, 44, 60, 65-66
    for Chinese civilians, 29-30, 44, 102
    climate. *See* weather
    clothing, 24-25, 30, 41, 44, 46, 52, 102, 106, 114, 143, 146
    food. *See* food
    living quarters, 4-5, 26, 36, 46, 68-70, 77-78, 80, 82, 93, 95-96, 141, **208**
    travel. *See* transportation
Lockhart, S. S., 30, *240*
Lovre, Harold O., 158, 162-63
Lungsheng, 126
Lun Yung, 33

M

M-1 rifle, 14, 17, **180**
Mackle, Corinne Saunders, 41, 43-44, 54, 72, 105, 151, **176**, **210**, *243*. *See also* Saunders, Corinne
Mackle, Jim, 72, 105, 151, **176**, *243*
Mackle, Nancy, 72, 107, 151, **210**

mail service, 40-42, 43, 45, 47, 79, 101, 104, 127, 128, 129-30, 143. *See also* censorship
Malta, 149
maps, **184, 186, 189, 190, 197, 200, 207**
MARS Task Force/5332d Brigade (Provisional), 121-22
Marshall, George, 89, 133, 138
Martin, Ed C., 160
Mauss, Jane Saunders. *See* Saunders, Jane
Mauss, Jessica, **226**, **227**
Mauss, Shelley, **227**
Mauss, Steve, **226**
Mauss, Trevor, **226**, **227**
Mayes, Larry, **221**
McCay, Terrence, 105
McClure, Robert B., 101, 147
McGovern, George, 163, 165
McKusick, Marshall, 41, 53
McNair, Lesley J., 128
Medal of Honor, 106, *235*
medical emergency, 55-57
Mediterranean Sea, 149
Miami, 1, 23
Milbank, 1, 2, 11, 23, 93, 149, 150, 151, 161, **176**, **183**, **222**, **223**
Milbank High School, 3, 7, **175**
military occupation specialty (MOS), 21
Miller, Paul R.M., 71-72, 81-82, 154
Minneapolis, 18, 23, 149, 151
Mitter, Rana, 87, *250*
Mong Yu, 102, *252*
morale (American) in CBI theater, 84-86
Mou Ting-fang, 117
Mountbatten, Louis, 34-35, 89, **193**
Mount Rushmore, 157, 158, 159, **219**
movies, 23, 72, 93, 109, 139, 145
Mueller, Don, 154
mules (pack trains), 23, 45, 52-53, 58
Mundt, Karl, 158, 162

N

Nagasaki, 135

National Labor Relations Act (Wagner Act), 166, 167, 168
National Labor Relations Board (NLRB), 166-69
National Young Republican Federation Convention, 159-60
Nationalist Chinese Army.
   Americans given commissions, 48, 51
   Americans working with Chinese officers, 31, 36-37, 102-03
   attitude toward war, 3-4, 94
   condition of troops, 3, 40, 127
   criticism of, 64-66
   defense drills, 69
   defense system, 94
   general performance in combat, 49-50, 64, 94, 95, 109-10, 117, 120, 125, 126, 127, 131
   living conditions, 3, 37, 40, 44, 60, 65-66
   mass execution, 66
   morale, 55, 65
   performance in during Burma offensive, 49-50, 64
   photos, **195, 198, 203, 204, 206, 209, 212**
   troop strength, 3, 77, 81, 82, 117, *241–42*
NCO Weapons Schools (in China), 40, 54
Nelson, Irwin L. ("Mow Em Down"), 44-45, 48, 51, 58, 67, 70, 75, 95, 121, 146, **192**
Nelson, Lieutenant, 44
New Year's Day (1944), 51
New Year's Day (1945), 97
New York City, 143, 147, 149, 169
94th Army, 113, 133, 142
94th Army Headquarters, 115, 117, 139
North African campaign, 18
North Dakota Administrative Service Group, 155
Northwestern University Law School, 153

note from Colonel Miller, 71-72
note from President Eisenhower, 158, **220**

O
Occoquan River, 169
Officers' Course (in China), 39-40
Officers Weapons Schools (in China), 40
Olson, Arlo, 105-06
Ostroot, Geraldine, **221**

P
paperwork demands, 109
Patton, George S., Jr., 11, 110, *235-36*
"Peanut," 87, 88
Pearl Harbor, 3, 34
Phillippi, Mr. (banker), 74
phonograph, 107-08
Pierre, 155, 162, 167
pigs, 4, 29, 43, 68, 69, 78, 107
play (theater), 54
point system for returning home, 119, 120, 131
police schools, 164
Port Said, 148
presidential election (1944), 82-83, 92
Priest, Ivy, 160
Pyle, Ernie, 17, *237*

R
Rapid City, 157, 159, 160, 170, 171, 172, **226**
rats, 4, 26, 68
recreation, 41-42, 50, 93-94, 138-39, 142, 145-46, 148, 168, 169-70, 171-72
Red Cross, 94, 114
Red Sea, 148
refugees, 91, **211**
Regular Army, 138, 153
replacements, 15-22, 75, 102, 104, 110, 121, **209**
reporting policy, 109
Republican conventions, 157, 159, 160, 161
Reserve Command, 101, 113

Reserve Officers' Training Corps (ROTC), 3, 7-8, 59, 105, 106, 163
Rest Camp, 93-94, **205**
returning home
  point system, 119-20, 131
  replacements unavailable, 102, 104
  trip back to the U.S., 139, 142-43, 145-49, **215**
Rhodes, Glen, 164
Rifle and Heavy Weapons Company Officers' Course No. 42, 12-15
road block in woman's back yard, 67-68
Roosevelt, Franklin D., 57-58, 79, 89, 92, 111, 133, *254*
ROTC (Reserve Officers' Training Corps), 3, 7-8, 59, 105, 106, 163
Russians, 135, 136

S
San Francisco, 167, 169
Saunders, Carina, **226**
Saunders, Carl, **226, 227**
Saunders, Corinne, 1, 2, **174**. *See also* Mackle, Corinne Saunders
Saunders, Debra, 156, **223, 224, 226**
Saunders, Emilie, **226, 227**
Saunders, Gene. *See* Saunders, Phil Walter
Saunders, Jane, 157, **223, 224, 226**
Saunders, Jean ("Jennie"), 1-3, 18, 82, 80, 149, 151, **176, 210, 223**
Saunders, John, 160, **223, 224, 226**
Saunders, Kevin, **226, 227**
Saunders, Leola, 1, 2, 18, 23, 42, 55, 105-06, 119, 149, 151, 172, **174, 176, 183**
Saunders, Lois Wilson, 154-57, 162, 168, 169, 171, **216, 223, 225, 226, 227**. *See also* Wilson, Lois
Saunders, Phil Crowley, 1-2
Saunders, Phil Walter
  awards and decorations
    American Theater Ribbon, 21
    Asiaitic-Pacific Service Ribbon, 75, 147
    Bronze Star ("campaign star"), 75, 147
    Bronze Star Medal, 125, 133
    Chinese Service Bar, 48
    Combat Infantryman's Badge (CIB), 128-29
    Commendation for service with the CCC, 147
    52nd Chinese Army Service Medal, 75
    overseas service bars, 147
    "Special Breast Order of Yun Hui with Ribbon," 153-54
    World War II Victory Ribbon, 147
  childhood, 1-3, **174**
  college
    '42 Coyote Yearbook description, 10, **177**
    as member of Law Association, Political Science League and Strollers, 9
    named in *Who's Who in American Colleges and Universities*, 9-10
    as president of fraternity, 9
    as president of the student senate, 8
    ROTC, 3, 7-8
    at the University of South Dakota, 3, 7-10
  death of, 172
  family life
    as an uncle, 43-44
    children's births, 155, 156, 157, 160
    at Corinne and Jim's wedding, **176**
    at family reunions, 170, **226, 227**
    high school graduation, 3, 7, **175**
    with his children, **224, 226**
    with his mother, **176, 223**
    international travel, 168, **225**
    in Leningrad, **225**
    with Leola before overseas assignment, **183**
    marriage, 154
    name changed from Gene, 2
    residence in Maryland, 167, **224**
    wedding photo, **216**
  health

amebic dysentery, 4, 141-42, *258*
bad cold, 130
and cleanliness, 112
eye exam, 114
fleas, 43
medical discharge not necessary, 130-31
no hay fever, 136
Pepto-Bismol, 4, 82
pills, 55, 74, 127
shots, 11, 23, 62
stomach aches, 50, 55, 74, 82, 114
stomach ailments, 4
tooth pain, 72
training accident, 21, *238*
law school, 118, 153, 155
legal and political careers
 as an Administrative Law Judge with NLRB, 168, 169
 as an Assistant Attorney General, 155, 157
 as Attorney General, 162-63, 164
 as candidate for governor, 164-65, **223**
 as chairman of S. D. Young Republicans League, 156-57
 as executive secretary for Governor Anderson, 156
 at the inauguration of Governor Foss, 162
 as instructor in local police schools, 164
 Juvenile Law Enforcement Committee, 164
 retirement from NLRB, 169-70
 speaking engagements after the war, 155, 156, 157, 159, 160, 161, **218, 222**
 as a Trial Examiner with the NLRB, 166-68
 White House meeting with Eisenhower and others, 158, **219, 220**
military career (during the war)

ambushed, 1, 34
appendectomy incident, 55-57, 74
in Burma, 70
at CCC Headquarters, 109
as Chief of Staff in 43rd Division, 117
with the Chinese and American officers, **203, 204**
and the Chinese language, 30
commissioned as a second lieutenant, 3, 8
as Company Commander at Camp Wheeler, 18, 21
as Executive Officer at Camp Wheeler, 16, 21
as Executive Officer for liaison group attached to 2nd Division, 77
as Executive Officer with 43rd Division Liaison Team, 133
finances, 138-39
on the French Indochina border, 52-53
frustration with Chinese troops, 64, 81, 94, 106-07, 109-10
Grant County Review articles, 80-81, 149-50
with his engineer officer, **205**
with his signal team, **196**
home visits before going overseas, 11, 18, 23
inspection of American living quarters in China, 119-20
interview with Phyllis Dolan, 149-50
Japanese prisoners, talk with, 117-18
Japanese surrender, reaction to, 136-37
journey from Kunming to convoy camp, 114-17
letters to editor of *Grant County Review*, 13-14, 118-19
as Liaison Officer in Central Command, 113
as Liaison Officer to the 52nd Army, 51
as Liaison Officer in TIG No. 4, 3, 40

military occupational specialty (MOS), 21
"90-mile march," 126-28, 130, 132
pistol stolen, 58
as Platoon Leader/Trainer at Camp Wheeler, 16
positive wartime experience, 139
promotions and pay, 16, 21, 78, 81, 96, 97, 131, 138-39
reading *Time* magazine, **208**
ruined uniform, 143, *259*
speech to Chinese generals, 54
with TIG No. 4 members, **192**
trip to China, 23-26
trip home from China, 139, 142-43, 145-49, **215**
as a Unit Training Officer, 21
visit to U. S. field installation, 87-88
wallet stolen, 62, 74
war bonds, 78
military career (post-war)
in the active reserve, 155-56
"date of relief from active duty"/"date of separation," 149, 153
honorable discharge, 163
on Inactive Status List of the Standby Reserve, 160, 163
as Lieutenant Colonel, 153, 155, 171, **217**
nomination as permanent officer in Regular Army, 153
personality, 9
post-war plans, 91, 110, 111, 118, 131, 137-38
Saunders, Phillip, 155, **223**, **224**, **226**
Savage, Dick, 119
2nd Division, 77, 81, 101
security for American soldiers, 77-78
Services of Supply (SOS), 26, 142, 143
Sewell, Luke, 93
Shanghai, 140, 142
Sharpe, Governor, *258*
Sigma Alpha Epsilon (SAE), 9, 59, 106
Signal Corps radio, 43, 140

Sims, Frank E., 8
Sinkai, 77
Situation in China, **197**, **200**
sleeping bags, 95, 96
Smith, Cristy, **227**
Smith, Debra. *See* Saunders, Debra
Smith, Gordon, **226**
Smith, Mr. (mail carrier), 53
social events, 48, 51, 54, 97, 99-101
softball ("kittenball"), 145, 148
South Dakota Young Republicans League, 156
Southeast Asia Command (SEAC), 35, 89-90
Southern Command, 101
Sun River, 170, **227**
Spates, Ken, 168
Spates, Suzan Wilson, 168
"Special Breast Order of Yun Hui with Ribbon," 153-54
Sputnik, 165
Squier, George Owen, 148
Stalin, Joe, 136
State Game Lodge, 159
Stilwell, Joseph W. ("Vinegar Joe"), 3, 26, 27, 32-35, 40, 76, 78, 80, 84, 87-91, **193**, *252*
Stilwell and the American Experience in China, 1911-1945, 3-4
Stimson, Henry, 89, 128
Strollers, 9
sub-machine gun accident, 79
Suez Canal, 148
Sultan, Daniel, 90
Sun Lou Yen, Mrs., 78
Sun Ti Lou, Mrs., 68
Supreme Commander for China theater, 3
Szechwan province, 27, **189**

T

Taft-Hartley Act of 1947, 166, 167
Taj Mahal, 25
Tang En-po, 131

tennis, 145, **205**
Thanksgiving (1943), 44-45
Thanksgiving (1944), 92
Thanksgiving (1945), 151
thefts, 58, 62
"tiger country," 24
30-division plan, 31-32
Thomas, Jesse, 154
Threshie, Robert, 148
Throckmorton, James, 8
Tibbs, Casey, 162
Time magazine, 86, 120-21, 123-24, **208**
Time Runs Out in CBI, 111, 131
train travel (in China), 104, 116-17
training (military)
    American air ground school, 77
    Army Schools, 32-33, 38-40, 51, 54-55
    basic infantry officers' course, 11-15, **178**, **179**
    "battle inoculation" courses, 18-20
    at Cadre School, 16
    Camouflage Demonstration Area, 22
    at Camp Wheeler, 16-22, **180**, **181**, **182**
    course by Fourteenth Air Force, 57
    courses after the war, 155-56
    field training at Camp Wheeler, 21
    at Fort Benning, 11-15, **178**, **179**
    infantry replacement, 15-22
    non-commissioned officers' course (for Chinese), 39, 40
    Officers' Course (for Chinese), 39
    overhead artillery fire, 22
    and reorganization in the China theater, 121
    by Traveling Instructional Groups (TIGs), 33, 36-37, 38-39
    unit training in 52nd Chinese Army, 54-55
    village fighting course, 19
transport plane, **185**
transportation
    airplanes, 24, 26, 109, 139, 142, 145, 146

    by bus, 149, 150
    by foot, 69, 124, 126-28, 142
    horses, 5, 43, 58-59, 66-67, 109
    jeeps, 45, 115, 139, 140
    mules, 23, 45, 52-53, 58
    off-trail, 110
    by ship, 148-49
    trains, 104, 116-17, 149, 151
    by truck, 48
Traveling Instructional Groups (TIGs)
    in general, 33, 36-39
    TIG No. 4, 33, 34, 39, 40, 43, 44, 49, 58, 59, 67, 69, **192**
troops. *See* American troops; Japanese troops; Nationalist Chinese Army
Truman, Harry S., 111, 136, 153, *254*
Tuchman, Barbara, 3-4, 135

U

unfair labor practices, 166-67, 168
unions, 166-67
unit training in China, 54-55
Unit Training Officer/MOS, 21
University of South Dakota, 3, 7, 41, 59, 105, 106, 108
U.S. China-Burma-India theater of operations. *See* China-Burma-India theater (CBI)
U.S. Forces Rear Echelon, 104
U.S. Forces Rest Camp, 93-94, **205**
U.S. Liaison Group, 51-52
USS General G.O. Squier (AP-130), 148-49, **215**

V

vaccines, 11, 23, 62
Vermillion, 3, 7, 74, 161
village fighting course, 18, 19
volunteers (U.S. civilian), 57-58
voting in 1944 U. S. election, 83

W

Wade-Giles system of romanization, *240*
Wade, Ralph M., 8
Wagner Act (National Labor Relations

Act), 166, 167, 168
Walker, Dixie, 93
war bonds, 78
war correspondent from America, 42
War Department, 27, 83, 91, 97, 104, 114, 119, 128, 129, 130
Warburton, Herbert, **219**
Ward, Ben, 59, **192**
Warner, Paul, 93
washing clothes, 43, **194**
Washington, D. C., 43, 89, 110, 127, 151, 158, 166, 167, 169
water buffalo, 35, 68, 69, 70, **199**
Waterbury obstacle course, 17
weapons, 14, 17, 39, 52, 58, 59, 63, 65, 78, 79, 81. *See also* training (military)
Weapons Maintenance Team No. 4, 39
weather
    cold, 4, 24-25, 30, 42, 44, 46, 54, 59, 87, 95, 96, 102, 104, 115, 128
    hot, 5, 14, 25, 67, 69, 73, 75, 114, 121, 123, 130, 139, 145
    rain, 69, 72-74, 78, 88, 106, 118, 128, 130, 132, 136
    snow, 44, 50
Wedemeyer, Albert C., 90, 99, 102, 107, 109, 110, 120, 123, 125, 142, **201**, *251*
Weeks, I.D., 7, 53, *234*
Wenshan, 34-35, 39-40, 54
Western Command, 101, 113
Whang, Mr. (interpreter), 62, 105, 119, 150
Whang So Gee, Mrs., 68-69
Wheaton, 167, 169

Wheeler, Joseph, 15
Wheeler, Raymond A., 90
Willey, John P., 121
Wilson, Allen, 59-60, 81, 150, 154, 168, **225**
Wilson, Barbara, 150, 154, 168, **225**
Wilson, Dorothy, 154
Wilson, Lois, 59-60, 108-09, 118, 140, 150, 154. *See also* Saunders, Lois Wilson
Wilson, Suzan, 150
Witsell, Edward F., 153
Wood, Howard, 156
World War II Memorial and Registry of Remembrances, 172
World War II Victory Ribbon, 147
wrist watch (for interpreter), 105, 119
Wukang, 117, 126

Y

Yangtze River, 27, 92, **189**
Y-Force (Yoke Force), 31-32, 80, 93
Y-Force Operations Staff (YFOS), 26, 32, 77, 92
YFOS Headquarters, 26, 33, 35, 36, 49, 55, 58, 59, 60, 62, 64, 72
Young Republican National Convention, 157, 159, 160
Young Republicans League, 156
Yung-fu, 131
Yunnan province, 26, 30, 31-33, 40, 65, 67, 70, **186**, **189**

Z

Ziolkowski, Korczak, 162

www.ingramcontent.com/pod-product-compliance
Lightning Source LLC
Chambersburg PA
CBHW032102090426
42743CB00007B/206